WISCONSIN
Hunting

WITH BRIAN LOVETT

YOUR IN-DEPTH GUIDE TO WISCONSIN'S PUBLIC HUNTING GROUNDS

S0-CFO-990

© 1993 by Krause Publications, Inc.

All rights reserved.

No portion of this book may be reproduced in any form without permission.

Published by:

krause
publications

700 E. State Street • Iola, WI 54990-0001
Telephone: 715/445-2214

Library of Congress Number 93-77542

ISBN: 0-87341-249-4

Printed in the United States of America

About the Author

Brian Lovett is the outdoors editor for the *Oshkosh Northwestern* newspaper, and a field editor for *Wisconsin Outdoor Journal* magazine.

He was raised in DeForest, Wis., and grew up hunting in the Columbia County and Mather areas.

Lovett graduated from the University of Wisconsin-Oshkosh in 1989. He resides in Oshkosh with his wife, Jennifer.

Acknowledgements

For Jenny.

I would like to thank everyone who made this project possible, including employees of the Department of Natural Resources, and county and federal personnel throughout Wisconsin. In addition, the information contained within wouldn't have been possible without the help of the folks who work at chambers of commerce statewide. I must also thank Jennifer, Mom and Dad for their encouragement; and Krause Publications for its support and faith.

Finally, I must thank the Milwaukee Map Service Inc., for allowing us to reproduce portions of its comprehensive state maps. For information on the complete set of maps, write: Milwaukee Map Service Inc., 959 N. Mayfair Road, Milwaukee, WI 53226.

State of Opportunity

"Hunting in Wisconsin," someone once said, "is going out to a public area and using your skills and know-how to pursue game."

It's true. No sportsman who studies what's available in public hunting lands in Wisconsin will complain about not having a place to hunt. Wisconsin contains millions upon millions of acres that are open to everyone. Whether it's warm-season grasses, thick tamarack swamps, dense aspen stands, majestic oaks, a river bottom or a cattail marsh, you can find good public properties to hunt.

It would be impossible to list all of Wisconsin's public hunting areas — even all of the exceptional ones — in one book. You will find the famous ones, such as Horicon and Necedah, listed here. You'll also find lands that many people have never heard of, let alone visited.

This book does not attempt to rank the areas in terms of perceived quality. As we all know, that will vary depending on the hunters and their interests. Rather, Wisconsin Hunting tries to provide the reader with up-to-date information on what they can expect if they are interested in hunting the properties that are described within.

Each chapter will discuss the major game species and types of wildlife habitat available to hunters at each property. Wildlife managers will tell you about game populations and the best times for hunters to pursue their favorite species. Maps will give you an idea of the area's configuration, as well as showing you how to reach each property.

It's important to remember that any property — public or private — has its ups and downs in terms of hunting opportunities, as well as its own unique features. "Wisconsin Hunting" will tell you about public hunting properties, but it's up to you to find your niche there. There's no substitute for scouting, and you'll likely be amazed at how few people you'll see even at popular public areas if you aren't afraid to walk a mile or two from the parking lots.

It's also important to remember that there are often private lands within the boundaries of many public areas. Also, some private lands are leased for public hunting within the area's boundaries. These leased areas may change year to year. Please respect posted areas, and check a county plat book for the latest information on land ownership.

In addition, it always pays to check the current state or federal regulations that apply to specific areas you plan to hunt.

With all of that in mind, use this book to enhance the enjoyment you receive from hunting. After all, that's what it's all about.

Len Rue Jr.

TABLE OF CONTENTS

NORTH

CENTRAL

EAST

WEST

SOUTH

Dunbar Wildlife Area

MARINETTE COUNTY

The Dunbar Wildlife Area in Marinette County provides hunters a unique setting for some familiar North-country game animals. The 1,320-acre area, which the DNR once leased but now owns, was formerly managed for sharptail grouse. Wildlife manager Roger Amundson said the sharptails are now gone, unfortunately.

However, the area has a new management focus. Dunbar is the home to a substantial and rare sand-barrens vegetation community. At one time, much of northern Wisconsin featured similar prairie habitat, but there are only a few such areas left.

The DNR's prime focus in the area now is to maintain its vegetative community. The grasslands featured in this habitat were ideal for sharptails. However, sportsmen know that their best chance for success now lies in the aspen and brush areas surrounding the grasslands. The sharptail's cousin, the ruffed grouse, can be found throughout Dunbar's thick stuff. Grouse populations here, as in the rest of Wisconsin, are cyclical. They hit a low in 1992, but their numbers should continue to rise through the end of the decade.

Amundson said ruffed grouse hunting in the area doesn't need to be complicated. In fact, his advice is simple.

"It's a big, wide-open area," he said. "The best hunting is probably around its edge. Hunters have to get away from the open stuff."

Amundson said grouse hunters should stick to the numerous aspen stands around the area. Aspen covers a great deal of the property's eastern section, and areas adjacent to the grasslands can be especially productive.

TRAVEL GUIDE

NEAREST SERVICE CENTER: Crandon.
LODGING: There are several resorts and other lodging opportunities in the Crandon area. The Crandon Area Chamber of Commerce lists about 13.
SPORTS SHOP OR HUNTING LICENSE OUTLET: Beef's Archery and Sports, 605 S. Forest Ave., Crandon, (715) 478-2646.
HOSPITAL OR EMERGENCY MEDICAL CLINIC: Rhinelander Medical Center-Crandon Office, 209 E. Elm St., Crandon, (715) 478-3318.
EMERGENCY VETERINARY CLINIC: Animal Health Care Center, 301 E. Pioneer St., Crandon, (715) 478-2500.
AUTO REPAIR OR TOWING: George's Self Service, 500 S. Lake Ave., Crandon, (715) 478-2221.

This edge cover at Dunbar is also attractive to whitetails. Deer are abundant throughout the property and, in general, through the Marinette County area. Aspen areas provide excellent cover and escape routes for deer. Spots where aspen thickets narrow or meet with evergreen stands often create deer funnels for north-country whitetails. Look for places where trails meet with bedding areas nearby.

Hunters should look around the aspen-grassland edge for likely spots to wait for deer. These areas not only provide the most likely habitat for the animals, but also give hunters an added advantage. The vast, open grasslands allow hunters — especially those in tree

Brush and aspen stands that surround the grasslands of the Dunbar Wildlife Area provide excellent hunting.

stands — to see long distances.

Dunbar also features good numbers of blueberry, juneberry and chokecherry plants. Depending on berry production during the growing season, this can attract good numbers of black bears, Amundson said. Berry picking can also be good.

Other northern Wisconsin mammals, including rabbits, also benefit from this cover. Coyote hunters also like Dunbar, Amundson said. The remnant prairie makes for good "brush wolf" habitat, and also allows hunters using high-powered scopes to get some wonderful shooting opportunities.

Whether you're going to the area to hunt or simply observe the unique prairie habitat, access to Dunbar is relatively easy. U.S. Highway 8 crosses the property along its southern edge, and a logging road allows people to reach the rest of the area.

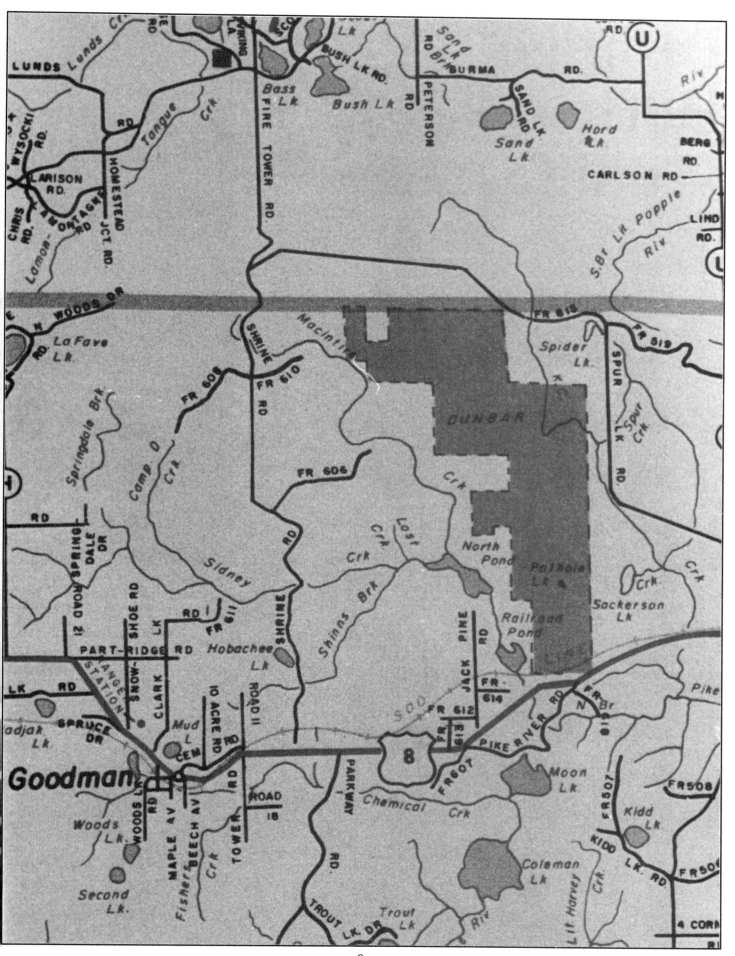

Peshtigo Harbor Wildlife Area

MARINETTE COUNTY

"I like to hunt ducks in the Green Bay area."

Waterfowlers need only hear that phrase to start dreaming of vast skeins of bluebills pouring into a decoy rig on the upwind side of an open-water marsh.

It's safe to say things aren't like they used to be. Nonetheless, area waterfowlers still know one of the best places to swing a shotgun over a spread is Peshtigo Harbor Wildlife Area.

Roger Amundson, DNR area wildlife manager, said Peshtigo Harbor is popular with water-fowlers because the area features a variety of wetlands for duck production and migratory flights. Peshtigo Harbor was once considered one of the best waterfowl breeding areas in Wisconsin. Amundson said production has dropped in recent years, mainly because of habitat losses along the bay itself.

"Our best production is in wood ducks and mallards," he said.

The DNR has worked with Ducks Unlimited to develop four small pot-holes on the property for duck breeding.

The area still sees migratory flights of ducks. However, Canada geese have become a bigger part of hunters' game bags than in the past. But hunters can still have shoots that remind them of the "glory days," Amundson said.

"Geese have become more and more important in the bag over the years, and ducks have probably become less important," he said. "But they have gotten some diver

---

TRAVEL GUIDE

NEAREST SERVICE CENTER: Marinette.

LODGING: There are numerous resorts, motels and inns in the Marinette area. The Marinette Area Chamber of Commerce lists seven and sent brochures for eight others.

SPORTS SHOP OR HUNTING LICENSE OUTLET: Jenquin's Ace Hardware, 2205 Hall Ave., Marinette, (715) 732-0571. Sportsman's Den, 1331 Main St., Marinette, (715) 735-5544. Marinette County Courthouse, 1926 Hall Ave., Marinette, (715) 732-7406.

HOSPITAL OR EMERGENCY MEDICAL CLINIC: Bay Area Medical Center, 3100 Shore Drive, Marinette, (715) 735-6621.

EMERGENCY VETERINARY CLINIC: Town and Country Veterinary Clinic, W 1292 Highway 41, Marinette, (715) 735-9511.

AUTO REPAIR OR TOWING: There are numerous auto repair places in the Marinette area. The Marinette Area Chamber of Commerce lists more than 10.

---

shooting in recent years."

Hunters typically use boats or skiffs to hunt the area's larger, open-water sections. Traditionally, one of the better spots for water-fowling is around the spot where the Peshtigo River meets Green Bay. Amundson said hunters should be aware of a 500-acre refuge that is marked at the mouth of the river.

The diverse habitat at Peshtigo Harbor offers hunters every-thing from waterfowl to white-tailed deer. Besides being a nest-ing grounds for wood ducks and mallards, it also attracts good numbers of migrat-ing waterfowl.

Hunters who seek puddle ducks and geese can also find success by jump-shooting or float-hunting the area's sloughs and the Peshtigo River.

About half of the almost 6,000-acre area is woodlands, Amundson said. Sportsmen who aren't inter-ested in pursuing game with webbed feet have plenty of acreage to seek out upland game. Amundson said the area holds a good local population of ruffed grouse and woodcock. Aspen areas along wetland edges often provide likely hiding spots for these birds. Woodcock will often choose wetter areas than partridge.

Peshtigo Harbor is also popular with deer hunters. With its mix of

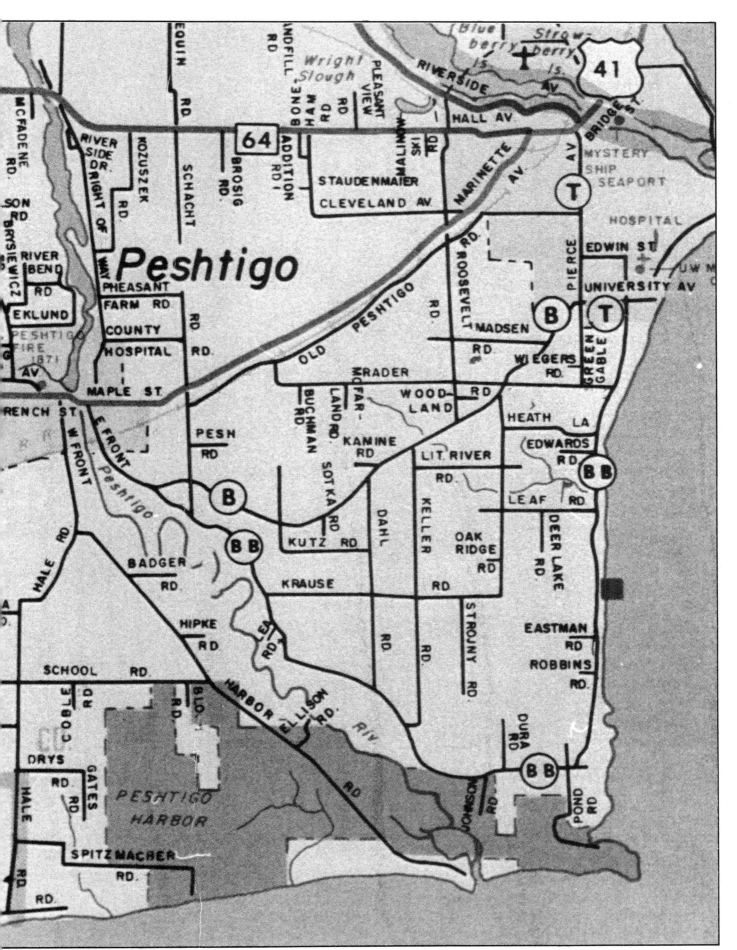

Peshtigo Harbor is popular with waterfowlers because the area features a variety of wetlands for duck produc- *tion and migratory flights.*

woodlands and wetlands, Peshtigo Harbor offers plenty of deer habitat. And Marinette County, overall, has made a name for itself in recent years for the high numbers and quality of its deer. Antlerless quotas were high during the late 1980s and early 1990s, and some nice racks are consistently taken from the area.

Archery and firearms hunters use the area, but hunting pressure is especially high during the first weekend of the gun season, Amundson said. However, it tends to drop off as the season progresses.

When the first snows of winter blanket the area, hunters can hit the brushy cover at Peshtigo Harbor in search of cottontail rabbits. Also, the area's marshy habitat offers good conditions for raccoons, although the animals are not pursued as much as they once were.

Access to the Peshtigo Harbor property is easy if you use County Trunk BB, which runs along northern part of the area's eastern half.

Nicolet National Forest

FOREST AND VILAS
COUNTIES

*f hunting holds more for you than simply stalking and bagging game, the Nicolet National Forest might be what you're ooking for in a perfect hunting site. More than 670,000 acres of ational forest land lie within the icolet's boundaries. Further, the tal acreage within the Nicolet's oundaries exceeds 900,000, includ-ng some state, county, tribal and rivate lands.

This vast forest sports a variety f northern Wisconsin vegetation nd wildlife habitat. Mature hard-ood forests, aspen plots, tamarack wamps, wetlands, uplands, lakes, vers and beaver ponds are scat-ered throughout the property. hite-tailed deer, ruffed grouse, oodcock, waterfowl, snowshoe are, varmints and squirrels are all ommon.

The Nicolet covers portions of six ounties: Vilas, Forest, Oneida, lorence, Oconto and Langlade. lthough each county offers its own nique recreational opportunities, his chapter will focus on Forest nd Vilas counties, basically the orest's northwestern portion.

Hunters visiting the Nicolet must o their homework. Because the roperty is so vast, finding the right rpe of habitat and cover for differ-nt game species requires a sharp ye and a good pair of walking oots.

Tony Rinaldi, forest biologist, aid the Vilas County portion of the icolet features sandy soils and few etland areas. Traveling east, how-ver, heavier soils become more ommon. The Forest County portion eatures more wetland areas. ypically, the forest vegetation ncludes aspen woods and some ardwood stands. In addition, scat-ered forest openings provide forage lants for wildlife.

TRAVEL GUIDE

NEAREST SERVICE CENTER: Eagle River.
LODGING: There are scores of lodging opportunities in the Eagle River area.
SPORTS SHOP OR HUNTING LICENSE OUTLET: Eagle Sports, 702 Wall St., Eagle River, (715) 479-8804.
HOSPITAL OR EMERGENCY MEDICAL CLINIC: Eagle River Memorial Hospital, 201 Hospital Road, Eagle River, (715) 479-7411.
EMERGENCY VETERINARY CLINIC: Eagle River Animal Hospital, 1720 Highway 45 North, Eagle River, (715) 479-7090.
AUTO REPAIR OR TOWING: Auto and Tire Clinic, 518 W. Pine St., Eagle River, (715) 479-9185. D&S Mobil, 223 S. Railroad St., Eagle River, (715) 479-2650. Eagle River Firestone-Mufflers Unlimited, 126 E. Division St., Eagle River, (715) 479-6737. Lakeland Motor Sales Inc. 1150 E. Wall St., Eagle River, (715) 479-4401.

Hunters visiting the Nicolet National Forest must do their homework. Because the property is so vast, finding the right type of habitat and cover for differ-ent game species requires a sharp eye and a good pair of walking boots.

Deer are probably the most popu-lar game species in the Nicolet, Rinaldi said. Deer numbers have been good throughout the forest, and the variety of thick cover and the area's large acreage give the animals numerous escape routes and hiding places.

Archery hunters make good use of the forest, Rinaldi said. And, since there is so much forest to use, the pressure is spread out, offering a quality hunt.

The forest sees substantially more hunting pressure during the November firearms season. Typically, the area south of Highway 70 gets more pressure

than the area to the north. However, deer numbers in both areas are similar.

Walking trails and roads provide good access to much of the forest. But access in some areas is diffi-cult. Also, the Nicolet's big blocks of land might intimidate some hunters, but sportsmen who have a compass and a good set of legs can outdistance the crowds.

The forest has several developed campgrounds, and camping is per-mitted throughout the area. Deer hunters will often make use of these opportunities by spending the season in a trailer or tent close to the area they hunt.

Coyotes are hunted throughout

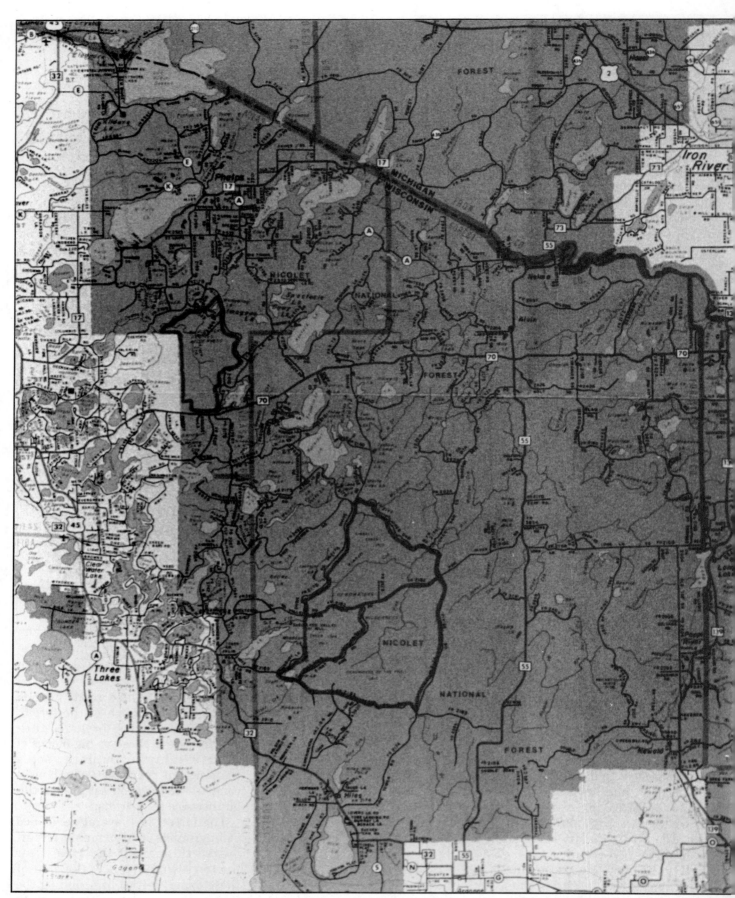

Nicolet National Forest, northwest. Detailed maps of the Nicolet National Forest are available at the main office in Rhinelander or district offices in Eagle River, Florence, Laona and Lakewood. They are also available by writing to Nicolet National Forest, 68 S. Stevens St., Rhinelander, WI 54501 or calling (715)-362-1300.

Patrick Durkin

Deer are probably the most popular game species in the Nicolet. Deer numbers have been good throughout the forest, and the variety of thick cover and the area's large acreage give the animals numerous escape routes and hiding places.

he forest, but deer hunters should ake note that the Nicolet holds ome timber wolves. Rinaldi said o packs are established, but lone volves travel through the area very year. Remember, these big redators are protected. Coyote unting season in the northern ortion of Wisconsin is closed during the firearms deer season to nsure wolves aren't shot accidenally.

With healthy stands of aspen cattered throughout the forest, rouse and woodcock hunters can lave good shooting in the Nicolet.

Walking trails south of Highway 0 provide good starting points for pland bird hunters. When the opulation cycle is up, good num-

bers of ruffed grouse reside in the forest. An aspen cutting program in the forest ensures new growth and a good age-mix of trees, which benefits the birds.

Woodcock nest in spots through the forest, and migrating birds also use the area. This migratory flight typically hits its peak around mid-October in much of Wisconsin, but may come earlier to northern areas, such as Nicolet.

Nicolet can also offer some duck hunting opportunities. Local ducks are present on some of the area's smaller lakes, streams and beaver ponds. Rinaldi said hunters can get some action early in the season, but these areas are known to burn out quickly.

The shorelines of most of the larger lakes in the Nicolet are mainly privately owned, Rinaldi said.

The forest is also known for its snowshoe hare hunting. These big bunnies prefer swampy areas where tamarack, cedar or aspen are present.

Hares don't receive a great deal of hunting pressure, Rinaldi said, so quality hunts are easily had.

Gray squirrels are also present in areas with mature oak stands. However, the squirrels receive little hunting pressure.

15

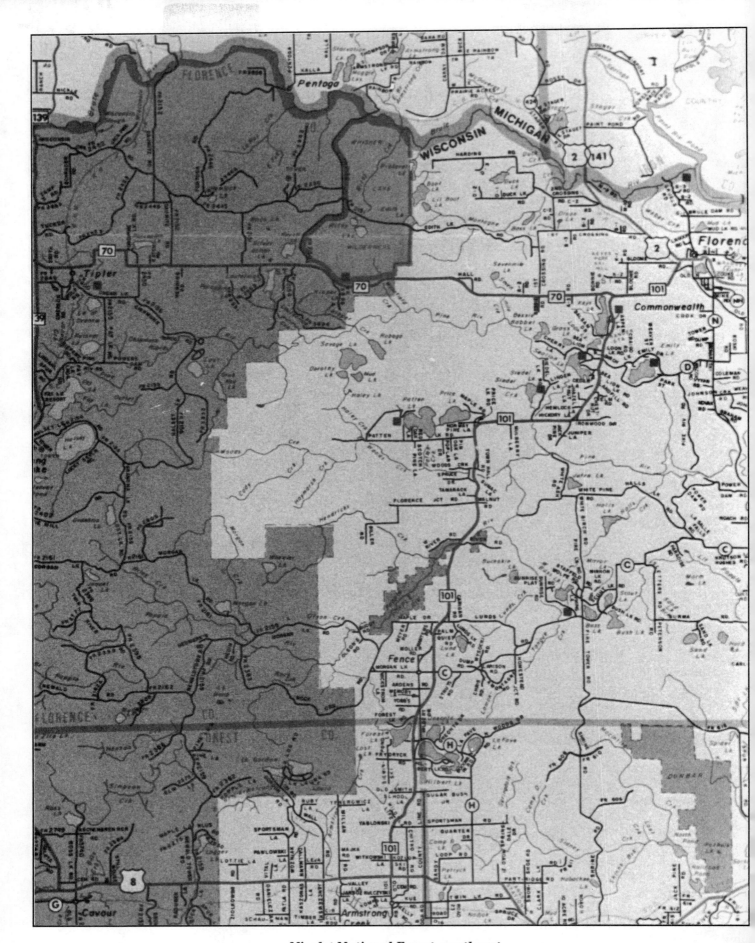

Nicolet National Forest, northeast

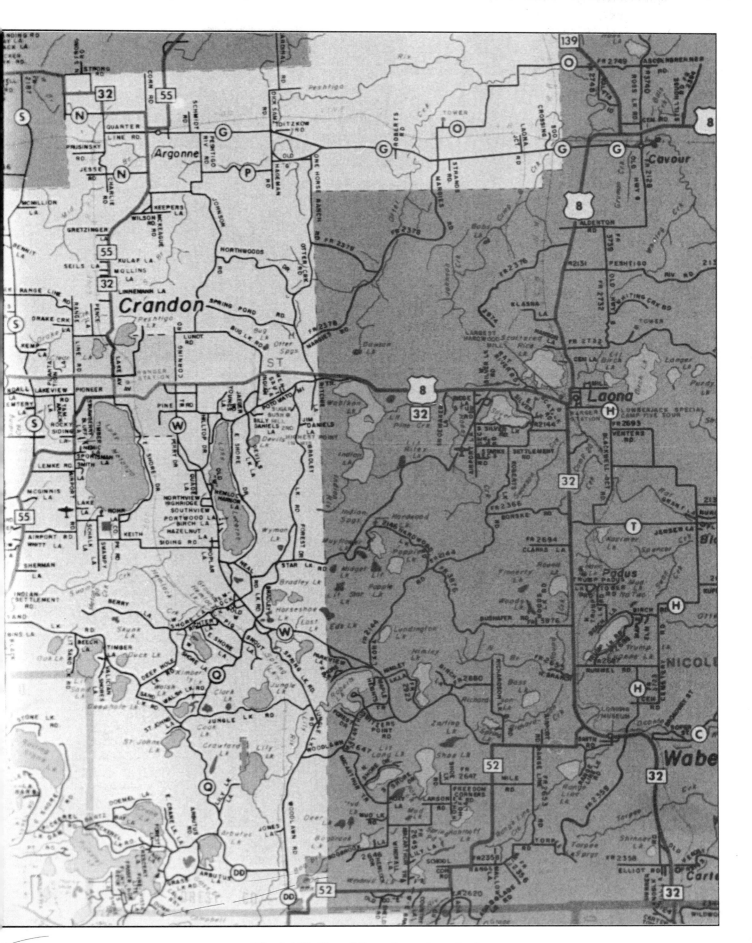

Nicolet National Forest, west central

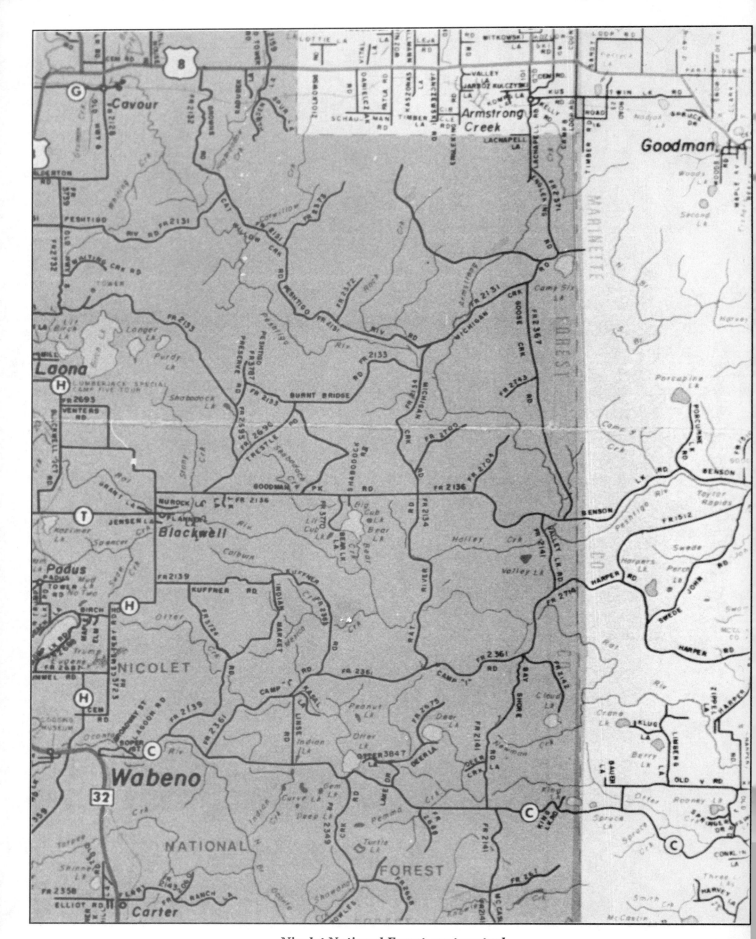

Nicolet National Forest, east central

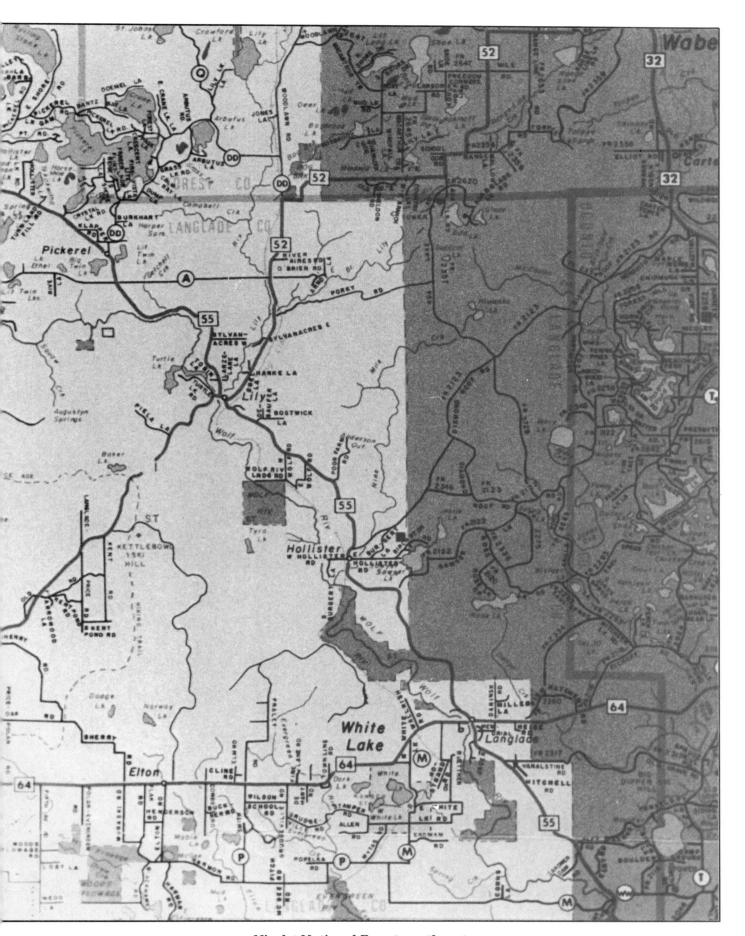

Nicolet National Forest, southwest

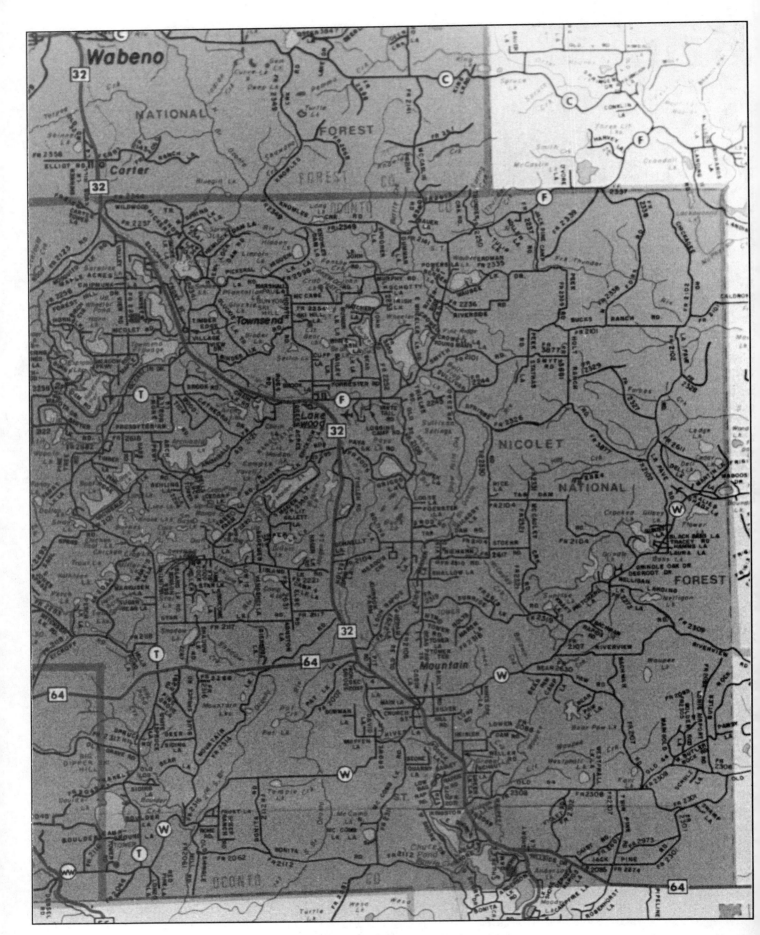

Nicolet National Forest, southeast

20

Brule River State Forest

DOUGLAS COUNTY

If you enjoy hunting northern Wisconsin, you can't get much more north than this. The 47,000-acre Brule River State Forest begins at the mouth of the famous Bois Brule River and follows its course southward for miles, providing sportsmen some of the finest hunting and fishing opportunities Wisconsin offers.

As with many Northern public hunting grounds, Brule River's most popular game species is the white-tailed deer. The forest offers a variety of habitat types and heavy cover for the animals.

Bruce Bacon, DNR wildlife manager, said the forest's southern portion is mainly jack pine, scrub oak and aspen, while the northern portion features some clay soils and boreal forests.

"The whole area is basically a big deer yard," Bacon said. Naturally, that means hunting opportunities are very good in years with early winters. It also means the area attracts a good share of hunters during the firearms season.

One of the keys to success at Brule River is to focus on the thick cover provided through much of the forest, Bacon said. Hunters seem to key on these areas because they attract whitetails during the winter. While many deer are content to spend their springs and summers in surrounding agricultural lands, they head for the thick stuff as temperatures fall and the snow piles up.

"That's what we have and it's what they want," Bacon said. "We have some super-heavy cover for deer."

The forest holds good populations of deer, Bacon said, and it holds good-sized bucks.

Because many sportsmen know the Brule River State Forest to be a

TRAVEL GUIDE

NEAREST SERVICE CENTER: Iron River.
LODGING: Lumbermen's Inn Motel Restaurant and Lounge, Box 127, Iron River, (715) 372-4515. Rustic Roost, Highway 2, Iron River, (715) 372-4426.
SPORTS SHOP OR HUNTING LICENSE OUTLET: Mr. T's Sport and Recreation, Iron River, (715) 372-4356.
HOSPITAL OR EMERGENCY MEDICAL CLINIC: Medical Associates, Ashland, (715) 682-2358.
EMERGENCY VETERINARY CLINIC: G. Wilson, Ashland, (715) 682-4199.
AUTO REPAIR OR TOWING: A&L Standard Service, Iron River, (715) 372-4700.

good spot during the firearms season, hunters may have to seek isolated patches to escape heavy pressure.

Although gun hunting pressure can be high, the bow season offers hunters an opportunity to chase whitetails in relative solitude, Bacon said. Few spots in the forest attract concentrated hunting pressure during archery season.

Ruffed grouse and woodcock are also abundant, especially in the forest lands that lie south of Highway 2, Bacon said. This region's scrub oak, aspen and jack pine areas can hold good numbers of birds.

Because the forest cover can be so heavy, grouse hunters must scout ahead and work for their birds, Bacon said. Likely areas include patches of aspen regrowth. The forest has an aspen cutting program, which helps ensure a good mix of tree age-classes.

The Brule River State Forest offers a variety of habitat types and thick cover, which provides for healthy populations of white-tailed deer, black bears and game birds.

Woodcock hunting can be excellent, Bacon said. Several potholes on the property feature alder and aspen edges, a traditional hot spot for timberdoodles.

The forest also holds local birds, Bacon said. These birds can provide good action for those who like to run their dogs in September. Also, some years bring a good flight of migrant woodcock. Because the area is so far north, the main flight might arrive earlier than many hunters expect.

The North country isn't often noted for duck and goose hunting, but Bacon said the Brule River Forest can provide good waterfowling for those who take the time to pursue them. Bacon said some birds fly up and down the Brule River itself, and the water holds some ducks. However, very few people really attempt to hunt it.

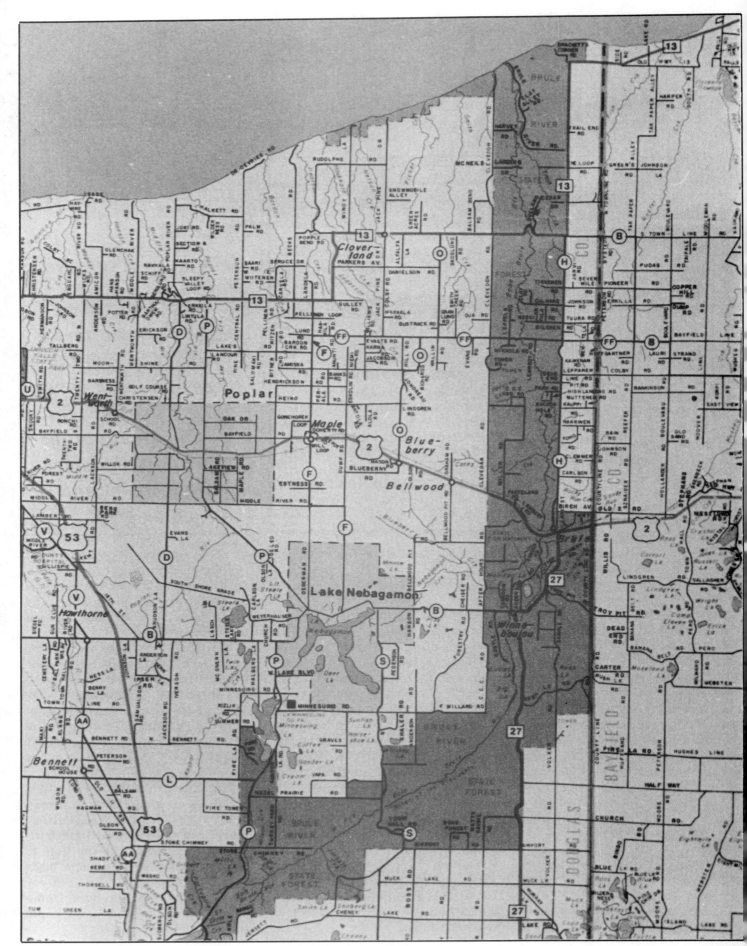

Leonard Lee Rue III

Though the Brule River State Forest is most noted for its excellent deer hunting, black bears are also common and offer hunters another form of big game hunting.

The forest also has about 20 small wetland impoundments north of Highway 2, Bacon said. These areas can offer some good puddle-duck hunting. In addition, hunters can get a crack at Canada geese occasionally. The DNR also does some management for short grasses, which geese will feed upon.

Squirrels are an underutilized game resource in the forest, Bacon said. Some good areas for squirrels can be found in the mature hardwood stands north of Highway 2.

The forest's thick cover and wet areas also make for excellent snowshoe hare habitat. Hare populations were down in the early 1990s, Bacon said, but even then hunters had some success with them. Swamps, conifer/aspen mixes, and old fields reverting to woods offer good hare hunting.

With plenty of small mammals around, fox and coyotes are abundant in the area. Bacon said some hunters come here to pursue these predators.

Black bears are also common throughout the forest, providing recreation for both bait and dog hunters.

Rusk County Forest

The Rusk County Forest provides hunters in the Ladysmith area with first-class opportunities for deer and upland birds, and also features unique natural beauty.

The forest covers about 85,000 acres, said Frank Vanecek, DNR wildlife biologist. The land is broken into three major blocks, the largest of which is the 50,000-acre Blue Hills portion.

The forest lands offer a variety of wildlife habitat, Vanecek said. The Blue Hills feature steep topography and stands of mature hardwoods, as well as second-growth areas of aspen. Other parts of the forest are comprised of flatter terrain, wetlands, and aspen and alder cover.

Rusk County is popular with deer hunters, and hunting pressure increased during the late 1980s and early 1990s because of high antlerless quotas in the area, Vanecek said. However, hunter concentrations are expected to drop as the herd is brought back into line with its habitat.

The county forest lands still feature good, solid deer populations. Deer are scattered throughout the different habitat types, Vanecek said. Early-season archery hunters can hedge their bets by hunting near forest openings planted with forage plants such as clover. Also, years that feature good acorn crops can draw concentrations of deer into mature oak areas.

Hunters have a good shot at bagging older bucks on the county forest lands, Vanecek said. The area holds decent numbers of older, larger animals. However, the rugged terrain of the Blue Hills and thick cover elsewhere give these animals the advantage.

Access to most of the county forest lands is good, Vanecek said. The

RUSK COUNTY

The Rusk County Forest covers about 85,000 acres, and is divided into three major blocks, the largest of which is the 50,000-acre Blue Hills portion. The Blue Hills feature steep topography and stands of mature hardwoods, as well as second-growth areas of aspen.

TRAVEL GUIDE

NEAREST SERVICE CENTER: Ladysmith.

LODGING: Davis Motel, 820 W. Miner Ave., Ladysmith, (715) 532-5576. Best Western-El Rancho Motel, W8490 Flambeau Ave., Ladysmith, (715) 532-6666. Evergreen Motel, 1201 W. Lake Ave., Ladysmith, (715) 532-5611. Hi-Way 8 Motel, 420 E. Edgewood Ave., Ladysmith, (715) 532-3346.

SPORTS SHOP OR HUNTING LICENSE OUTLET: T&T Sport Marine, W8646 Highway 8 West, Ladysmith, (715) 532-7422. James Sport Shop, 206 W. 2 N., Ladysmith, (715) 532-6016.

HOSPITAL OR EMERGENCY MEDICAL CLINIC: Rusk County Memorial Hospital, 900 W. College Ave., Ladysmith, (715) 532-5561.

EMERGENCY VETERINARY CLINIC: Information unavailable.

AUTO REPAIR OR TOWING: Jim's Mobile, 300 W. Lake Ave., Ladysmith, (715) 532-7885. Goffin Oil Co., 407 W. Lake Ave., Ladysmith, (715) 532-7866. Ladysmith Standard Station, 112 W. Lake Ave., Ladysmith, (715) 532-7291. Bill Stearns Motors, 215 E. Worden Ave., Ladysmith, (715) 532-3333.

forest is accessible through a good system of county and town roads, as well as some trails.

Grouse and woodcock hunters will want to focus on the many aspen areas throughout the forest. Local and migrating woodcock are also common.

Vanecek said upland bird hunting pressure increased during the late 1980s and early 1990s. Nonetheless, scouting will help hunters find areas where they can pursue birds with little competition.

Black bears are common on Rusk County Forest lands, Vanecek said. Hunting opportunities for bruin are good. The eastern portion seems to be the preferred spot. During the record-setting 1992 bear season, Rusk County Forest hunters bagged some large bears, including animals in the 400- to 500-pound range.

Hound hunting for bears is popular in this portion of the state, Vanecek said. Bait hunters also use the area, but this technique seems to be more popular in areas farther north.

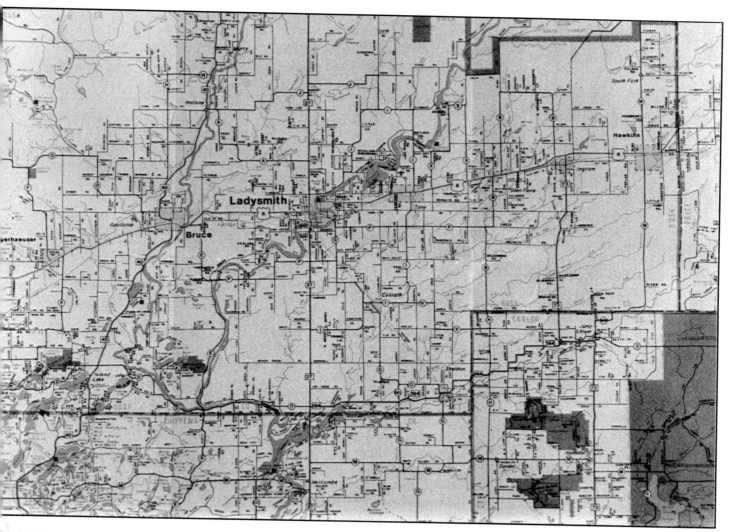

Rusk County Forest land is scattered across the county. A map showing the public land is available by writing to Paul Teska, Rusk County Forestry Dept., 311 Miner Ave., Ladysmith, WI 54848, or by calling (715)-532-2113.

Mature oak stands in the Blue Hills area offer some good hunting for gray squirrels, Vanecek said. Not many people pursue the animals in northern Wisconsin, so competition is light.

Snowshoe hares also offer small-game hunters a chance for some shooting. Hares in the county forest lands seem to prefer new aspen and clear-cut areas. Tamarack swamps are also a likely bet. Hare season is open year-round in Wisconsin, but many gunners wait until the animals' coats start to change from brown to white — usually in November — before pursuing them. In years of low snowfalls, hunting the white hares against a drab background can greatly increase success rates.

Waterfowling opportunities in the Rusk County Forest are limited, Vanecek said. Beaver ponds throughout the area offer early shooting for mallards and wood ducks, but that's usually the extent of the forest's duck hunting opportunities.

Pershing Wildlife Area

TAYLOR COUNTY

The Pershing Wildlife Area, located in northwestern Taylor County, covers 7,400 acres. The property is comprised of two units, giving waterfowlers good chances at ducks and geese. In addition, deer hunters will find whitetails in abundance.

But it's grouse — both ruffed and sharptail — that make the area unique.

Pershing is one of the few areas in Wisconsin that features sharptail grouse hunting. About 3,000 acres of the property consist of brush prairie, which is managed for the birds. The DNR uses controlled burns to maintain sharptail habitat.

Frank Vanecek, DNR wildlife biologist, said the sharptail population at Pershing is stable, and consisted of about 200 birds in the early 1990s.

Still, few sportsmen pursue sharptails. Their numbers are simply too few to attract the same amount of interest as more common species. However, Vanecek said a few hunters carry on the sport simply for the unique recreation and tradition it supplies.

To an outside observer, the hunt's final reward might seem small. The state's sharptail season is only three weeks long, and the bag limit is one bird per day. Sharptail hunting involves lots of walking, and the birds often flush wildly.

However, sharptail chasers will tell you that the hunt — not the kill — is the finest aspect of pursuing these birds. And every one bagged can be counted as a trophy. Sharptails also attract a great deal of attention in spring, when they perform their courtship dances.

The sharptail's abundant cousin, the ruffed grouse, is another star performer at Pershing. The area

---

TRAVEL GUIDE

NEAREST SERVICE CENTER: Medford.

LODGING: Americinn Motel, located on Highway 13, 1-800-634-3444. Malibu Inn, Highway 13, 1-800-676-3995. Royal 8 Motel, Highway 13, (715) 748-5040.

SPORTS SHOP OR HUNTING LICENSE OUTLET: Z's Sport Shop, 1281 N. 8th St., Medford, (715) 748-2855. Ben Franklin, 142 S. Main St., Medford, (715) 748-4770. Holiday Station, 442 S. 8th St., Medford, (715) 748-9924. Taylor County Courthouse, Roger Emmerich, county clerk, 224 S. Second St., Medford, (715) 748-1460.

HOSPITAL OR EMERGENCY MEDICAL CLINIC: Memorial Hospital of Taylor County, emergency room located at 135 S. Gibson St., (715) 748-8100.

EMERGENCY VETERINARY CLINIC: Medford Vet Clinic, 233 S. 8th St., Medford, (715) 748-2341.

AUTO REPAIR OR TOWING: H&H Motors, 312 S. Wisconsin Ave., Medford, (715) 748-4969 or (715) 748-2745. Krug's West Side Service, 549 Billings St., Medford, (715) 748-3194 or 748-4083.

The Pershing Wildlife Area in northwestern Taylor County gives waterfowlers good chances at ducks, geese and deer. But it's grouse — both ruffed and sharptail — that make the area unique.

---

features about 3,000 acres of predominately aspen habitat for the birds. Vanecek said the DNR performs extensive clear-cutting to obtain a good mosaic of tree types for the birds. The management emphasis in these areas is focused directly on ruffed grouse.

The success of these efforts, which began about 1987, has been difficult to gauge because of the grouse's natural population cycles, Vanecek said. When the cycle is up, however, birds will thrive in the quality habitat.

Woodcock also use the are: Vanecek said, and many of th ruffed grouse management pra tices also benefit these birds.

Pershing can offer hunters top quality northern Wisconsin duc and goose hunting, Vanecek sai The property features many acr of wetlands, including numerou impoundments and beaver ponds.

The area produces a good numb of local ducks and Canada gees Vanecek said. The main duc species are mallards, blue-winge teal and ringbills. As the fall migra tion progresses, Northern ducks – mainly puddlers — will also use th area heavily.

Vanecek said much of the wate fowl hunting is done over decoys

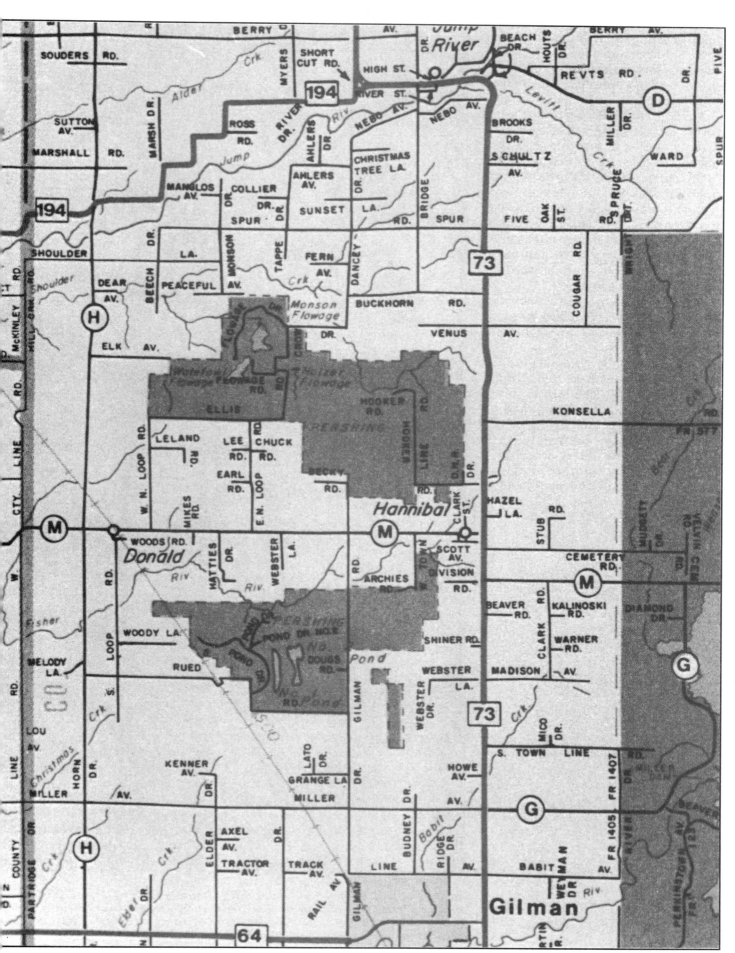

jump-shooting. Many hunters park their vehicles and then walk into the area, but thick cattails and bog in the wetland areas can make for rough going.

A refuge covers the northwestern corner of Pershing's northern unit. This is closed to hunting except during the firearms deer season.

Of course, white-tailed deer are also abundant at Pershing. Vanecek said good populations exist throughout the different types of habitat. Firearms hunters can improve their odds by hunting game trails on the edges of woods and open grassy areas.

Access to some areas of Pershing can be difficult, Vanecek said, especially lowland and wetland spots.

Both units of Pershing Wildlife Area can be entered by using County Trunk M. The larger unit lies directly north of the road, while the smaller unit is directly south. Town roads running north and south provide direct access to the lands; many hunters simply pull off the roads and park, and then walk into the area.

Grouse — both ruffed and sharptail — make the Pershing Wildlife Area unique. Pershing is one of the few areas in Wisconsin that features sharptail grouse hunting. About 3,000 acres of the property consist of brush prairie, which is managed for the birds.

Flambeau River State Forest

SAWYER COUNTY

When you visit Flambeau River State Forest, it may seem as if you've walked into a picture post card.

Without exaggeration, the area is simply one of Wisconsin's natural treasures. The 88,000-acre forest is home to the wild Flambeau River, northern wilderness and abundant wildlife. Sight-seers and hunters alike will find something in the forest to their liking.

The property, which lies mainly in Sawyer County but also covers portions of Rusk and Price counties, is basically a northern upland forest. Much of the vegetation is maple and basswood trees, remnant oak stands, aspen stands and conifer swamps.

The northern and southern forks of the Flambeau River run through the forest. The river features some excellent sections of whitewater rapids. The forest also holds several smaller lakes and creeks.

Cliff Wiita, the DNR's area wildlife manager, said aspen is the key to the forest's hunting success. Quite simply, new-growth stands of aspen attract wildlife.

Aspen stands are mainly associated with woodcock and ruffed grouse hunting. Wiita said Flambeau is no exception. A timber management program ensures there is plenty of diversity in aspen age classes.

Grouse are focused in areas of aspen. Wiita said when the grouse population cycle is up, the area offers good hunting. The cycle was near its low point in 1992, but the forest's quality habitat provides birds excellent cover when the cycle rises.

Woodcock production was down in the early 1990s, Wiita said, mainly because of harsh spring weather. However, local birds can

TRAVEL GUIDE

NEAREST SERVICE CENTER: Park Falls.

LODGING: There are numerous lodging opportunities available in the Park Falls area. The Park Falls Area Chamber of Commerce lists almost 30.

SPORTS SHOP OR HUNTING LICENSE OUTLET: South Side True Value, Park Falls, (715) 762-2402. Dave's Fletching and Archery, Park Falls, (715) 762-2272. Scully's Inc., Park Falls, (715) 762-3363. Bridge Bait, Highway 13 South, (715) 762-4108.

HOSPITAL OR EMERGENCY MEDICAL CLINIC: Flambeau Medical Center, Park Falls, (715) 762-2484.

EMERGENCY VETERINARY CLINIC: Park Falls Pet Clinic, Highway 13 North, Park Falls, (715) 762-2079. Phillips Veterinary Service, W6891 Liberty Lane, Phillips, (715) 339-2605.

AUTO REPAIR OR TOWING: Information unavailable.

The 88,000-acre Flambeau River State Forest is home to the wild Flambeau River, abundant wildlife and north-country wilderness. Sightseers and hunters alike will find something in the forest to their liking.

still provide early-season shooting.

The area also sees migratory flights. When the "flight" is in, hunting can be excellent. Wiita said the top spots to hunt are aspen areas, especially those in or around wetland areas.

Upland bird hunting received a great deal of promotion in the late 1980s and early 1990s, Wiita said, and its popularity rose substantially.

However, the top hunting draw for the area is still the white-tailed deer. Flambeau offers good deer habitat and a healthy population of animals. The area saw an increase in hunting pressure in recent years,

Wiita said, mainly because of high quota levels in the early 1990s. However, hunting pressure will likely return to low levels when the herd is at population goals.

As hunting pressure drops, Flambeau could regain its reputation as one of the state's top trophy buck areas. Wiita said he expects isolated areas — ones that hunters need to work at to reach — will again provide high-quality buck hunting opportunities.

Black bear hunting is also popular in the forest. The number of hunters using bait or hounds is split about 50-50. Bait hunters usually experience higher success rates, but the Sawyer County area

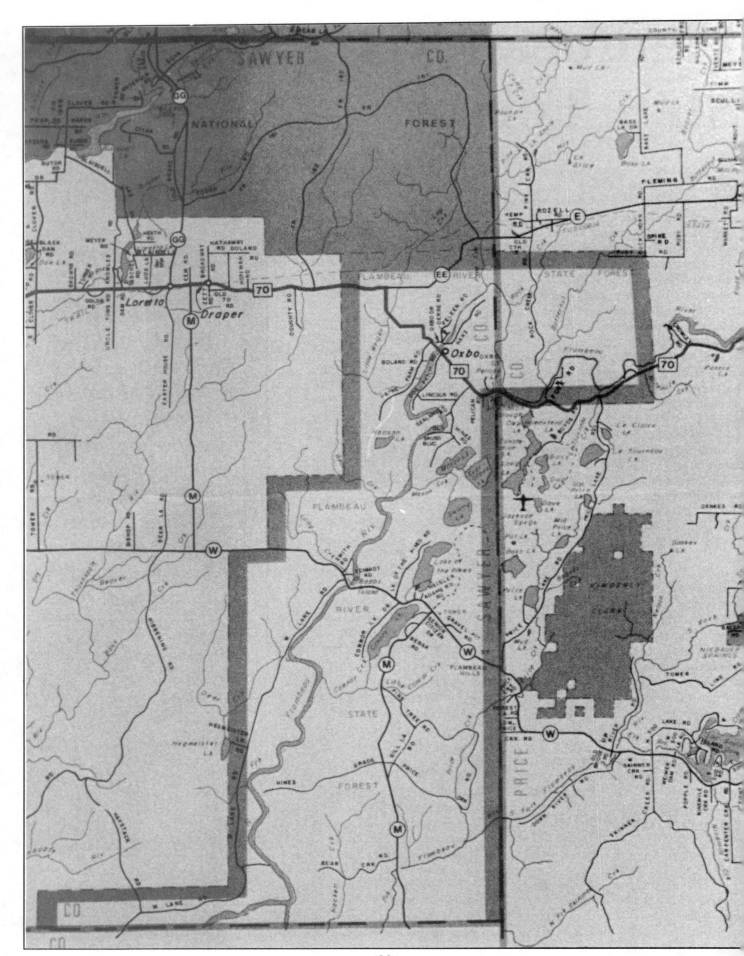

is traditionally a stronghold for hound hunters. Wiita said this may be because of the huge amount of public land that's available to dog hunters in the area.

Hound hunters also pursue predator species such as bobcats, coyotes and fox. The area features a high coyote population, and there are more bobcats in the area than most people realize. Red fox aren't common in the timbered areas, but can be found along edge areas. Wiita said winter predator hunting is a big activity in the forest, and varmint chasers usually experience good success.

The forest's aspen areas are also home to another popular northern small game species: snowshoe hare. Wiita said hares zero in on aspen areas. Many sportsmen make hare hunting a top winter activity.

The forest offers some duck hunting, but Wiita said they are limited. Waterfowl habitat on the property is scarce. Most of the duck hunting is in the form of jump-shooting along the rivers and creeks.

Access to the forest is good, and the area offers several campgrounds.

A timber management program at the Flambeau River State Forest ensures there is plenty of diversity in aspen age classes.

Northern Highland State Forest

VILAS COUNTY

No matter what aspect of northern Wisconsin hunting you enjoy most, the Northern Highland-American Legion State Forest in Vilas and Oneida counties holds something for you.

This area is actually two state properties: The Northern Highland State Forest and the American Legion State Forest, and it covers a 200,000-plus-acre chunk of prime land.

DNR wildlife manager Chet Botwinski said the area is sort of a cross-section of typical North-country habitats. It ranges from light sandy soils with jack pine to heavier soils and hardwoods. It consists mainly of a rolling, pitted outwash, dotted with small lakes and bogs.

The forest is highly recreation-oriented. Access to most portions of the property is very good, and the forests draw quite a few people at all times of the year.

Not surprisingly, deer hunting is the major attraction, Botwinski said. The forests see some of the highest hunter densities in northern Wisconsin during the gun season. Nonetheless, the area's great mix of habitat and its large size can make for quality hunts for those willing to scout and get away from the crowds.

The entire mix of habitat types in the forest — which include mature oak stands and different year-classes of aspen stands — make for all-around good deer populations. The whitetails benefit from the mix. Of course, some areas are better than others.

Two deer management units in the northern part of the area, units 36 and 37, have some of the highest winter deer population goals in northern Wisconsin — about 25 per square mile of habitat.

Generally, bucks in the forest are killed at a fairly high rate, Botwinski said. However, the excellent escape routes and safe havens provided by the forest result in many bucks living longer.

The area also features a great deal of water, which takes many forms. Lakes are numerous in the forests, and the Wisconsin and Manitowish rivers flow through different parts of the properties. As a result, the forests feature some of the best waterfowling opportunities available in northern Wisconsin.

With all these waters, the area holds relatively good breeding populations of ducks, Botwinski said. The area isn't on par with the Mississippi River for waterfowling, but it can be good. The main breeding species are mallards, wood ducks, teal and black ducks. Most area lakes have resident populations of ducks. About six or seven lakes hold good stands of wild rice, which attract migrating waterfowl and offer a natural staging area for birds preparing to head south in fall. These bodies of water probably provide the most consistent hunting.

Also, beaver ponds abound in the forests. Hunters can find good opportunities here, either in the

TRAVEL GUIDE

NEAREST SERVICE CENTER: Rhinelander.
LODGING: There are numerous lodging opportunities in the Rhinelander and Woodruff areas.
SPORTS SHOP OR HUNTING LICENSE OUTLET: Mel's Trading Post, 105 S. Brown St., Rhinelander.
HOSPITAL OR EMERGENCY MEDICAL CLINIC: Rhinelander Medical Center, 1040 Kable Ave., Rhinelander.
EMERGENCY VETERINARY CLINIC: Dunn Animal Hospital, in Sunrise Plaza on Lincoln St.
AUTO REPAIR OR TOWING: Gateway, 1911 N. Stevens St., Rhinelander. Shoeder's Auto Center, 2226 N. Stevens St.

The Northern Highland State Forest and the American Legion State Forest cover a 200,000-plus-acre chunk of prime land. These lands range from light sandy soils with jack pine to heavier soils and hardwoods.

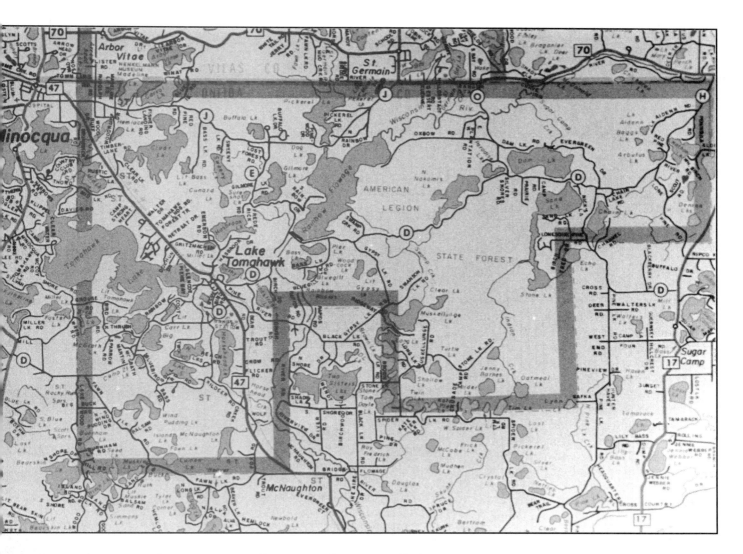

form of jump-shooting or decoy hunting for mallards and woodies.

Some of the larger lakes and flowages on the properties attract good flights of migrating diving ducks, Botwinski said. The main visitors are bluebills and ringbills.

The forests also sustain an active timber-cutting program, which makes for a healthy age-class mix of timber. Ruffed grouse are the main beneficiaries of this practice, and Botwinski said the forest features good grouse populations.

When the birds' population cycle is up, good hunting can be found throughout the properties. Hunters should scout the area to locate the best stands of aspen.

Woodcock hunting is somewhat spotty. Some woodcock are locally produced, but this area probably wouldn't rank with the North's true hot spots because it features lighter, sandier soils.

Hunters will occasionally hit some good concentrations of migrating birds. These migrators tend to disperse throughout the area, and seek out the best-quality habitat. Scattered drainage areas throughout the forest provide good hunting.

Snowshoe hares provide sportsmen with good winter hunting. Botwinski said the population is cyclic, and there haven't been great numbers of hares in the forests recently. However, people can still enjoy decent hare hunting in some areas.

Peshtigo Brook Wildlife Area

OCONTO COUNTY

Oconto County is well known for its upland bird hunting. And while its central characters may have changed, the Peshtigo Brook Wildlife Area is certainly among the top public bird hunting properties in the area.

The area, which covers about 2,100 acres in central Oconto County, features good grouse and woodcock habitat. Young aspen areas that border marshlands act as magnets for the birds. But this wasn't always the area's primary focus.

The DNR purchased most of the land in Peshtigo Brook during the 1950s. Originally, it was to be a management area for sharptail grouse, which were once common throughout the area. Within a decade, however, sharptails were essentially gone. The management focus then shifted to waterfowl, and impoundments were built. These plans were also abandoned when game managers found the area's light soils made it financially impractical to maintain the impoundments.

Today, the area resembles much of the other land in that part of the state. Hills slope down to marshy lowlands and into the Peshtigo Brook itself. The area features much forest land, including many stands of young alder and aspens.

Roger Amundson, DNR wildlife manager, said that means grouse and woodcock.

"It's a pretty popular upland game bird hunting area," he said. "The habitat is pretty good."

Grouse hunters know well the attraction that aspen holds for their favorite birds. Maintaining the young aspen areas at Peshtigo Brook is a big part of the property's management, Amundson said. Aspens are harvested periodically

to ensure that mature-forest tree species don't replace them. The DNR has used clear-cutting to regenerate the areas.

"And we will be doing some habitat work in the future with logging jobs," Amundson said. "They will be designed to improve the habitat for grouse."

The area also provides good woodcock hunting. Aspen and alder thickets — especially those that closely border moist lowland areas — offer birds an inviting spot.

Amundson said Peshtigo Brook sees good numbers of woodcock when "the flight is on." Conventional wisdom holds that this magical time is usually around mid-October, but experienced bird

chasers know it's best to occasionally check their hunting spots to when the migrants have arrived.

Peshtigo Brook usually produsome woodcock hatches each ye Amundson said, which mea hunters can get some shooting the area on opening day, insteawaiting until the leaves turn smgold.

The forest habitat also makes dandy deer hunting.

The area receives substant hunting pressure during firearms deer season, Amundsaid. Often, hunters who have treled to the area and can't find

TRAVEL GUIDE

NEAREST SERVICE CENTER: Oconto Falls.
LODGING: The Coachlight Motel, 248 N. Main St., Oconto Falls, (414) 846-3424. Mercier's Oconto Falls Hotel, 172 N. Main St., Oconto Falls, 846-2229.
SPORTS SHOP OR HUNTING LICENSE OUTLET: Magnin's Hardware, 167 N. Main St., 846-2711.
HOSPITAL OR EMERGENCY MEDICAL CLINIC: Community Memorial Hospital, 855 S. Main St., Oconto Falls, 846-3444.
EMERGENCY VETERINARY CLINIC: Falls Animal Health, 171 N. Franklin St., Oconto Falls, 846-3574. Dr. Paul Yatso, 204 Meadow Road, Oconto Falls, 846-4280.
AUTO REPAIR OR TOWING: Peterson Ford, 300 N. Main St., Oconto Falls, 846-2826. Jim Kane Chevrolet, 325 Van Buren St., Oconto Falls, 846-3211.

The Peshtigo Brook Wildlife Area, which covers about 2,100 acres in central Oconto County, features good grouse and woodcock habitat, which also is home to white-tailed deer. Young aspen areas that border marshlands act as wildlife magnets.

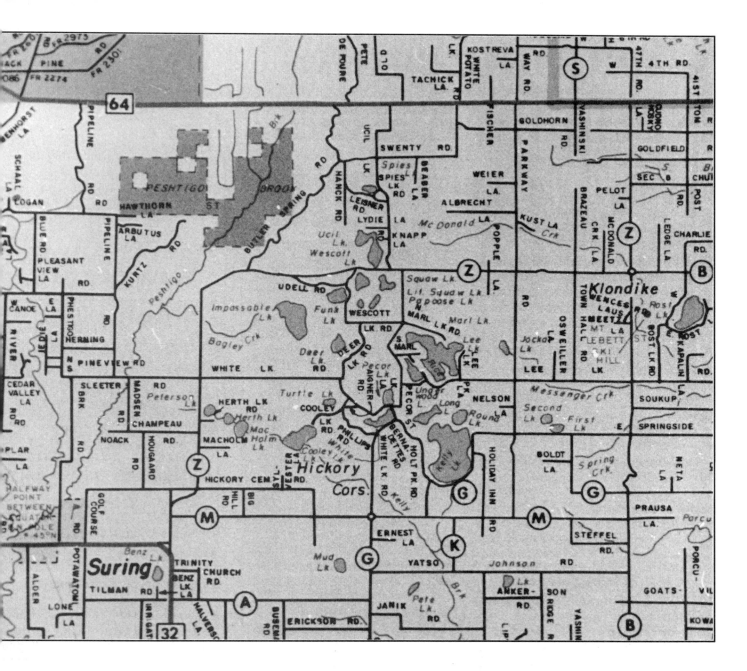

ate land to hunt on will end up in public areas such as Peshtigo Brook.

However, one plus — depending on your perspective — is that few roads border the property. Amundson said Peshtigo Brook is a fairly wild area. Hunters unafraid of a little walk can locate areas with little pressure.

Waterfowling opportunities at Peshtigo Brook are limited, Amundson said. The area also holds some beavers, and their dams can produce ponds or small spillways that attract birds. Also, wet autumns can result in standing water through lowland areas.

Because the area is relatively wild, Amundson said, it also is home to a few black bears and bobcats.

And although few people pursue them, predators are also common. Wet areas bordered by timber make for excellent raccoon habitat. Foxes and coyotes are also common.

Chequamegon National Forest, Washburn Unit

PRICE COUNTY

The Washburn Ranger District of the Chequamegon National Forest has one main attraction for sportsmen: Big white-tailed bucks.

Because of the forest's habitat, the area doesn't feature the numbers of deer — or deer hunters — like other areas in northern Wisconsin. But if you're willing to work for a wall-hanger, the Washburn unit might be willing to oblige.

Don Bilyeu, public affairs officer for the Chequamegon National Forest, said the Washburn unit — which covers about 150,000 acres — has different types of cover than the forest's other four ranger districts. The land is at higher elevations, so it has fewer wet areas than the other districts. Its rolling hills feature mainly sandy soils dotted with jack pine and oak barrens.

"It reminds me of the Western states," Bilyeu said. "You can see across vistas. It's not as brushy as other areas because of the nature of the vegetation."

Because of the district's habitat, the state once considered reintroducing elk into Wisconsin at the Washburn unit. That plan was abandoned, but hunters can still hope to see Wisconsin's equivalent of an elk rack — thick, wide, white-tailed deer antlers.

Deer populations aren't high, but the unit's habitat and large expanses of land are ideal for producing older, larger bucks. Part of this is because of the relatively light firearms hunting pressure, Bilyeu said. Because bucks stand a decent chance of surviving the November

TRAVEL GUIDE

NEAREST SERVICE CENTER: Washburn.
LODGING: Nohl's Mission Springs Resort, Route 3, Ashland, (715) 682-5014. Super 8, Harbor View Drive, Washburn, (715) 373-5671. Redwood Motel, 26 W. Bayfield St., Washburn, (715) 373-5512.
SPORTS SHOP OR HUNTING LICENSE OUTLET: Leinos Gas and Goods, 137 W. Bayfield St., Washburn, (715) 373-5722. Holiday Station, 606 Bayfield St., Washburn, (715) 373-2305. Langford Snyder Drugs, 128 W. Bayfield St., Washburn, (715) 373-5588.
HOSPITAL OR EMERGENCY MEDICAL CLINIC: Memorial Medical Center, 1615 Maple Lane, Ashland, (715) 682-4563.
EMERGENCY VETERINARY CLINIC: Bay Area Animal Hospital, Highway 13, Washburn, (715) 373-5474.
AUTO REPAIR OR TOWING: Frenchies Auto Repair, 115 W. Bayfield St., Washburn, (715) 373-5301. Ray's Automotive, 605 W. Bayfield St., Washburn, (715) 373-2669.

season, the area holds a good percentage of 3- to 5-year-old animals. With the right genetics and nutrition, these deer are capable of producing racks most hunters only dream of.

"This area does not get the hunting pressure you get farther south," Bilyeu said. "But we do grow them big.

If you're willing to work for a wall-hanger of a buck, the Washburn unit of the Chequamegon National Forest might be willing to oblige.

"Just being in that area is nice. You're up out of the swamps, with no bugs, and you can see across valley or up onto a hillside."

Since the district's land and vegetation differ from many other areas in the region, hunters should be prepared to do some pre-season scouting to locate deer. The wide open nature of the country won't offer as many likely looking spots for whitetails as an area that features thicker cover.

By locating food plots and trails, sportsmen can hedge their bets for deer hunting. Scouting and observing deer behavior will also give hunters an added edge after opening day.

One factor in the deer hunter's favor is the wide-open visibility the area provides. Sportsmen shouldn't have trouble finding good shooting lanes, and whitetails will be easier to see than in thick lowland or aspen areas.

Bilyeu pointed out that dee

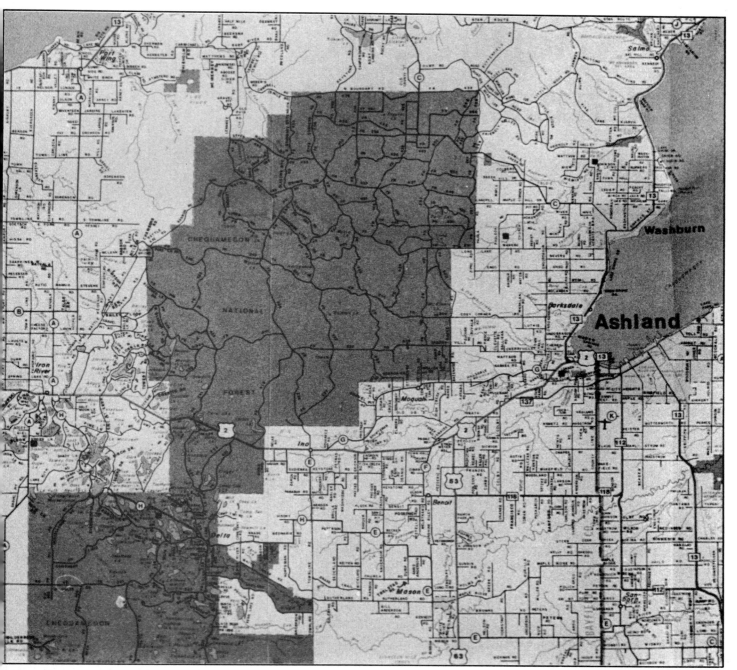

Detailed maps of the Washburn Unit of the Chequamegon National Forest are available by writing *or calling the Park Falls Ranger Station, 1170 4th Ave. South, Park Falls, WI 54552, (715) 762-2461.*

hunters in the Washburn unit or any other public hunting areas are prohibited from building permanent blinds or tree stands for deer hunting.

"We don't want to appear to be bad hosts, but it must be adhered to because of safety factors," he said. "We have many people who come up and build deer blinds or tree stands in the forest. That is illegal. They will be cited."

Grouse, woodcock or snowshoe hare hunters won't find too many opportunities in the Washburn Ranger District. However, Bilyeu said the district's wet areas could produce some waterfowl hunting.

"Potholes up in that area could hold some lost migratory ducks," he said. "It's something to check out on a fall weekend when you have nothing else to do."

Chequamegon National Forest, Medford Unit

TAYLOR COUNTY

The Medford Ranger District of the Chequamegon National Forest features more than enough land for anyone to get lost in.

The 123,384-acre district, located in Taylor County, is one of five ranger districts in this forest. The Medford unit is known mainly for its many small outwash and pothole areas, and also for the fine upland bird hunting it produces each autumn.

Don Bilyeu, public affairs officer with the Chequamegon, said the Medford unit's reputation for game birds extends beyond Wisconsin's borders.

"It's actually quite a popular area for bird hunters from the South," he said. "We get a lot of folks who come up to hunt birds. They bring their big pickups and their dog kennels and their dollars to come up and spend a week or two hunting ruffed grouse."

The Chequamegon has plenty of birds to go around, Bilyeu said. Although hunters should call ahead to check on the grouse's cycle, the Medford area is hard to beat for bird hunting. The district has an active timber harvest program throughout its area. The cuttings vary in size from small wildlife openings of an acre or less to much larger aspen-harvest areas. As aspen areas regenerate, ruffed grouse are drawn to the habitat, which in turn attracts the hunters.

Scouting for areas that hold good numbers of grouse can pay off in the huge forest. The property offers a wide variety of habitat types, so locating good cover can save miles

TRAVEL GUIDE

NEAREST SERVICE CENTER: Medford.
LODGING: Americinn Motel, located on Highway 13, 1-800-634-3444. Malibu Inn, Highway 13, 1-800-676-3995. Royal 8 Motel, Highway 13, (715) 748-5040.
SPORTS SHOP OR HUNTING LICENSE OUTLET: Z's Sport Shop, 1281 N. 8th St., Medford, (715) 748-2855. Ben Franklin, 142 S. Main St., Medford, (715) 748-4770. Holiday Station, 442 S. 8th St., Medford, (715) 748-9924. Taylor County Courthouse, Roger Emmerich, county clerk, 224 S. Second St., Medford, (715) 748-1460.
HOSPITAL OR EMERGENCY MEDICAL CLINIC: Memorial Hospital of Taylor County, emergency room located at 135 S. Gibson St., (715) 748-8100.
EMERGENCY VETERINARY CLINIC: Medford Vet Clinic, 233 S. 8th St., Medford, (715) 748-2341.
AUTO REPAIR OR TOWING: H&H Motors, 312 S. Wisconsin Ave., Medford, (715) 748-4969 or (715) 748-2745. Krug's West Side Service, 549 Billings St., Medford, (715) 748-3194 or 748-4083.

of fruitless walking.

Woodcock go with grouse like jelly with peanut butter. Therefore, Bilyeu said, the forest can feature some good timberdoodle hunting. Many wet areas throughout the unit give woodcock chasers likely spots to look for birds. Patches of young aspen and alder in these

The Chequamegon's Medford Unit offers excellent hunting for deer, grouse and woodcock. Besides its abundant wildlife, the Medford Unit also includes a trail that enables disabled people to hunt many parts of the forest.

boggy spots are traditional producers. The unit holds some local birds early in the season, and then plays host to the traditional mid-fall flight of migrants.

With the forest's many types of cover, deer are also abundant. They benefit from the mix of lowlands spruce, hardwoods, aspen regrowth and tag-alder swamps.

Because the area is so large hunting pressure during the November firearms season is often dispersed over a wide area. Some spots tend to draw hunters each year, of course, but Bilyeu said any one willing to scout and walk should have no trouble getting away from crowds. "You're not going to trip over other people," he

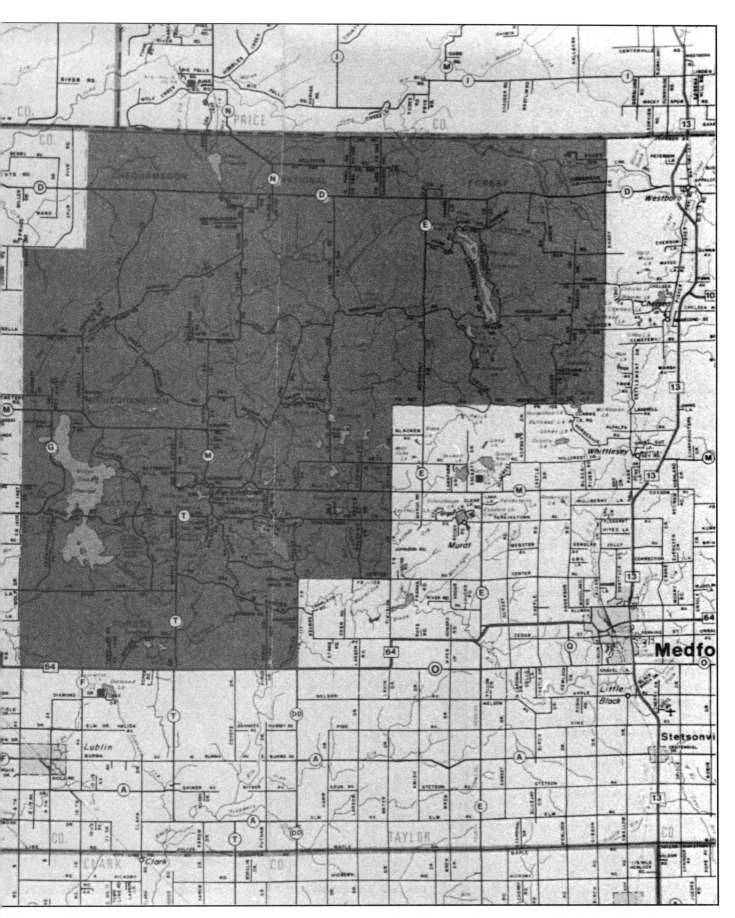

Detailed maps of the Medford Unit of the Chequamegon National Forest are available by writing or calling the *Medford Ranger Station, 850 N. 8th St., Hwy. 13, Medford, WI 54451, (715) 748-4875.*

said.

Although the area is known more for its good-sized deer populations, Bilyeu said the Medford unit still produces big bucks each year. The huge area and thick cover provide plenty of escape routes and hiding places for deer to grow old.

The Medford unit's many mature timber stands also feature some good North-country squirrel hunting. When he first came to the area, Bilyeu asked about a good spot to hunt bushytails. He was told to go to Medford.

Because the Medford unit of the Chequamegon contains abundant water, it offers some waterfowl hunting. Still, ducks and geese don't receive a lot of attention from sportsmen, Bilyeu said. People who enjoy pothole hunting or jump-shooting can probably find success in the forest. The Medford unit also offers nesting sites for mallards, wood ducks and mergansers, Bilyeu said.

"Some folks hunt them," he said. "When they do that they're getting away from the large groups of duck hunters that go other places. Sometimes it pays off."

Some likely areas for waterfowl hunters include the Upper Steve Creek Waterfowl Area in the unit's northwestern corner, Chequamegon Waters Flowage in the district's southwestern portion, and Bear Creek and Beaver Creek waterfowl areas in the south.

The Medford Ranger District also features the White Birch Hunter's Trail for the Disabled. This trail allows disabled sportsmen to hunt many areas of the unit.

An active timber harvest program in the Medford Unit of the Chequamegon National Forest is one of the reasons the ruffed grouse is one of the most popular game species in the area.

Navarino Wildlife Area

SHAWANO COUNTY

If you're interested in a near-north location that offers good hunting for whitetails, upland birds and waterfowl, the answer might be the Navarino Wildlife Area.

Navarino is a 14,500-acre property in Shawano County. Despite receiving a lot of hunting pressure because it's located near the heavily populated Fox River Valley, this wildlife area consistently rates as one of Wisconsin's top public hunting grounds.

John Huff, the DNR's area wildlife manager, said Navarino is primarily a forest wildlife area. Yet the area is also home to a variety of waterfowl and other non-game species.

The area is well known by deer hunters, who use Navarino heavily during the archery and firearms season. The area is in use from the opening bell of the bow season through the last big chill of the December archery season. Huff said the area supports excellent deer populations, and produces some big racks at times.

Navarino provides whitetails with a complete mix of habitat: new and mature forest, grasslands, sedge meadows and wetlands. This provides deer with a great deal of cover and food.

Access to Navarino is easy. Many state, town and county roads run along or through the property, and parking areas are abundant. Huff said bow hunting pressure has increased in recent years. The area has always been popular with gun hunters. Nonetheless, good hunting is available. Navarino features some almost impenetrable brush and cedar areas where deer easily escape hunters to live another year.

This thick, brushy cover also makes Navarino a prime spot for

TRAVEL GUIDE

NEAREST SERVICE CENTER: Shawano.
LODGING: There are numerous lodging opportunities in the Shawano area. The Shawano Area Chamber of Commerce lists about 20.
SPORTS SHOP OR HUNTING LICENSE OUTLET: There are several sporting goods stores in the Shawano area. The chamber of commerce, via the Yellow Pages, lists six.
HOSPITAL OR EMERGENCY MEDICAL CLINIC: Shawano Community Hospital, 309 Bartlette St., Shawano, (715) 526-6464 for emergencies.
EMERGENCY VETERINARY CLINIC: There are several veterinary services in the Shawano area. The Yellow Pages provided by the chamber of commerce lists seven.
AUTO REPAIR OR TOWING: There are numerous auto repair shops available in the Shawano area.

grouse and woodcock. Both species are abundant on the property.

Huff, himself an upland bird hunter, said about 8,500 of the area's 14,500 acres are forested. Of that, about 4,500 acres are covered primarily with aspen.

Navarino has an active timber-management program, which strives to create a diversity in age classes and forest types for wildlife. Grouse are a direct beneficiary of this, as they thrive in the younger aspen areas.

Hunters heavily pursue the grouse populations at Navarino, Huff said. However, good hunting opportunities exist throughout the bird season. Hunters may simply have to walk a bit farther from the parking lot later in the year.

Grouse numbers at Navarino were down in the early 1990s, just as they were throughout Wisconsin, Huff said. But when the cycle is up, grouse can be abundant.

Woodcock shooters should find excellent hunting throughout Navarino. The aspen areas, alder thickets, and heavy and moist soils make ideal habitat for the little game birds.

Huff said hunters should find birds in traditional spots, such as alder thickets adjacent to wetlands, or aspen areas with good ground cover, such as hazel brush. Other good spots to check are old farm fields on the property where natural brushy vegetation has become re-established. The DNR used to stock

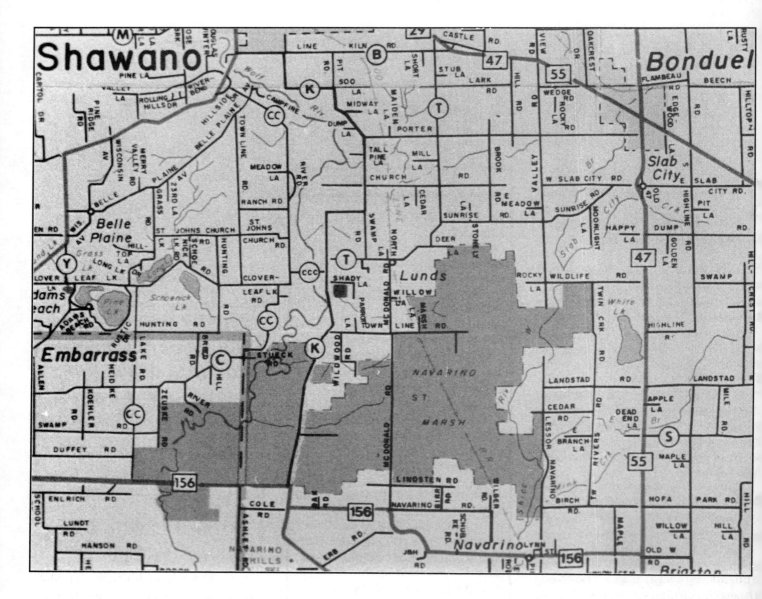

pheasants in some of these areas on a put-and-take basis. But these areas are now devoted to providing better woodcock habitat.

Waterfowlers also know Navarino to be a good spot to hunt puddle ducks and Canada geese. The area features seven main flowages, several ponds and two rivers: The Wolf and the West Branch of the Shioc.

Production at the area is good, Huff said. The DNR has worked to establish grasslands adjacent to flowages, which benefit nesting birds. The main species are mallards, wood ducks, teal and, to a lesser extent, ringbills and hooded mergansers. Some local Canada geese are also present.

One problem with production at Navarino is that its flowages dry up during drought years, so there's no

dependable source of water at these times. However, Huff said he's been pleasantly surprised by the numbers of birds that have returned to the area since the long drought of the late 1980s.

A 1,000-acre refuge is located in the south-central part of Navarino, and is closed to all hunting during the waterfowl season. Huff said the area sees a good influx of migrant birds — mainly mallards and Canada geese — which make good use of this area.

Waterfowl hunting at Navarino takes two main forms: decoy hunting and pass shooting. Reaching Navarino's flowages with a canoe or skiff is easy. Many spots are available for dropping in a boat.

Pass shooters often walk into brushy points, dikes or other likely

looking areas near the refuge. Navarino has its share of sky-busting problems, but Huff said the area's wooded, brushy nature results in closer-range birds for pass shooters.

Squirrel hunters also love Navarino. Depending on the acorn crop, the area can produce some excellent opportunities for bushytails.

Navarino's best oak areas are located along the bottomlands of the Wolf and Shioc rivers. Some good oak stands can also be found north of Highway 186 and along the area's high ridges.

Sawyer County Forest

SAWYER COUNTY

County forests can offer good hunting opportunities, but they're sometimes limited because the areas can be relatively small plots of land.

That's not the case with the Sawyer County Forest. This forest covers about 98,000 acres, and it offers hunting for deer, upland birds, waterfowl and small game.

The forest offers something for everyone, said DNR wildlife manager Sam Moore. The habitat varies from rolling, hilly terrain with maple-basswood forests to mature oak forests, and young aspen and alders. Throw in wetlands, and hunters can pursue almost every type of game found in northern Wisconsin.

"There's a great deal of variety," Moore said. "It's a very aesthetically pleasing forest."

The area has always been popular with deer hunters, and with good reason. With its variety of habitat, whitetails are abundant throughout the property. Moore said the area consistently produces good racks.

"There's an awful lot of country here," Moore said. "That's why it's good hunting."

Roads in the area have been vastly improved in recent years. However, much of the forest remains inaccessible. Hunters who walk into remote blocks of country improve their chances. The limited hunting access is directly related to the number of 2- to 3-year-old bucks in the area, Moore said.

The forest's thick, heavy cover gives the deer an extra advantage. Whitetails love dense, new aspen stands, which give them security. Also, the area is wet enough that deer will use islands or hummocks to escape and find sanctuaries.

The forest has few agricultural

TRAVEL GUIDE

NEAREST SERVICE CENTER: Hayward.

LODGING: There are several resorts, motels, hotels and campgrounds in the Hayward area. The Hayward Area Chamber of Commerce lists 10, but there are assuredly more.

SPORTS SHOP OR HUNTING LICENSE OUTLET: Hayward Bait and Tackle, 404 E. 1st St., Hayward, (715) 634-2921. Hayward Super Sports, Highway 63S, Hayward, (715) 634-4800. Pastika's Sport Shop, 214 S. Dakota St., Hayward, (715) 634-4466. Ubbie's Sport Shop, 142 Main St., Hayward, (715) 634-4000.

HOSPITAL OR EMERGENCY MEDICAL CLINIC: Hayward Area Memorial Hospital, Route 3, Hayward, (715) 634-8911.

EMERGENCY VETERINARY CLINIC: Care Animal Clinic, Highway 27 South, Hayward, (715) 634-5050. Hayward Animal Hospital, Highway B, (715) 634-8971. Timberlawn Pet Care Center, 635 Gehrts Road, Hayward, (715) 634-8712.

AUTO REPAIR OR TOWING: There are several auto repair shops in the Hayward area. The chamber of commerce lists seven.

areas inside or outside its borders. Hunters need to look for natural deer funnel areas, and determine which natural browse species deer are eating. The southern and western portions of the forest tend to hold higher deer populations, Moore said. Northern and eastern portions of the forest have more mature timber.

Grouse and woodcock fanatics

The Sawyer County Forest covers about 98,000 acres, and it offers good hunting for deer, upland birds, waterfowl and small game.

can also find wonderful hunting, Moore said. The area south of Winter features a great deal of aspen and alder habitat for the birds.

The area's aspen pulp market has been strong over the years, so cutting programs on the property remain active. This ensures a good mix of year classes. The young aspen stands, particularly those 1 to 12 years old, offer grouse protection from predators, and food supplies in the form of insects and buds.

The grouse population hit the low end of its cycle in 1992, but bird numbers should continue to climb through the end of the decade.

The aspen and alder cover mixes — especially those adjacent to wet or lowland areas — offer excellent habitat for woodcock. The area features good woodcock production. The forest doesn't see large migratory flights of timberdoodles. Moore said this is probably because it lies

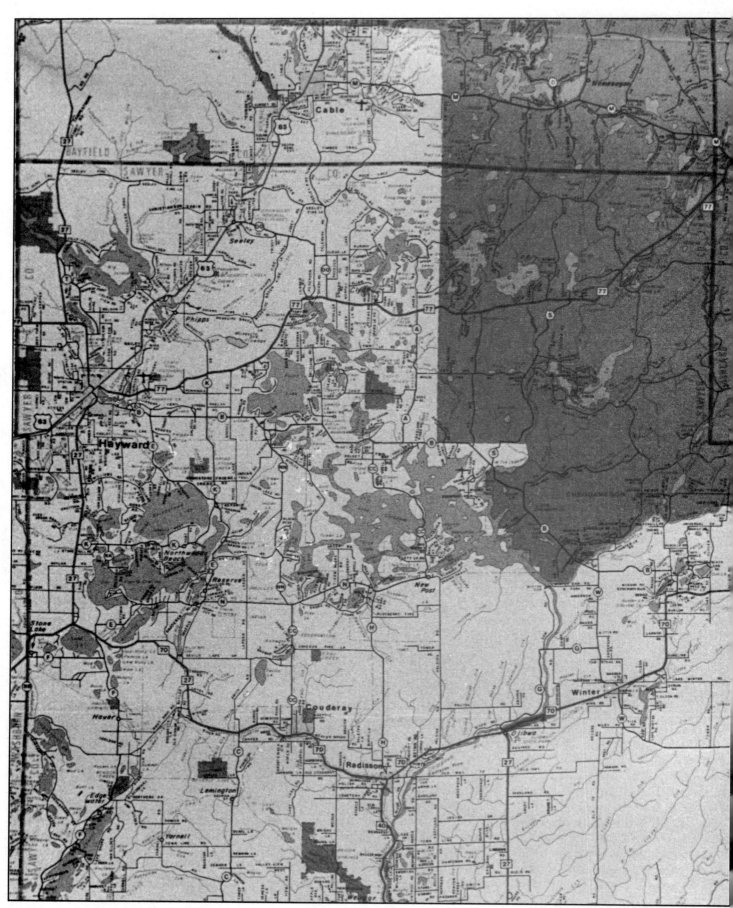

Sawyer County Forest land is scattered across the county. A county plat book showing public land is available by writing to Sawyer Co. 4-H Clubs Inc., P.O. Box 351, Hayward, WI 54843, or by calling (715)-634-4839.

Gregg Gutschow

Much of the Sawyer Co. Forest remains inaccessible. Hunters who walk into remote blocks of country improve their chances. The limited hunting access is directly related to the number of 2- to 3-year-old bucks in the area.

directly south of Lake Superior, and birds usually fly around the lake and end up congregating in areas south of the forest.

"But we do get pretty good hunting," Moore said.

The forest's northern and western portions can also offer good waterfowling. Lakes in this area tend to be less developed than in the south, and gunners can have some good hunting.

The forest also features loads of beaver ponds, where hunters can have good days shooting mallards and wood ducks. Creeks throughout the area offer jump-shooting opportunities.

Moore said the area doesn't see a great deal of migrant duck activity. But if the weather is right, hunters can find success on lakes or flowages with diving ducks.

Mature oak stands south and west of Hayward — especially those near the Blue Hills — can produce some good squirrel hunting, Moore said.

Also, snowshoe hares are common throughout the lowland and alder- thicket areas of the forest. The animals usually haven't grown their all-white coat by the time sportsmen are tromping around the woods, and they can be a welcome addition to the game bag.

Coyotes are also common. The coyote season is closed during gun deer season throughout much of the north, but hunters willing to scope out open areas in winter can find success with the predators.

Langlade County Forest

LANGLADE COUNTY

S ome say forestry and wildlife can't work together, but the Langlade County Forest proves otherwise.

The 130,000-acre forest, made up of several blocks of land in scenic Langlade County, supports a good variety of wildlife, most of which benefits from the property's progressive forestry techniques.

The county land consists mainly of deciduous forest blocks, according to Carl McIlquham, wildlife biologist for the DNR. The forest contains large blocks of aspen, as well as maple-basswood areas, but conifer areas are few.

The county has an active timber-management program, McIlquham said. Clear-cut areas of pulp trees, such as aspen and birch, provide for aspen regrowth and a variety of timber age-classes throughout the forest. As is the case with much of northern Wisconsin, a good mix of forest types is a key for wildlife.

McIlquham said white-tailed deer are probably the No. 1 species for hunters in Langlade County, and the county forest supports good numbers of them. Whitetails are found throughout the forest, but tend to concentrate in areas with young aspens, which provide not only cover but a good food source. Deer love to nibble on young aspen shoots.

McIlquham said that while the county's timber management has benefited deer, it also provides sort of a quandary. As more areas are logged, access on logging roads improves. As a result, hunters can reach more of the large blocks of forest land, and can put more pressure on deer.

Overall, the forest is hunted relatively hard during the gun and archery seasons, McIlquham said. Yet with all of the acreage, people

---

The 130,000-acre Langlade County Forest supports a good variety of wildlife, most of which benefits from the property's progressive forestry management.

TRAVEL GUIDE

NEAREST SERVICE CENTER: Antigo.

LODGING: There are numerous lodging opportunities available in Antigo. The Antigo Area Chamber of Commerce motel list lists 10 places.

SPORTS SHOP OR HUNTING LICENSE OUTLET: There are numerous license outlets in Langlade County. The chamber of commerce lists more than 30. Also, DNR office is at 1635 Neva Road, Antigo.

HOSPITAL OR EMERGENCY MEDICAL CLINIC: Langlade Memorial Hospital, 112 E. Fifth Ave., Antigo, (715) 623-9225.

EMERGENCY VETERINARY CLINIC: Antigo Vet Clinic, 610 Amron Ave., Antigo, (715) 623-4116.

AUTO REPAIR OR TOWING: Wagner Shell Service, 738 Superior St., Antigo, (715) 623-4681. Bob's Standard Service, 335 Superior St., Antigo, (715) 623-2709.

---

have plenty of room to enjoy their favorite sport without rubbing elbows with neighbors.

The county forest has yielded some nice bucks in the past, McIlquham said. In fact, some legitimate trophies have been bagged, but they're fairly uncommon.

Timber management and the resulting new-growth aspen also greatly benefit ruffed grouse. McIlquham said grouse hunting can be very good, especially when population cycles reach their peak. In the early 1990s, grouse populations statewide were close to the low point in their cycle.

Because of the forest's large size,

some grouse probably never see a hunter who's after them, McIlquham said. On the other hand, some popular spots are hunted hard for birds. Hunters should try to locate pocket areas that will hold concentrations of birds.

The forest produces good numbers of woodcock to keep the local population healthy. In fact, hunters often enjoy good hunting for these birds during the early part of the season. But these locals tend to be poorly distributed. That is, tight concentrations of them can be found in some spots while other areas are devoid of birds.

Once Oct. 1 arrives, woodcock hunting tends to be boom or bust. Many local birds have moved out, and hunters rely on migratory flights of woodcock. This migration traditionally peaks around mid-October.

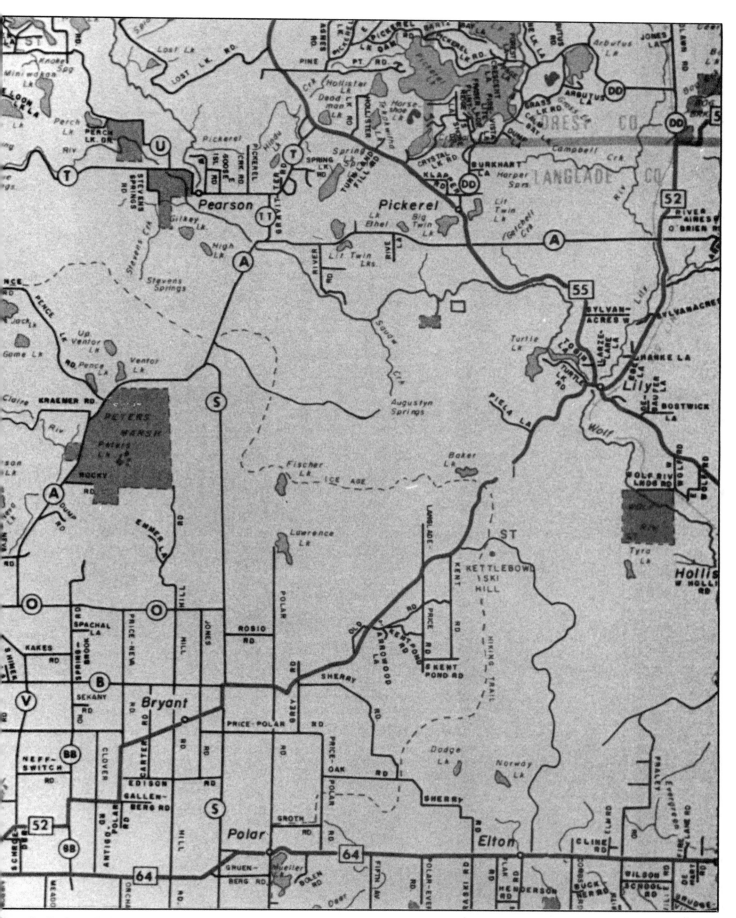

Langlade County Forest land is scattered across the area shown in the map above. Detailed maps of these areas are available by calling 1-800-288-6236, or writing to Forestry Dept., P.O. Box 460, Antigo, WI 54409.

47

Whitetails are found throughout Langlade County Forest land, but tend to concentrate in areas with young *aspens, which provide not only cover but a good food source.*

Waterfowlers can also find shooting around the forest. McIlquham suggests they concentrate on or around the state-owned Ackley Wildlife Area. This 1,000-acre property is bordered by the Langlade County Forest and contains about five flowages.

In addition, the country forest holds about 20 flowages, as well as many beaver ponds. These ponds tend to be transitory in nature. They may produce good shooting one fall but then be non-existent the next.

Black bears also offer some decent opportunities. The property is on the edge of what's considered bear country, but hunters who properly use bait have a good chance to kill an animal.

Another popular game animal is the snowshoe hare. Hare populations, like grouse, are cyclical, and their numbers were down in the early 1990s. However, McIlquham said pockets of hares can be found scattered throughout the property if hunters do their homework.

Lincoln County Forest

LINCOLN COUNTY

Lincoln County offers sportsmen about 100,000 acres of land on which to roam in search of deer, upland birds, bear and snowshoe hares.

The forest is contained in several major blocks, all of which feature good wildlife populations. Pat Rominski, DNR wildlife technician, said that the county lands feature a variety of habitat.

Most of the land is forested, Rominski said. County forest lands in the western part of the county feature a great deal of aspen, mixed with some oak stands and large swamp areas. Property along the eastern portion of the county features more hardwood stands and some lakes.

Deer can be found throughout county forest lands, Rominski said. Before 1992, the area featured very high populations of whitetails. Populations have fallen, but still remain healthy.

Because of the great variety of habitat on forest lands, deer can be found throughout the public property. Different pockets of cover tend to concentrate deer during different seasons, Rominski said. Hunters will want to scout ahead to identify these areas.

Hunting pressure on county forest land varies, Rominski said. Surveys have shown that pressure is significantly lower in the western portion of the county. This might be because access to the county's western portion is difficult. Also, the area features quite a few timber cutover areas, and the young forest is difficult to hunt.

A number of large bucks are taken from the area, Rominski said. Opportunities for mature deer are good.

Rominski said deer hunters should be aware that this area does

TRAVEL GUIDE

NEAREST SERVICE CENTER: Tomahawk.

LODGING: There are numerous bed and breakfasts, motels and resorts in the Tomahawk area. The Tomahawk Chamber of Commerce lists more than 40 total.

SPORTS SHOP OR HUNTING LICENSE OUTLET: There are several sports shops in the Tomahawk area. The chamber of commerce lists nine.

HOSPITAL OR EMERGENCY MEDICAL CLINIC: Sacred Heart Hospital, Tomahawk, (715) 453-7700. Tomahawk Medical Center, Division of Rhinelander Medical, (715) 453-7200.

EMERGENCY VETERINARY CLINIC: Animal Health Care Center, (715) 453-8448. Tomahawk Veterinary Clinic, (715) 453-5070.

AUTO REPAIR OR TOWING: There are several auto repair shops in the Tomahawk area. The chamber of commerce lists six.

Because of the great variety of habitat on forest lands, deer can be found throughout the public property.

have a population of timber wolves. The protected predators are very wary of human activity, so your chances of seeing one are not great. However, it is important to note that coyote hunting in the northern portion of the state is closed during the gun deer season in order to protect wolves from accidental shootings.

Grouse and woodcock hunters will also find the Lincoln County Forest to their liking. Rominski said the property features some good aspen and alder areas, which the birds use heavily.

There is some local production of woodcock. These birds can offer hunters some good September action.

Migratory birds can be plentiful here. The area offers some good, moist ground, which attracts timberdoodles. Woodcock like to use their long beaks to probe these areas for nightcrawlers. Hunters can locate areas that hold birds by looking for their small, chalk like droppings marks.

Snowshoe hares are also attracted to young aspen and alder areas, especially those in and around lowland areas and conifer swamps.

Hares are cyclical, and their populations are currently down. However, Rominski said that the animals still receive a fair amount of hunting pressure, especially during winter. Many sportsmen use snowshoes for travel since snowfalls in this region can be quite heavy.

Bear hunting opportunities in the county forest can be quite good. Rominski said that populations here are healthy, so strong, in fact, that some archery deer hunters have complained that bears are hitting their bait piles. Bait hunters who do their scouting probably have a good shot at taking a bruin.

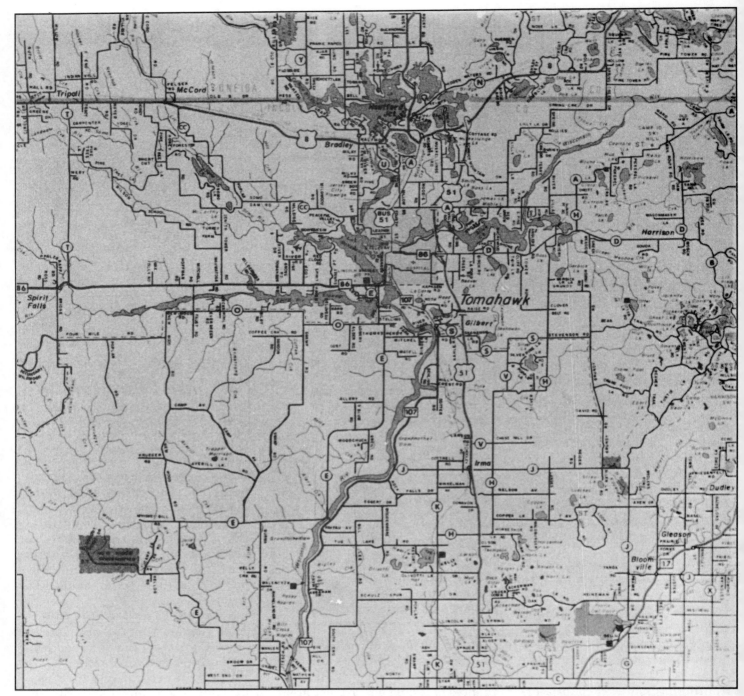

Lincoln County Forest land is scattered across the county. Plat books showing this public property are avail- *able by writing the Lincoln County Clerk Office, courthouse, 1110 E. Main, Merrill, WI 54452.*

Waterfowlers can also find some shooting opportunities throughout the forest lands. Rominski said that most of the duck hunting here is done along the Wisconsin River, which flows south through the center of the county.

Also, the forest has a high population of beavers, and some beaver ponds can provide some good early season shooting. Rominski said that there are also several lakes on the eastern portion of the forest that can offer some duck hunting.

There are also coyote hunting opportunities in the county forest, Rominski said.

CENTRAL

Sandhill Wildlife Area

WOOD COUNTY

W arning: After reading about Sandhill Wildlife Area, you might think this place is heaven on earth.

Trophy white-tailed bucks, thousands of migrating waterfowl staging in carefully managed flowages and upland birds aplenty, are all here. The only thing absent is the crowds.

Sandhill, which covers roughly 10,000 acres in Wood County, is governed by special regulations and is managed for quality hunting. Hunter numbers here are regulated. Small game and waterfowl seasons differ from the general state hunts, and the area is home to special deer hunts.

"We try to provide for quality hunting," said Mike Zeckmeister, superintendent of the Sandhill-Meadow Valley work unit.

Since 1979, Sandhill has been managed for older, larger white-tailed deer. Zeckmeister said education for youths and for beginning adult hunters plays a big role in the deer program.

Sandhill holds several summer workshops for youths and beginning adult hunters. These include field exercises, orienteering courses, a rifle range and other practical hunting skills. After individuals successfully complete these courses, they have an opportunity to participate in a special firearms deer hunt, generally held one or two weeks before the general state gun season.

Applications for the summer workshops are available at local and district DNR offices.

No bow hunting is allowed at Sandhill. The area is closed during the traditional November gun deer season, Zeckmeister said.

Since hunter numbers and the deer harvest are carefully con-

TRAVEL GUIDE

NEAREST SERVICE CENTER: Wisconsin Rapids.
LODGING: There are several lodging opportunities in the Wisconsin Rapids area. The Wisconsin Rapids Chamber of Commerce lists seven.
SPORTS SHOP OR HUNTING LICENSE OUTLET: Edgewater Resort, 1674 Apache Lane, Nekoosa, (715) 886-3488. Freeman's Bait and Tackle, 346 Wood Ave., Nekoosa, (715) 886-3541. Joe's Bait Shop, 1549 South Hollywood Road, Nekoosa, (715) 886-4932.
HOSPITAL OR EMERGENCY MEDICAL CLINIC: Riverview Hospital, 410 Dewey St., Wisconsin Rapids.(715) 423-6060.
EMERGENCY VETERINARY CLINIC: Information not available.
AUTO REPAIR OR TOWING: There are several auto repair shops in the Wisconsin Rapids area. The chamber of commerce lists 11.

trolled at Sandhill, the area can be successfully managed for older bucks. Zeckmeister said Sandhill features a greater density of older deer, although the overall population density isn't any different from surrounding areas.

Sandhill is surrounded by a deer-proof fence, which often gives hunters the impression that a deer season there could resemble a chicken shoot. Not so, Zeckmeister said. Hunters will have to scout and work for their deer at Sandhill.

Generally, about 150 to 200 deer are harvested every year at Sandhill, Zeckmeister said. Whitetails harvested on the property are aged, weighed and have their

Sandhill, which covers roughly 10,000 acres in Wood County, is governed by special regulations and is managed for quality hunting.

antlers measured. This data helps with deer management.

Also, Sandhill cooperates with the University of Wisconsin to do hunter behavioral studies at the area, Zeckmeister said.

Small game and waterfowl seasons are a little different at Sandhill than the rest of the state. The hunts generally begin at the same time the general state seasons open, but are usually closed at the end of October. The northern one-half of Sandhill is a wildlife refuge.

Also, hunter numbers are limited. Sportsmen must check in at the area's headquarters and receive a permit to hunt there. Only a set number of waterfowl and upland hunters are allowed on Sandhill each day. This allows managers to offer good hunting and keep a good handle on game harvest.

Hunters who arrive at Sandhill after the daily hunter quota has been reached might want to check out nearby Meadow Valley Wildlife Area. This 60,000-acre area fea-

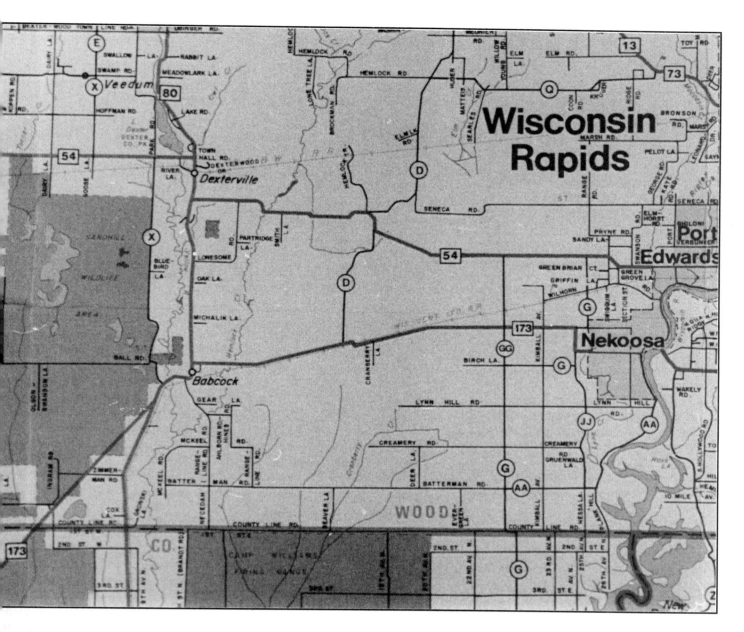

ures good opportunities for deer, waterfowl and upland bird hunting.

There is a lot of waterfowl management activity on the many impoundments at Sandhill. The area doesn't feature much in the way of waterfowl production, Zeckmeister said, but it is a major staging area for waterfowl.

The major species that use the area include mallards, wood ducks, blue-winged and green-winged teal, bluebills, mergansers and other common North American ducks. Canada geese also utilize Sandhill, and some snow geese come through every year.

The area has become a major staging area for sandhill cranes. The huge, noisy birds make good

use of the refuge. Also, Sandhill recently embarked on a trumpeter swan rearing project.

Grouse and woodcock also offer good shooting opportunities at Sandhill. Zeckmeister said there is a great deal of diversity in age classes of aspen on the property. Local grouse populations are good, but are subject to statewide population cycles.

Woodcock also thrive here. Zeckmeister said Sandhill has an alder management program, which benefits the tiny gamebirds.

Much of the activity every year at Sandhill is not related to hunting. The area features nature trails that allow bird watchers or hikers an opportunity to enjoy the land.

Sandhill isn't reopened for hunting after its special deer hunt ends, Zeckmeister said. Instead, the area's cross-country ski trails are opened up, giving people a unique opportunity to enjoy the winter landscape.

Wood County Wildlife Area

WOOD COUNTY

Wood County hunters can count themselves among the luckiest in the state. Waterfowl, deer and upland bird hunters have thousands of acres of public land on which to pursue their favorite game.

Wood County Wildlife Area features about 21,000 acres of prime central Wisconsin wildlife habitat. Nearby areas, such as Meadow Valley Wildlife Area and Wood County Forest lands, ensure that sportsmen won't lack for places to go when they're in the area.

Mike Zeckmeister, superintendent of the Sandhill-Meadow Valley work unit, said that Wood County Wildlife Area is comprised mainly of wetlands, but also features good diversity in the form of aspen and oak forests.

Waterfowling opportunities here are very good, Zeckmeister said. The DNR has an active wetlands management program at Wood County, which helps improve habitat for ducks.

The area is a prime wood duck spot. Zeckmeister said Wood County Wildlife Area features many ditches, some of which are adjacent to groves of oak. The fat acorns that drop from these trees act like a magnet for wood ducks, especially during times of staging and migration. The property is quite popular with wood duck hunters.

Most of the duck hunting at Wood County Wildlife Area is jumpshooting or decoy hunting. Many decoy hunters park on roads and then walk to areas they're going to hunt. Zeckmeister said jumpshooters and decoy hunters will want to use hip boots or chest waders at the property.

There are also some fairly inaccessible areas on the property,

TRAVEL GUIDE

NEAREST SERVICE CENTER: Wisconsin Rapids.
LODGING: There are several lodging opportunities in the Wisconsin Rapids area. The Wisconsin Rapids Chamber of Commerce lists seven.
SPORTS SHOP OR HUNTING LICENSE OUTLET: Edgewater Resort, 1674 Apache Lane, Nekoosa, (715) 886-3488. Freeman's Bait and Tackle, 346 Wood Ave., Nekoosa, (715) 886-3541. Joe's Bait Shop, 1549 South Hollywood Road, Nekoosa, (715) 886-4932.
HOSPITAL OR EMERGENCY MEDICAL CLINIC: Riverview Hospital, 410 Dewey St., Wisconsin Rapids.(715) 423-6060.
EMERGENCY VETERINARY CLINIC: Information not available.
AUTO REPAIR OR TOWING: There are several auto repair shops in the Wisconsin Rapids area. The chamber of commerce lists 11.

which gives adventurous hunters an advantage. Zeckmeister said sportsmen who work hard to reach out-of-the-way wetland areas have reported excellent shooting on mallards and other migrating ducks.

Zeckmeister said the area is also pretty good for Canada geese. Crop fields and cranberry bogs provide much of the action, but many of these are on private lands around the public areas.

People who plan on traversing wetland areas at Wood County Wildlife Area should be aware that there is a resident population of sharptail grouse there.

Zeckmeister said Wood County

The DNR has an active wetlands management program at Wood County, which helps improve habitat for ducks.

Wildlife Area's sharptail flock is the core of the central Wisconsin population. The birds, which traditionally thrive in upland prairie areas have adapted to the wetlands of the property. Sharptails are not legal game in this part of the state, and hunters should be able to distinguish the birds from other game when at the property.

There are good opportunities at Wood County Wildlife Area for deer hunters. Bow hunting and firearms hunting are both popular here.

Surprisingly, Zeckmeister said gun hunting pressure at the property has actually decreased in recent years. He believes this may be in response to the large numbers of hunter's choice and bonus tags that were offered in northern units during the late 1980s and early 1990s.

Although that decline in pressure may change, it was good news for sportsmen who hunted the property. The area does offer the opportunity to harvest a nice, mature buck.

Zeckmeister said that registration stations record 8- and 10-point

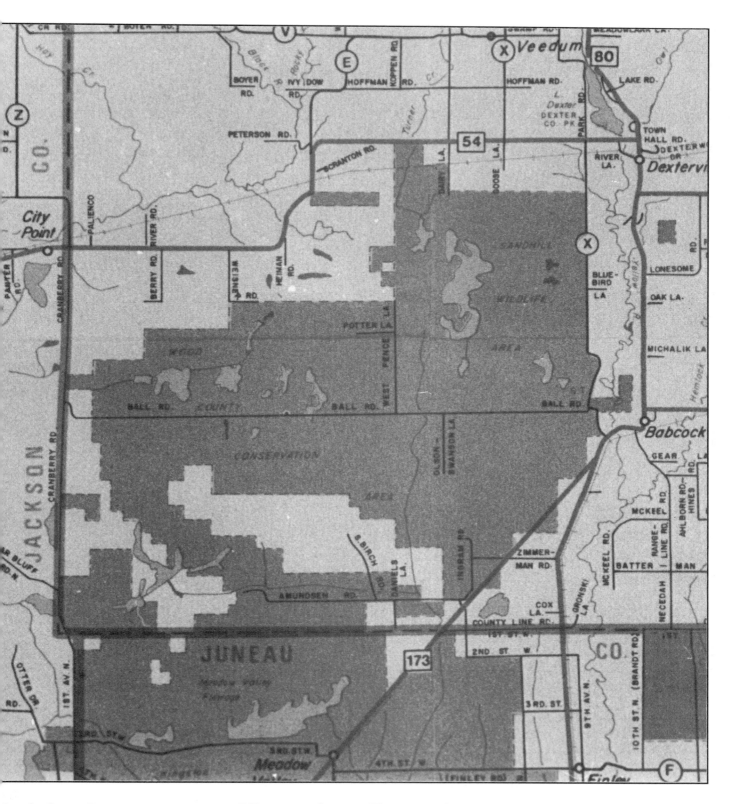

imals from the property every ar.

Grouse and woodcock hunters can so find shooting at Wood County ildlife Area. Zeckmeister said at there is a good timber manage- ent program at the property. mber sales throughout the forest ake for an excellent mixture of different aged trees. That suits the local grouse population just fine.

Woodcock also make use of the area. Alder and aspen areas around the abundant wetlands here make prime spots for timberdoodle.

Wood County itself also offers more than 30,000 acres of county forest land. These areas, which are divided into several blocks, provide good deer and upland bird hunting, as well as some waterfowling oppor- tunities along the Yellow River.

The vast Meadow Valley Wildlife Area is also a first-class public hunting spot. Hunters here can find good numbers of deer, upland birds and some good jump-shooting

The Wood County Wildlife Area is a popular waterfowl hunting area which supports a good number of wood ducks. Some of the wetland areas are relatively difficult to reach and provide excellent shooting for the adventuresome hunter.

opportunities for mallards and wood ducks. There are also some wild turkeys in the area.

Juneau County Forest

JUNEAU COUNTY

It's likely that many people reading this don't live in Juneau County. After hearing about the fantastic hunting opportunities available there, however, they might want to move.

The county is full of land that is open to public hunting. County forest lands total about 13,000 acres; there are also several other wildlife areas in the county.

DNR wildlife manager Jim Keir said county forest land is scattered in many blocks throughout Juneau County. Most plots contain a relatively small amount of acreage when compared to the total. Habitat on the tracts varies from oak to red pine plantations to aspen.

Keir said that scouting will be a key to almost every kind of hunting people want to pursue on Juneau County Forest lands.

Because the area isn't contiguous, it's best to start with a county plat book to learn the boundaries of the plot you plan to hunt. Then, scout the area to find out what kind of habitat, and game, it features.

Generally, upland game species are the most commonly hunted here, Keir said. This area of Wisconsin is well-known among upland bird hunters, who often travel here from the southern part of the state to chase grouse and woodcock.

Keir said there is a fairly aggressive timber harvest program on county forest lands. Wildlife management needs are built into the timber harvest recommendations in an attempt to maintain forest lands that are attractive to wildlife. These practices result in a regeneration of oak, jack pine and aspen.

Regrowth areas of aspen and other types of cover provide ideal habitat for grouse. Keir said

The county is full of land that is open to public hunting. County forest lands total about 13,000 acres; there are also several other wildlife areas in the county.

TRAVEL GUIDE

NEAREST SERVICE CENTER: Mauston.
LODGING: Alaskan Motor Inn, I90 and 94 and Highway 82, Mauston, (608) 847-5609. Country Inn by Carlson, Highway 82 East, Mauston, (608) 847-5959. City Center Motel, 315 E. State St., Mauston, (608) 847-5634. Willows Motel, 1035 E. State St., Mauston, (608) 847-6800.
SPORTS SHOP OR HUNTING LICENSE OUTLET: Juneau County Courthouse, 220 E. State St., Mauston.
HOSPITAL OR EMERGENCY MEDICAL CLINIC: Hess Memorial Hospital, 1050 Division St., Mauston, (608) 847-6161.
EMERGENCY VETERINARY CLINIC: Mauston Vet Clinic, Highway 82 East, Mauston, (608) 847-6024.
AUTO REPAIR OR TOWING: There are several auto repair places in the Mauston area. The Mauston Area Chamber of Commerce lists nine.

hunters will want to check around different areas of the forest to find localized hotspot areas where birds are concentrated.

Woodcock hunting in the area tends to be secondary to grouse hunting, Keir said. However, if hunters find the right spots, they can get some shooting. Alder areas, especially those that border wet areas, will often concentrate birds during the annual fall migration.

Upland bird hunters can also find success at Meadow Valley Wildlife Area, also located in the county.

Deer also find good habitat on much of the county forest lands, Keir said. Whitetails will use a variety of different cover types ranging from young aspen stands to wetland areas, so hunters will need to locate deer before the season in order to ensure a good hunt.

The western and southern portions of Juneau County offer hunters some steep hills to climb. These spots can provide good vantage points for scouting or hunting. Areas where timber and grass or wetland areas meet also provide good vantage spots.

Meadow Valley and Kingston Conservation Area, located in the northwest part of the county, also offer hunters plenty of land on which to pursue whitetails.

Waterfowling opportunities around the county can be good, depending on the spot. Keir said. Beaver dams can offer good puddle duck shooting at scattered locations. Meadow Valley offers good

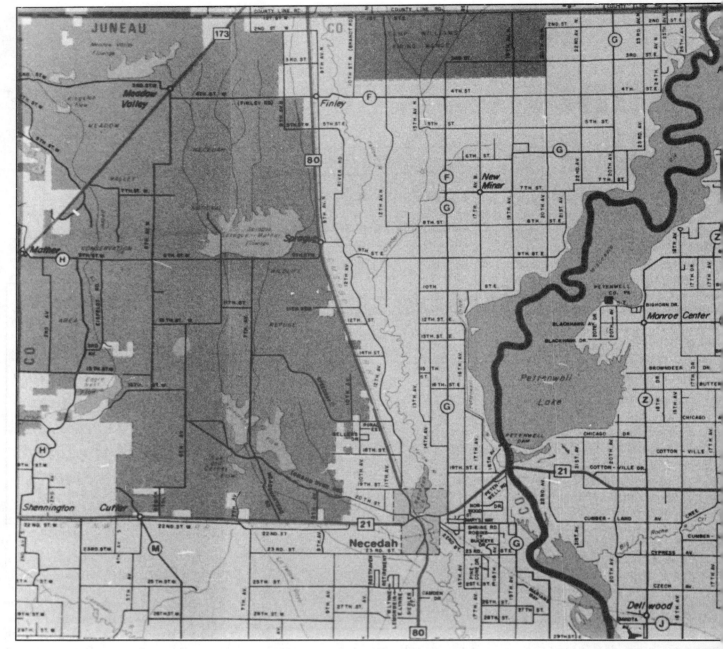

Juneau County Forest lands are scattered across the county. Plat books showing public land boundaries are available by calling (608) 847-9389, or writing Juneau County Title Co., 221 E. State, Mauston, WI 53948.

jumpshooting opportunities for mallards and wood ducks. Other spots include various flowages around the county, as well as the large Petenwell and Castle Rock flowages on the county's eastern half.

Oak stands in Juneau County Forest lands offer good habitat for wild turkeys. The big birds often roost in mature trees, then fly down in the morning.

Squirrels are also abundant in oak areas throughout the county. Keir said squirrel hunters can find some quality hunting in the area.

During the winter, many hunters enjoy pursuing coyotes and other predators on public hunting grounds. Again, hunters will want to scout county forest lands to find suitable areas to pursue these animals.

Necedah National Wildlife Refuge

JUNEAU COUNTY

As September closes and the cool winds of October begin blowing over the state, flocks of waterfowl grow to peak proportions on the lakes and marshes of Wisconsin.

Necedah National Wildlife Refuge is no exception. This 40,000-acre property, located in Juneau County, is managed by the U.S. Fish and Wildlife Service for migratory birds.

The property offers good hunting opportunities for waterfowl, as well as deer, upland birds, wild turkeys and small game. Also, the area features thousands of acres of refuge for migratory birds that stop there on their migration south.

Bud Oliveira, refuge manager, said the area is a mixture of habitats. The property features about 12,000 acres of wetlands, including streams, ditches and marshes. There are about 23,500 acres of forest lands, and around 6,300 acres of grasslands. Also, there are less than 1,000 acres of croplands.

The property is divided into six separate areas for hunting. Areas 1, 2, 4, 5 and 6 are open to hunting for migratory gamebirds, small game, gun and bow deer hunting and wild turkey in spring and fall. These areas are located on the outside boundaries of the property. A refuge map will pinpoint their specific boundaries.

Area 3, which makes up most the property's center, is open only for gun deer hunting, bow hunting during the late archery season, wild turkey in spring and small game hunting after the gun deer season.

There is also an area near the

TRAVEL GUIDE

NEAREST SERVICE CENTER: Mauston.

LODGING: Alaskan Motor Inn, I90 and 94 and Highway 82, Mauston, (608) 847-5609. Country Inn by Carlson, Highway 82 East, Mauston, (608) 847-5959. City Center Motel, 315 E. State St., Mauston, (608) 847-5634. Willows Motel, 1035 E. State St., Mauston, (608) 847-6800.

SPORTS SHOP OR HUNTING LICENSE OUTLET: Juneau County Courthouse, 220 E. State St., Mauston.

HOSPITAL OR EMERGENCY MEDICAL CLINIC: Hess Memorial Hospital, 1050 Division St., Mauston, (608) 847-6161.

EMERGENCY VETERINARY CLINIC: Mauston Vet Clinic, Highway 82 East, Mauston, (608) 847-6024.

AUTO REPAIR OR TOWING: There are several auto repair places in the Mauston area. The Mauston Area Chamber of Commerce lists nine.

south part of the property that is permanently closed to hunting.

Oliveira said there are also several special regulations for hunting on the property. The construction of permanent blinds, stands or ladders is prohibited. Also, except for named species — deer, migratory birds, turkey, gray and fox squirrels, cottontail rabbits, snowshoe hare, ruffed grouse and raccoon — all other wildlife species, including coyotes, may not be killed.

The area also serves as a major stopover area for migrating birds. Puddle ducks are the most common visitors. In 1992, the peak duck usage of the area was Oct. 21, when about 14,000 birds were inhabiting the area.

Oliveira said Necedah is a pretty good waterfowl production area, turning out about 1,000 birds each year. Blue-winged teal make up about 51 percent of the total, while mallards account for 36 percent. Widgeon and black ducks are also produced. In addition, quite a few wood ducks are raised locally.

The area also serves as a major stopover area for migrating birds. Puddle ducks are the most common visitors. In 1992, the peak duck usage of the area was Oct. 21, when about 14,000 birds were inhabiting the area.

The area does attract some divers, Oliveira said. Ringnecks are the most common species, but they make up only about 7 percent of the total birds at Necedah.

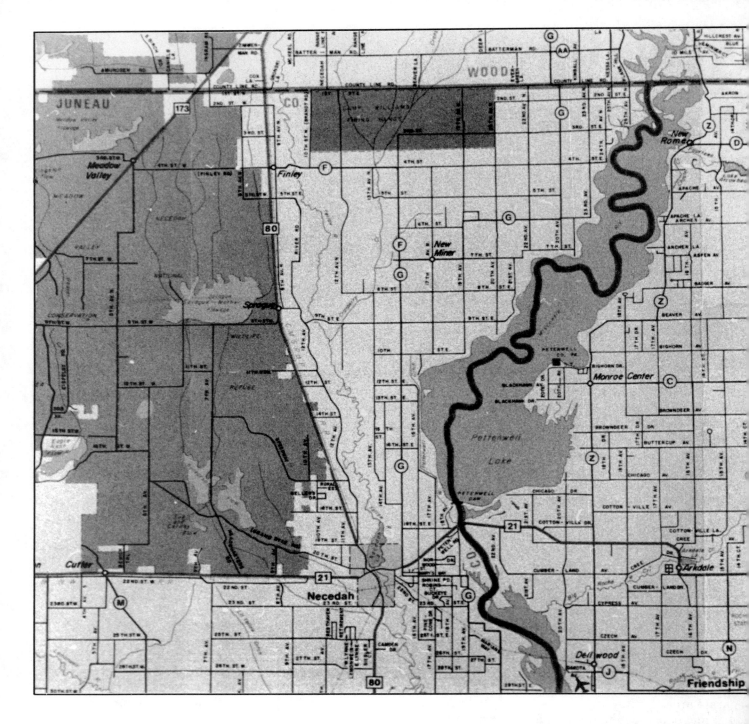

Canada geese are also a common migrant at Necedah, Oliveira said. There were about 250 geese at the area on Sept. 20, 1992. That number rose to about 9,000 on Oct. 1 and just shy of 14,000 on Oct. 21.

Waterfowl hunting methods at Necedah vary. Oliveira said many gunners walk ditches and creeks in huntable areas in an attempt to jumpshoot wood ducks. Many sportsmen use boats or wade into Suk-Cerney Flowage, then set up decoys and call to birds. Motorboats are allowed on the flowage.

Oliveira said there aren't too many pass shooting opportunities around refuge boundaries.

Necedah also has a good white-tailed deer population, according to Oliveira. That, coupled with the refuge status of much of the property prior to the November firearms season, draws quite a few gun hunters to the area on opening weekend.

In 1992, 1,855 hunters were counted at Necedah on opening day.

On the second day, around 1,60 were counted. However, pressur dropped off substantially after that

Ruffed grouse and woodcock als offer very good hunting opportun ties at Necedah, Oliveira said.

Selected cuttings and clear cut are part of a timber managemer program at the area, which leads t good aspen regeneration and, i turn, good grouse habitat.

Some local woodcock are pr duced at Necedah, and some migra tory birds use the area. Howeve

Patrick Durkin

Canada geese use Necedah as a stopover during their fall migration. In 1992 the number of geese on

Necedah's wetlands exploded from 250 in late September to around 14,000 by late October.

he property doesn't feature the dense alder stands and similar cover that the birds prefer, so timberdoodle action is sporadic.

Wild turkeys also provide hunting action at Necedah. Oliveira said the property is in Zone 9. In 1992, 74 birds were harvested in Zone 9 during the spring hunt, and 5 were taken during the fall hunt.

Squirrels and rabbits are also abundant at Necedah. Mature oak

stands and brushy hedgerows, respectively, should provide sportsmen with ample opportunities for these small game species.

Also, less popular species such as jacksnipe and raccoons can also provide action for sportsmen who want to experience different forms of hunting.

Camping is not permitted in the refuge, but the nearby Meadow Valley Wildlife Management Area

does feature camping sites. Also, except on designated trails in Area 5, motorized vehicles are restricted to township roads.

Colburn Wildlife Area

ADAMS COUNTY

Mention central Wisconsin and you'll likely conjure up images of white-tailed deer and grouse hunting. Colburn Wildlife Area, located in Adams County, offers sportsmen just that.

The property, which is about 4,900 acres, contains a mixture of scrub oak uplands, sedge meadows and willow-tag alder wetlands. Carter Creek runs through the area.

DNR wildlife manager Jim Keir said that Colburn has a very good population of deer. The property lies in management Unit 53, and the overwinter goal there is about 30 deer per square mile of habitat. That results in a pre-hunting season population of about 40 deer per square mile of habitat in the area.

Whitetails are spread throughout the property, Keir said. In spite of a restriction on vehicle travel in Colburn and the numerous wetland areas there, hunters find that they can gain access to almost all parts of the property. The area doesn't offer enough sheer size to discourage hunters from tromping back to relatively remote places.

Keir said hunting pressure during the opening weekend of the November firearms season is very heavy. Many hunters concentrate their efforts on wooded areas, but some will also stake out spots along the open sedge meadows in hopes that they will intercept deer that use the areas as escape routes.

"I would guess if somebody wanted to find a trophy that's not the place to look," Keir said.

Archery hunters will find Colburn much less crowded, both during the early fall portion of the season and during the late hunt.

Bow hunters in many parts of the state like to position their stands next to crop fields. However, Keir

TRAVEL GUIDE

NEAREST SERVICE CENTER: Friendship.
* The Adams County Chamber of Commerce prefers that anyone in need of information about the greater Adams County area contact: Adams County Chamber of Commerce, (608) 339-6997, or Box 301, Friendship, Wisc., 53934.

said that hunters at Colburn will want to hunt on oak ridges and along trails that come out of wetlands.

Colburn also offers upland wingshooters some good gunning opportunities for ruffed grouse. Keir said that the property does feature quite a bit of aspen, which acts as first-rate habitat for the fancy-flushing gamebirds.

The DNR has done a lot of small area cuttings around the property, which leads to a good, mixed age of timber. There is fairly good aspen regrowth.

Grouse populations are expected to rise as the end of the decade nears, but Keir said that grouse numbers at Colburn and much of central Wisconsin "missed" the high point of the last cycle. That is, bird numbers in the area didn't really reach a peak.

Keir said the phenomenon is unexplained, but he expects bird numbers to be good again.

There is some local production of woodcock at Colburn, Keir said. The area has never been a true woodcock hotspot, and Keir doubts whether many people travel to the area specifically for timberdoodle. However, many birds are taken incidentally by grouse hunters. The best time to encounter migrating

In spite of a restriction on vehicle travel in Colburn and the numerous wetland areas there, hunters find that they can gain access to almost all parts of the property.

woodcock is generally mid-October, depending on weather patterns.

Good waterfowling can be had at Colburn, but Keir said it's often dependent on water conditions during a given year. Hunting opportunities change annually with beaver dam locations along Carter Creek.

Keir said hunters will need to do some pre-season scouting to determine whether substantial numbers of birds are utilizing the area. If ducks have taken up residence at a beaver pond area, it could offer some quality hunting. The walk to the creek can be difficult, which should result in less competition for birds.

Squirrel hunters can also find opportunities for their favorite game at Colburn. Mature oak stands on the property, particularly near the eastern edge, offer good habitat for squirrels. These craft

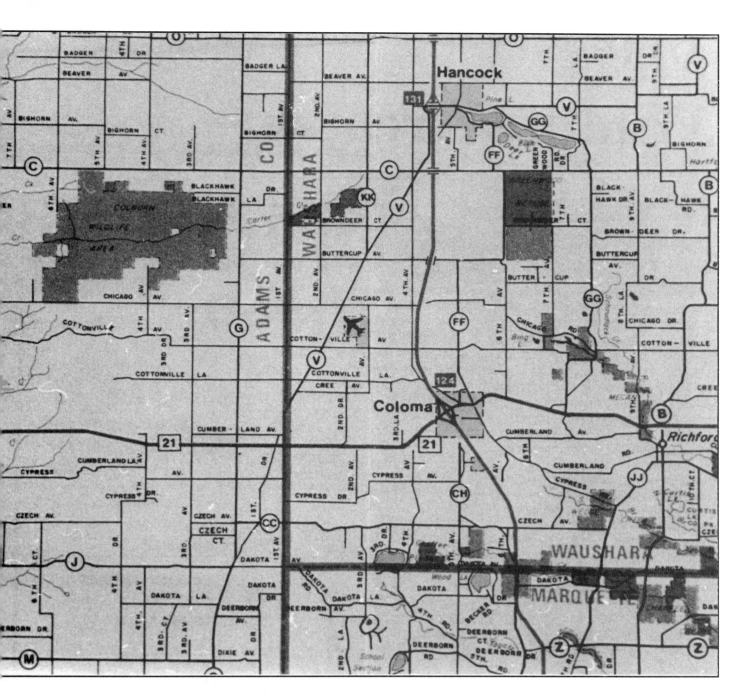

animals are often overlooked by hunters, even on popular public areas.

Rabbit hunting opportunities at Colburn are limited, Keir said.

Hunters may also find some coyote hunting at Colburn. The large open areas at the property will give sportsmen good spots from which to call for the predators. Access to the interior of the property generally improves as wetlands begin freezing.

Access to the property is fairly good, and can be gained by nearby county roads.

Mead Wildlife Area

MARATHON, WOOD AND PORTAGE COUNTIES

Bird and deer hunters in Marathon, Wood and Portage counties can count themselves lucky: Mead Wildlife Area provides good hunting opportunities in both categories.

Mead covers about 28,000 acres of land in the three counties. And although it's certainly no secret among outdoor enthusiasts, its thriving wildlife populations and top-notch habitat make it a quality area.

"It's got pretty much everything, which makes it a little bit unique," said Brian Peters, wildlife technician for the DNR. "The main thing we like to stress is our diversity of habitat."

Mead features a mixture of different timber and grass areas in its uplands, as well as a patchwork of creeks, rivers, wetlands and impoundments.

With all of its water, Mead is a natural area for waterfowl. Peters said the main management emphasis for the wetland areas is for duck production. Quite a few local birds, mainly mallards, wood ducks and teal, are produced annually at the area.

As fall wears on, the property will also see some very good flights of northern ducks. Good numbers of gadwall and widgeon will join other puddle duck species at the area, and ringnecks, bluebills, redheads and canvasbacks also use the waters.

In addition to ducks, there are some Canada geese that nest at Mead. Peters said the area used to see a substantial build-up of about 2,000 to 3,000 geese before the waterfowl season, but the September opening of goose hunting has reduced that number to about 500 to 1,000 birds. The area is part of the Exterior Zone for

TRAVEL GUIDE

NEAREST SERVICE CENTER: Stevens Point.
LODGING: There are numerous lodging opportunities in the Stevens Point area. The Stevens Point-Plover Area Chamber of Commerce lists 13.
SPORTS SHOP OR HUNTING LICENSE OUTLET: Cliff's Bait and Tackle, 706 Post Road, Stevens Point, (715) 344-4371.
HOSPITAL OR EMERGENCY MEDICAL CLINIC: St. Michael's Hospital, 900 Illinois Ave., Stevens Point, (715) 346-5000.
EMERGENCY VETERINARY CLINIC: Oakview Pet Hospital, 201 Post Road, Plover, (715) 344-6311.
AUTO REPAIR OR TOWING: There are numerous auto service places in the Stevens Point area.

geese.

Waterfowlers can use a variety of methods to find success at Mead. The area features three refuges, which are heavily utilized by migrating birds in fall, so pass shooting is popular.

In addition, there are many dikes that provide access to good wetland areas. Hunters also have an easy time putting in canoes or skiffs in order to hunt over decoys, and many areas on the property can be reached with waders.

Peters advised hunters to obtain a map of the area and do some scouting before hunting. Not only are some of the property boundaries irregular, but hunters should also be aware of all refuge boundaries. The areas are closed to access from Sept. 1 through Dec. 10, except during the gun deer season.

With all of its water, Mead is a natural area for waterfowl. ... Quite a few local birds, mainly mallards, wood ducks and teal, are produced annually at the area. As fall wears on, the property will also see some very good flights of northern ducks.

The mixture of habitat at Mea benefits the solid white-tailed dee population. The area does receiv heavy hunting pressure during th gun deer season, and is also hotspot during archery seasor Many hunters experience good su cess on the area's southeastern se tion.

However, the area does featur some secluded spots, Peters saic Hunters willing to put in the homework, don hip boots and wal a few miles can experience som excellent deer hunting opportun ties.

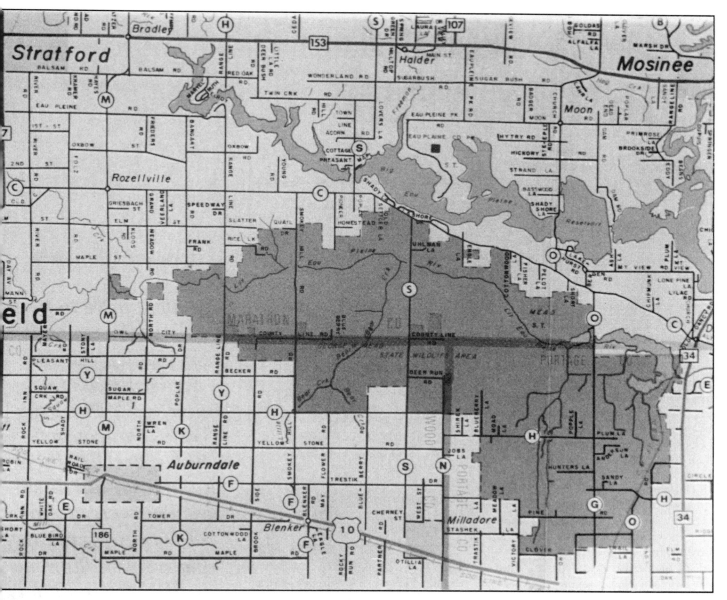

Many of the deer taken at Mead are 1.5-year-old animals. But hunters willing to get away from the crowds probably have the best shot at harvesting an older whitetail.

The timber areas at Mead also provide wingshooters with fine grouse and woodcock opportunities. Peters said there is a timber program at the property, which results in a good variety of aspen year classes.

Peters said the area features a good grouse population. There is some fairly heavy hunting pressure on the birds, but the area can be counted on to provide good shooting opportunities.

Mead also features an excellent woodcock flight. When the birds are "in" — typically around mid-October — shooting can be fast and furious. Young aspen or alder areas near wet or bog areas can provide the best action.

Peters said Mead also produces some local woodcock, which can provide gunning opportunities when the season opens in mid-September.

Bunny hunters should also find Mead to their liking. The area features cottontail rabbits and snowshoe hares, and plenty of habitat for both.

Mead also features some mature hardwood stands, which make ideal sites for squirrel hunting. Hunters who can locate areas of hickory or oak will likely find bushytails waiting.

Although Mead features some grassland areas, there is no pheasant stocking program here. There are prairie chickens on the property, and hunters should be able to identify the birds, especially if they are hunting open fields or edge areas that the protected birds might find appealing.

Dewey Marsh Wildlife Area

PORTAGE COUNTY

Y ou can thank the fires.

That might seem an odd statement at first glance. However, it was wildfires in the late 1970s that played a big role in creating good upland wildlife habitat at Dewey Marsh Wildlife Area.

Located in Portage County north of Stevens Point, Dewey Marsh offers hunters about 5,100 forested acres, and about 3,900 of lowland swamp or brush. The property features quite a bit of aspen, some alder areas, some oak and swampy bog areas.

DNR wildlife manager Joe Haug said grouse hunting at Dewey Marsh can be very good. Naturally, the thick aspen areas at the property are key spots for ruffed grouse.

Haug said the big fires at the area in 1977 burned most of the marsh over. This led to regeneration of aspen in many areas. This also led to a lot of aspen stands of the same age.

"Once you hit that 15-to 20-year bracket, an aspen stand has pretty well lost its habitat characteristics that make it so good for upland gamebirds," he said. "Still, there are enough areas of the younger stuff, so to speak, that make it a good area for hunting."

Haug said the DNR tries to break up the age classes of aspen at the area by clear-cutting and holding timber sales.

Woodcock are also available in good numbers at Dewey Marsh. Haug said there is some local production on the property, but migrating birds make up the bulk of the shooting opportunities.

The best areas at Dewey Marsh will be traditional hotspots such as the fringes of tag alder thickets and

TRAVEL GUIDE

NEAREST SERVICE CENTER: Stevens Point.
LODGING: There are numerous lodging opportunities in the Stevens Point area. The Stevens Point-Plover Area Chamber of Commerce lists 13.
SPORTS SHOP OR HUNTING LICENSE OUTLET: Cliff's Bait and Tackle, 706 Post Road, Stevens Point, (715) 344-4371.
HOSPITAL OR EMERGENCY MEDICAL CLINIC: St. Michael's Hospital, 900 Illinois Ave., Stevens Point, (715) 346-5000.
EMERGENCY VETERINARY CLINIC: Oakview Pet Hospital, 201 Post Road, Plover, (715) 344-6311.
AUTO REPAIR OR TOWING: There are numerous auto service places in the Stevens Point area.

aspen areas, Haug said.

Since Dewey Marsh is close to Stevens Point, the area does receive a great deal of hunting pressure for upland birds. Pressure is high during the early part of the season, Haug said, but the area is large enough that sportsmen can find birds and have a quality hunting experience.

Deer hunting at Dewey Marsh is also good. Haug said the area usually goes into the hunting season with about 45 deer per square mile of habitat. Normally, the harvest for bow and gun seasons combined will be about 15 deer per square mile of habitat.

Archers like Dewey Marsh, Haug said. Spots where thick aspen stands meet open marsh areas can prove productive during the early season.

Firearms hunters also make good

Hunters have to hike back to the center of the property to find the best waterfowl hunting. ... The property features potholes, creeks and a number of old ditches. The water found at Dewey Marsh is relatively shallow, so hunters use hip boots or chest waders to reach it.

use of the area. Hunting pressure tends to scatter whitetails throughout the property during this time, Haug said.

Like many areas of the state, Dewey Marsh sees a fairly high harvest — about 75 to 80 percent — of 1.5-year-old bucks. With that kind of turnover, there aren't a lot of trophy bucks available to sportsmen.

Intrepid hunters can get some good duck shooting at Dewey Marsh. Waterfowl production at the area is basically limited to wood ducks, Haug said. The area also

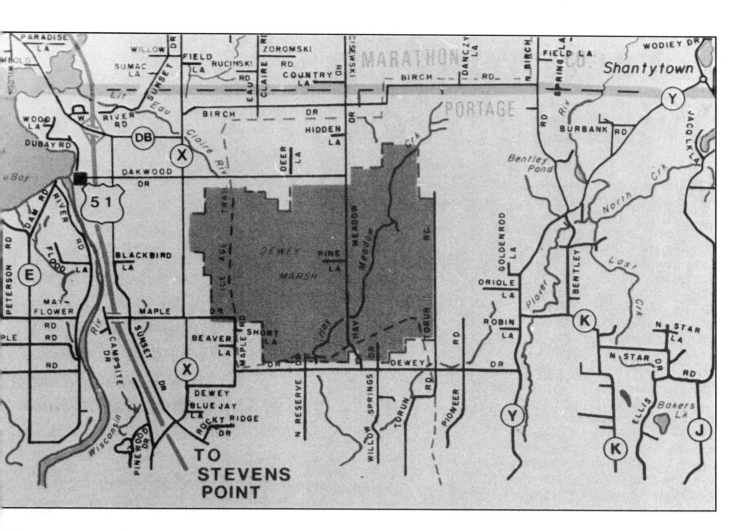

serves as a staging area for woodes.

Hunters have to hike back to the center of the property to find the best waterfowl hunting. Haug said there are opportunities for decoy hunting as well as jumpshooting. The property features potholes, creeks and a number of old ditches. The water found at Dewey Marsh is relatively shallow, so hunters use hip boots or chest waders to reach it.

"It is truly a swamp type of situation," he said. "(People) have to trek back quite a ways to get any decent duck shooting."

Although the wildfires destroyed much of the mature timber at Dewey Marsh, there are still some good stands on the western and eastern fringes of the area. Squirrel hunters will find good populations of their favorite game in these spots.

Access to Dewey marsh is very good, Haug said. State and county roads either run through or adjacent to the property, and there are parking lots available to hunters.

The area is large enough, however, that hunters can get lost in it, Haug said. A compass could prove to be a handy tool there. Also, there is a fair amount of private land within the project boundary, so hunters will want to pay strict attention to posted areas.

Greenwood Wildlife Area

WAUSHARA COUNTY

T hick, ancient oaks stretch high toward the sky as gray squirrels rustle their green leaves. That's probably one of the earliest images that many hunters take home from days afield as a youngster.

It's that type of experience that Greenwood Wildlife Area in Waushara County can provide. The 1,438-acre area, which lies at the edge of an open pitted outwash plain, features large expanses of top-quality oak.

You would expect this property to feature good opportunities for white-tailed deer, wild turkey and squirrel hunters. DNR wildlife technician Jim Radtke said sportsmen can also find ruffed grouse, cottontail rabbits and Canada geese at the area.

The area north of Brown Deer Court is a wildlife refuge. Archery deer hunting, squirrel and rabbit hunting area allowed there until Nov. 15. The area is then closed through Dec. 31.

The area south of Brown Deer Court is open to public hunting. Much of this area is covered with mature stands of oak, with some brushy and pine areas mixed in.

Greenwood also features several fields, which are maintained by area growers. Combined with the large oak stands, these two types of cover make for excellent wild turkey habitat.

The big birds often use tall oaks for roosting areas. Fields provide food in the form of crops and insects. Radtke said turkeys are often observed in the oak and field areas.

The first turkey hunting season in the Greenwood area was held in the spring of 1993. A limited number of permits were available to hunters, Radtke said, but those

TRAVEL GUIDE

NEAREST SERVICE CENTER: Wautoma.
LODGING: There are numerous campgrounds, bed and breakfasts and motels in the Wautoma area. The Wautoma Area Chamber of Commerce lists a total of 10.
SPORTS SHOP OR HUNTING LICENSE OUTLET: Information unavailable.
HOSPITAL OR EMERGENCY MEDICAL CLINIC: Associated Family Physicians of Wautoma and Berlin, (414) 787-4613.
EMERGENCY VETERINARY CLINIC: Information unavailable.
AUTO REPAIR OR TOWING: Charles Chevy, (715) 228-2911.

opportunities should increase with time.

Deer are also abundant in the Greenwood area. The whitetail population at the property is good, thanks in part to the refuge. Heavy pressure during the annual November firearms season can force many animals into the refuge.

Radtke said archery hunters have experienced good success in recent years at Greenwood. However, as the area became more popular with bow hunters, harvest rates have tapered off somewhat.

The refuge area at Greenwood was closed to bow hunting at one time. However, managers opened up the opportunity after sharecroppers complained of high deer densities in the area.

Since the area is dominated by one habitat type, hunters should scout ahead to find natural funnel areas or heavily used trails. Locating these areas where deer will likely be found will help make for a more successful hunt.

Squirrel hunters should find Greenwood to their liking. Simply, oak means fox and gray squirrels. Mature oaks provide squirrels with den trees and a great source of food: acorns.

Squirrel hunters should find Greenwood to their liking. Simply oak means fox and gray squirrels. Mature oaks provide squirrels with den trees and with a great source of food: acorns.

Unlike many areas, squirrel hunting is quite popular at Greenwood, Radtke said. Still, with such ideal habitat, hunting opportunities here remain good.

Greenwood can also provide waterfowlers with a unique hunting opportunity. The farm fields in the property attract some Canada geese every year. Geese often roost a nearby Mecan Springs Refuge, and use the area as sort of a stopping off spot.

Since most of the farm fields are within the refuge area, pass shooting is really the only form of hunt

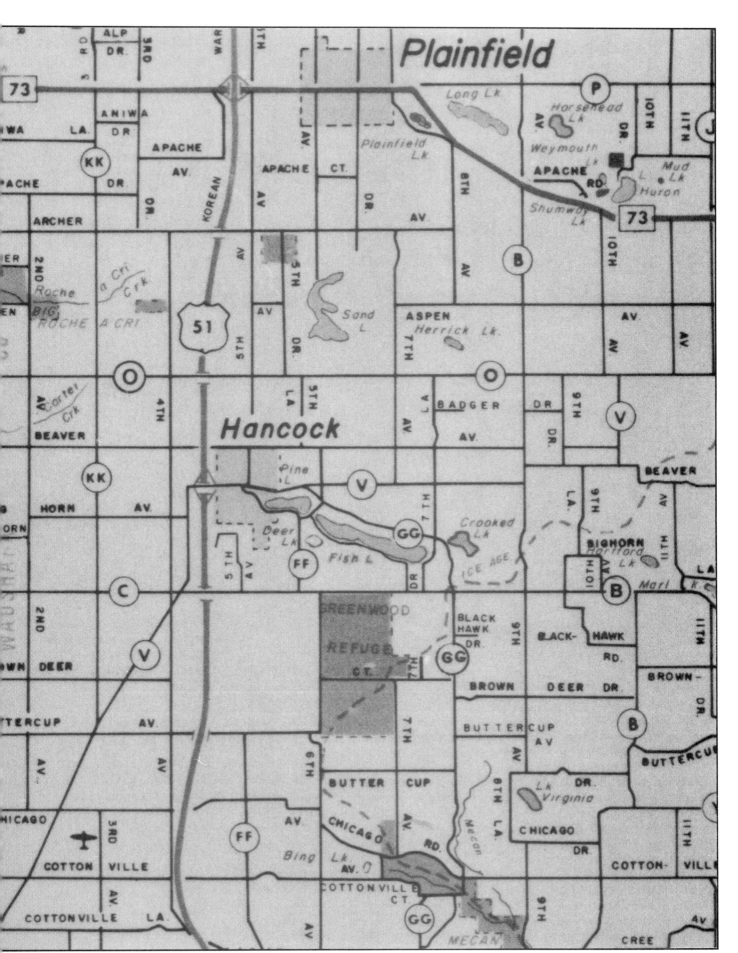

Plainfield

Hancock

An abundance of mature oak trees makes for an abundance of acorns and both gray and fox squirrels at the *Greenwood Wildlife Area in Waushara County.*

ing for geese. There is little or no water on the property in most years, so decoy hunting or jump shooting is out of the question.

Radtke said the DNR has cut about 10 five- to 10-acre openings around Greenwood, mainly to facilitate the regrowth of aspen and other plants. Ruffed grouse are attracted to these areas, and the birds provide some gunning for upland shooters.

Some woodcock also visit Greenwood during migrations, but the lack of water on the property limits the number of timberdoodle that use the property.

In the new growth and brushy areas, some cottontail rabbits can be found. Hunters who scout and locate likely hiding spots can get some shooting on bunnies during the generous season, which runs through February.

White River Marsh Wildlife Area

GREEN LAKE COUNTY

ind the right kind of food and you'll likely find wildlife. That old axiom holds true at the White River Marsh Wildlife Area.

The area, located in Green Lake and Marquette counties, is a sprawling 10,908-acre mix of habitats. The White River and Sucker Creek run through the property, and the Fox River marks the southeast boundary. The central part of the area is marsh, consisting mainly of cattails, sedges, reed canary grass and wild rice. Brush marshes and lowland forests are also found around the property, and upland areas feature mature woodlots, grasslands and crop fields.

Pheasants and deer are the most sought-after species here, and both benefit from the many food plots in the area.

Tom Hansen, DNR wildlife manager, said about 1,000 acres of land are share-cropped in the wildlife area. Local farmers share-crop the fields, and the crops are then left standing, providing food and cover for wildlife. Payment for the services is usually in the form of leaving food patches and establishing grass lands for use by wildlife.

Corn and alfalfa fields draw lots of deer, especially in hard winters or years when farmers are able to harvest the majority of their corn. The DNR doesn't do a great deal of direct management for whitetails at White River, but Hansen said the food plots there can be magnets.

White River features a good population of deer, and there are some decent-sized racks in the area, Hansen said. Because of that, the

TRAVEL GUIDE

NEAREST SERVICE CENTER: Princeton.

LODGING: There are numerous resorts, guest houses, motels and campgrounds in Princeton. The Princeton Chamber of Commerce lists a total of 11.

SPORTS SHOP OR HUNTING LICENSE OUTLET: Corner Bait, Highway 73 and County Trunk D, west end of Green Lake, (414) 295-6547. Princeton Mobil Mart, 933 W. Main St., Princeton, (414) 295-6500.

HOSPITAL OR EMERGENCY MEDICAL CLINIC: Princeton Family Medical Clinic, 502 W. Water St., Princeton, (414) 295-6432.

EMERGENCY VETERINARY CLINIC: Information unavailable.

AUTO REPAIR OR TOWING: Ken's Amoco, 531 S. Fulton St., Princeton, (414) 295-3511 days, or 295-6426.

area is popular with archery and gun hunters.

Hansen described deer hunting pressure at White River as moderate. Hunting pressure at the area apparently peaked during the 1970s, but has leveled off in recent years. Areas around crop fields can be very good, Hansen added. Much of the deer hunting pressure takes place in the central and southern portions of the property, where thicker cover exists.

Pheasant hunting is probably the second biggest activity at White River, Hansen said. The area fea-

Pheasants and deer are the most sought-after species here, and both benefit from the many food plots in the area.

tures very little natural reproduction, but is heavily stocked twice a week for three to four weeks into the season. During the first two weeks of the season, pheasant hunting at the property is closed at 2 p.m. After that, the season hours return to normal.

White River's croplands greatly benefit pheasants since they are in close proximity to the areas that are stocked. Hansen said no birds are stocked in grasslands, which are more accessible to hunters than thick marsh or other heavy cover.

Grass and cropland areas along County Trunk D, which runs through the north-central portion of the area, and South Road are the best places for hunters to check, Hansen said. There are several parking areas along both roads.

Since the area is more heavily stocked than other local hunting grounds and is close to population centers, it receives a lot of attention from pheasant chasers.

"It attracts people," Hansen said. "There's competition for the birds."

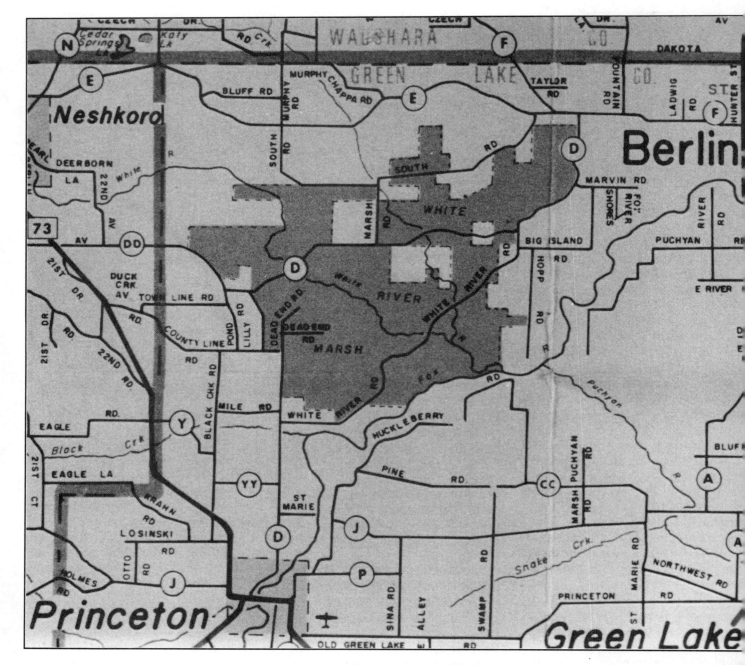

Although stockings end three to four weeks into the season, there are usually birds available to hunters, Hansen said. This also contributes to the area's popularity.

White River features a lot of water, in the form of natural marshes, rivers and some small impoundments. However, Hansen said it isn't managed as heavily for waterfowl as some other area marshes.

The area is about 95 percent natural wetlands, Hansen said. Therefore, if water levels in fall are low, it won't attract as many waterfowl as some other properties,

which may feature water control structures. If the water level is high, more birds will use the area. Nonetheless, White River is generally a great migration stop for waterfowl.

Birds can be found in the rivers and creeks through the marsh, as well as in marsh areas.

There isn't a lot of decoy hunting at the area, Hansen said. One reason might be that there are few roads and no boat access areas at White River. It retains a wilderness-like atmosphere, Hansen said.

Hunters mainly walk into the areas they are going to hunt,

Hansen said. Jump shooting is popular, but some hunters float the rivers or creeks in the area. This can be very productive, but ducks and geese will eventually wise up to the method.

The main duck species at White River are mallards and wood ducks. Hunters also bag green-winged and blue-winged teal. The area sees almost no diving duck use, since there is little open water habitat for the birds.

Canada geese use the area heavily, but hunters might have to walk long distances to reach them, Hansen said. They often roost in

Patrick Durkin

The White River Marsh Wildlife Area features very little natural reproduction of pheasants, but is heavily stocked twice a week for three to four weeks into the sea- *son. White River's croplands greatly benefit pheasants since they are in close proximity to the areas that are stocked.*

river oxbows far from the roads.

If duck or goose hunting proves slow during the fall, hunters can always enjoy the spectacle of sandhill cranes, which use the area in great numbers as a migration stop and staging area. Hansen adds that spring duck viewing at White River is very good.

Wild turkeys have done well around the White River area, but there aren't many of them in the public property itself, Hansen said.

Grouse are present at White River, but the population is usually low. This could be because birds in public hunting areas are hunted heavily.

Woodcock numbers, for whatever reason, are very low.

Hunters looking for squirrels can find loads of them in the oak wood lots around the property. Hansen suggested that people look for stands on higher ground around the marsh.

Some cottontail rabbits are also present.

The area was once heavily used by raccoon hunters. However, most of the predator hunting activity at the area has died down, possibly because of low fur prices.

Grand River Marsh Wildlife Area

GREEN LAKE AND
MARQUETTE COUNTIES

Grand River means geese, and lots of them. There are loads of ducks here, too, including plenty of divers for those not afraid of pushing their way out into the main water body.

Many successful Wisconsin waterfowlers are the keepers of an important bit of information: The best goose hunting in the Horicon Zone isn't necessarily near Horicon.

Grand River Marsh, a 7,300-acre marsh located in Green Lake and Marquette counties, heads the list of several central Wisconsin areas that continue to provide outstanding waterfowl hunting opportunities.

Ask local sportsmen. Grand River means geese, and lots of them. There are loads of ducks here, too, including plenty of divers for those not afraid of pushing their way out into the main water body.

The area, which had been partially drained during the 1950s, was restored beginning in 1958, when sportsmen's clubs, local and state authorities championed the creation of the wildlife area. Since then, the property has grown to include the vast wetland basin and the upland habitat surrounding it. About 3,000 acres have been impounded to provide a mix of vegetation and open water habitat. Water levels are managed to provide optimum conditions for vegetation and invertebrates for breeding and migratory birds. Periodic carp treatments have also helped.

Tom Hansen, area wildlife manager for the Department of Natural Resources, said Grand River Marsh will hold between 40,000 and 100,000 geese every fall.

There is a 3,000-acre refuge on the west half of the property that is closed to hunting during the waterfowl season. This area attracts

TRAVEL GUIDE

NEAREST SERVICE CENTER: Princeton.
LODGING: There are numerous resorts, guest houses, motels and campgrounds in Princeton. The Princeton Chamber of Commerce lists a total of 11.
SPORTS SHOP OR HUNTING LICENSE OUTLET: Corner Bait, Highway 73 and County Trunk D, west end of Green Lake, (414) 295-6547. Princeton Mobil Mart, 933 W. Main St., Princeton, (414) 295-6500.
HOSPITAL OR EMERGENCY MEDICAL CLINIC: Princeton Family Medical Clinic, 502 W. Water St., Princeton, (414) 295-6432.
EMERGENCY VETERINARY CLINIC: Information unavailable.
AUTO REPAIR OR TOWING: Ken's Amoco, 531 S. Fulton St., Princeton, (414) 295-3511 days, or 295-6426.

many of the geese using the area, which lends itself to a great deal of "firing line" hunting. In fact, Hansen said most of the goose hunting done on the property itself is pass shooting near the refuge. There are some decent decoy hunting opportunities in the eastern part of the marsh, however.

Also, the area surrounding Grand River Marsh is heavily farmed. As growers cut their corn through the fall, the area attracts huge squadrons of Canada geese. Nearby Big Green Lake and Lake Puckaway also serve as open water

roosting spots for the birds. Since these large bodies of water don't freeze up quickly, the entire region has become a late-season goose hotspot.

Duck hunting at Grand River is generally good, Hansen said. However, the area is heavily used. No motorboats or electric motors are allowed on the impoundment, so hunters willing to pole or paddle their way to secluded spots can experience some quality hunting, he added.

Grand River is a major waterfowl breeding area. Hansen said the area generally produces 2,000 to 3,000 ducks a year. There's a good mix of ducks here. The most popular puddle ducks are mallards, teal, widgeon and gadwall. Ringnecks also pour into the area each fall. A DNR count during the fall migra-

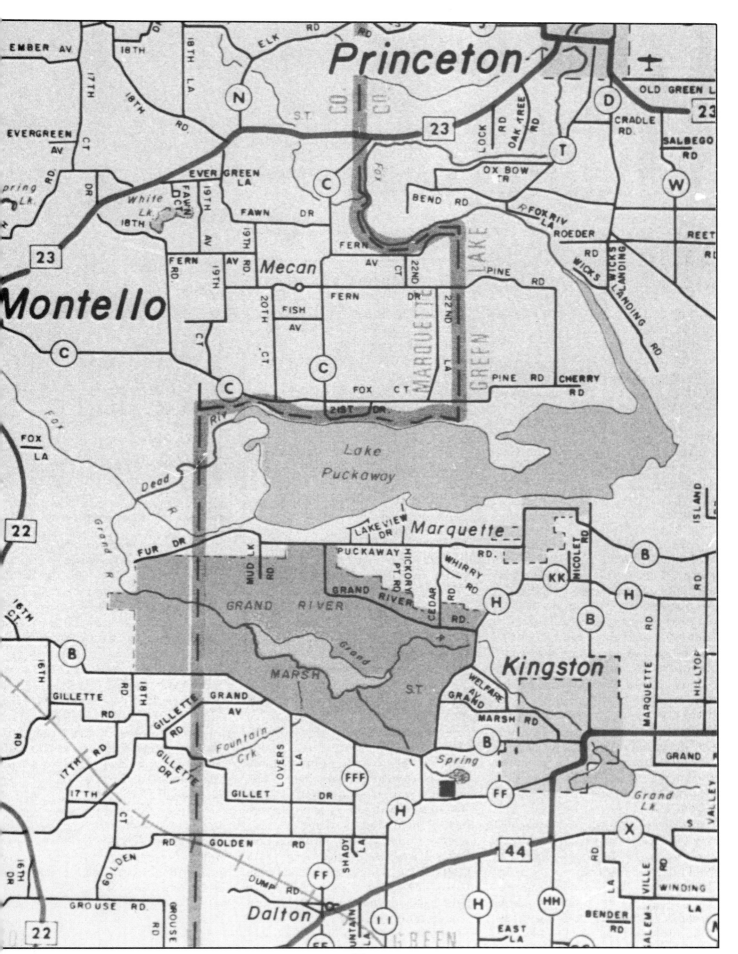

The Grand River Marsh, which had been partially drained during the 1950s, was restored beginning in 1958, when sportsman's clubs, local and state authorities championed the creation of the wildlife area.

tion in 1992 put the number of "blackjacks" at Grand River at about 7,000. Hunters pursuing diving ducks can have some good days here, especially during the week, when hunting pressure is lighter.

Hansen cautions hunters to be up on their duck identification, though. The area usually attracts a few canvasbacks each fall. The big birds have been protected.

Quality habitat is the main reason the area attracts birds. Hansen said it features lots of open water, coupled with very good submergent vegetation, consisting mainly of sago, wild celery and some wild rice. Wild rice and cattails are the primary emergents. Continuing carp treatments are a key to maintaining the quality vegetation at Grand River, he added.

There are several parking areas around the central and eastern portions of the marsh. There are also water access points on the

northern and southern ends of the marsh for hunters with canoes, skiffs or johnboats.

Since the area is about 80 percent marsh, it doesn't attract many archery hunters, Hansen said. Gun hunters make full use of the area, though. The waterfowl refuge is opened up during the firearms season, and many firearms hunters concentrate their efforts on the area's south end.

Hansen said the eastern portion of Grand River actually may be under-utilized during gun season. It features thick cover and hard walking, but deer are there.

There is a good population of deer in the Grand River area, Hansen said. In fact, Grand River has produced some nice racks.

The DNR stocks pheasants at Grand River for the first three or four weeks of the season. Birds are planted in grassy areas near cropped public lands, Hansen said.

Grand River isn't stocked as heavily as some other nearby wildlife properties such as White River Marsh Wildlife Area.

Predator hunting activity at Grand River is minimal, but there are plenty of foxes and raccoons in the area. Squirrel hunting is also limited, but hunters can find some bushytails in oak and other hardwood patches surrounding the marsh.

Hansen said Grand River features a larger cottontail rabbit population than other similar areas. The best spots are the upland edge areas along Town Road.

EAST

Brillion Wildlife Area

CALUMET COUNTY

If it's upland bird hunting your heart desires, Brillion Wildlife Area in Calumet County won't disappoint.

Ringneck pheasants are the main focus of hunters' attention at Brillion, according to Dick Nikolai, wildlife manager for the DNR. The area, the primary emphasis of which is habitat restoration, features about 2,000 acres of marsh and around 1,500 acres of upland grass cover, giving it some of the best pheasant planting habitat in the state.

Because the area is so conducive to pheasant stocking, and is so close to the heavily populated Fox River Valley, it does see a lot of hunter activity, especially early in the pheasant season.

However, as the season wears on, pressure subsides and people looking to get away from heavily hunted plots of land can find Brillion a likely looking spot.

Pheasants are planted here twice a week for the first two weeks of the pheasant season. They are planted once a week for another one or two weeks. Local sportsmen's groups also release pheasants around the area.

Roosters are stocked in upland grass cover at Brillion, such as switch grass or canary grass. Hunters can often locate the birds in these areas, especially soon after stockings, but hunting pressure tends to push them toward the marsh and heavier cover. A parking lot off Bastian Road in the northeast corner of the area is a traditional access point to grassy areas on the northern half of the property.

Because of the grassland habitat Brillion provides, another great, albeit less popular, gamebird thrives there: Hungarian partridge,

TRAVEL GUIDE

NEAREST SERVICE CENTER: Brillion.
LODGING: Sandman Motel, Highway 10, Brillion, (414) 756-2106.
SPORTS SHOP OR HUNTING LICENSE OUTLET: Schad's True Value, 205 N. Main St., Brillion, (414) 756-3231.
HOSPITAL OR EMERGENCY MEDICAL CLINIC: Brillion Clinic, 133 Wisconsin Ave., Brillion, (414) 756-2055.
EMERGENCY VETERINARY CLINIC: Veterinary Associates, 1922 Highway 10, Reedsville, (414) 754-4307.
AUTO REPAIR OR TOWING: Horn Ford Mercury, 666 W. Ryan St., Brillion, (414) 756-2115. Pietroske Chevy-Olds, 109 S. Main St., Brillion, (414) 756-2133. Enneper Garage, 417 W. Ryan St., Brillion, (414) 756-2243.

also known as gray partridge.

Nikolai, who hunts Huns himself, said he knows of at least five coveys of the birds on the Brillion property. A covey can consist of anywhere from six to 25 birds.

Huns prefer short native grasses as their No. 1 habitat. Unlike running roosters, they tend to shun the thick red willow or cattail marshes. The birds also seek out harvested fields, and hunting along the edges of these areas can be productive.

Nikolai said most of the Huns at Brillion are located on the north and southeast ends of the property. Hunters seeking them out will have to walk a while in between flushes, but the action can be fast once a covey is located.

Initial flushes often involve the entire covey. This can mean more

Because of the grassland habitat Brillion provides, another great, albeit less popular, gamebird thrives there: Hungarian partridge, also known as gray partridge.

than a dozen birds exploding out of the grass, and Nikolai said many surprised hunters often can't decide which bird to take.

Nikolai said he often marks where individual or pairs of birds set down after the initial flush. He then seeks these birds out for second flushes. However, the birds, which are strong flyers, can often become skittish after being raised once, and may flush at long distances the second time around.

Often, Huns are taken incidentally by pheasant hunters. There aren't too many people who seek them out exclusively.

Quality waterfowl hunting is also available at Brillion, Nikolai said. The marsh areas and upland grasses mix nicely to enhance good natural reproduction of ducks, mainly mallards, wood ducks and teal. When the fall migration is on, wid-

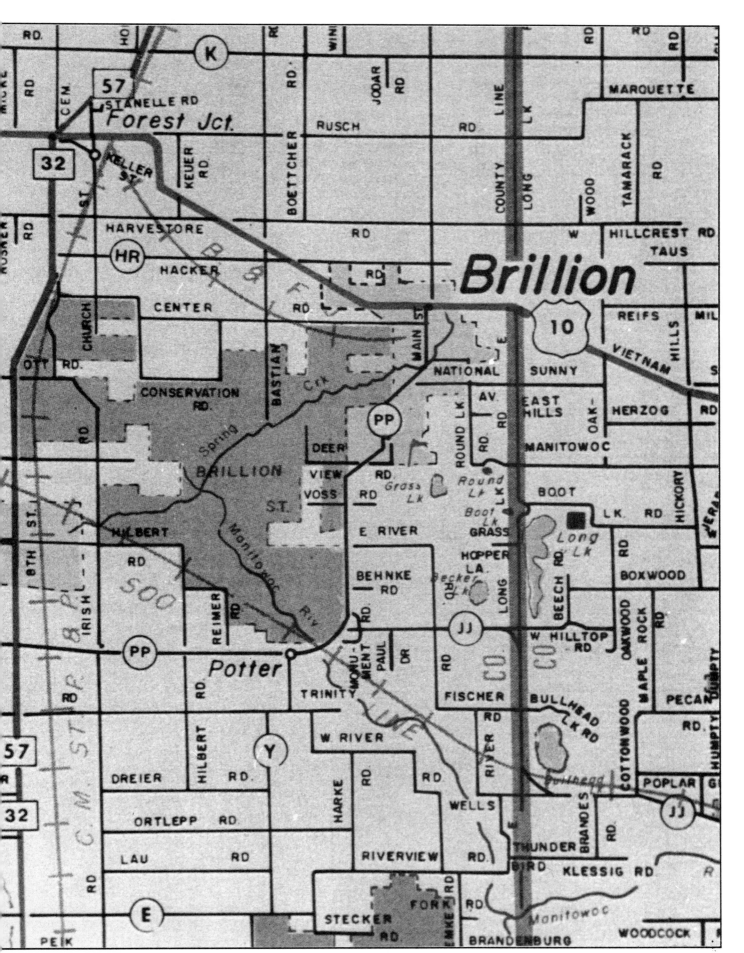

Pheasants are stocked at the Brillion Wildlife Area twice a week for the first two weeks of the season. The *birds are stocked in upland grassy areas, but hunting pressure tends to push them toward the marsh.*

geon and shovelers are also common at the area. The number of migrating birds using the area is increased in years when heavy fall rains flood the area and create large expanses of water.

The confluence of the Manitowoc River and Spring Creek in the center of the property is a traditional hotspot for duck hunters. These waters, plus Black Creek, also offer good hunting throughout the property.

There are also potholes around the area that provide good hunting opportunities. There is also a proposal to construct a 250-acre impoundment at the area.

White-tailed deer are abundant at the property, Nikolai said. It is a very good bow hunting spot, and archers often use a series of hiking trails at the area for easier access to hunting spots.

Gun hunting pressure at Brillion is very heavy, Nikolai said. People planning on hunting here during the firearms season should use caution, and seek out remote, lightly hunted areas if possible.

Nonetheless, hunters do take good bucks from the area now and then. Some parts of Brillion are almost inaccessible to humans

because of the heavy marsh, and there is a chance for bucks to survive the hunting season.

There is also a deer yard on the property where whitetails spend much of the winter when snow depths and cold temperatures make their lives difficult.

Killsnake Wildlife Area

CALUMET AND
MANITOWOC COUNTIES

H abitat restoration is the primary emphasis for Killsnake
Wildlife Area, but hunters
know it as a place where
upland birds, waterfowl, deer and
wild turkeys thrive.

The 5,550-acre property, located
in Calumet County, features a variety of habitat. There are about
2,500 acres of canary grass flats,
2,000 acres of uplands (of which
about 1,500 are grasses) as well as
some cedar and tamarack swamps
and wetlands.

Big, gaudy pheasants are the
main hunter attraction here,
according to DNR wildlife manager
Dick Nikolai. The grassland cover
on the property makes for excellent
stocking areas.

Hunting pressure on the birds is
high for the first two weeks at
Killsnake, Nikolai said. After that,
the crowds dwindle, and sportsmen
can find quality opportunities without going elbow to elbow with fellow
gunners.

Birds are stocked twice a week
for the first two weeks of the pheasant season. During this time, the
area has a 2 p.m. closure to pheasant hunting. After that, birds are
stocked once a week for one or two
weeks, Nikolai said.

Birds are stocked in the grassy
upland areas where hunters can
access them. These include waterfowl nesting areas consisting of
switch grass and big blue stem.
However, the birds are often
pushed into thick, dense marsh
areas when pressured heavily. Still,
hunters with dogs stand a good
chance of raising birds throughout
the season, Nikolai said.

Roosters are the only fair game at
the area; hen shooting is not
allowed.

You won't hear many bird
hunters talking about it, but

TRAVEL GUIDE

NEAREST SERVICE CENTER:
Chilton.
LODGING: Thunderbird Motel,
121 E. Chestnut St., Chilton, (414)
849-4216. Lakeview Motel and
Restaurant, N4111 Highway 55,
Stockbridge, (414) 439-1130.
**SPORTS SHOP OR HUNTING
LICENSE OUTLET:** Calumet
County Courthouse, 206 Court St.,
Chilton, (414)849-2361. Farm and
Home Supply, 519 N. Madison St.,
Chilton, (414) 849-9391.
**HOSPITAL OR EMERGENCY
MEDICAL CLINIC:** Calumet
Medical Center, 614 Memorial
Drive, Chilton, (414) 849-2386.
**EMERGENCY VETERINARY
CLINIC:** Information unavailable.
AUTO REPAIR OR TOWING:
Bunnell Auto Body and Repair,
1021 E. Chestnut St., Chilton,
(414) 849-4822 or 849-4487.
Vande Hey Brantmeier, 516 N.
Madison St., Chilton, (414) 849-
9331.

Killsnake does feature a very good
population of gray partridge, more
commonly known as Hungarian
partridge, or Huns. The fast flyers
do very well in the short grass cover
abundant on the property.

Nikolai, who hunts Huns, said a
study once showed that Killsnake
had one of the highest populations
of Huns in the state. Currently,
Nikolai said he knows of at least six
coveys of Huns on the property. A
covey can consist of six to 25 birds.

Private lands in the region formerly featured coveys of the birds,
but intensified agriculture resulted
in those populations crashing. As a
result, public lands often have some
of the larger concentrations of
birds.

> *Wild turkeys congre-
> gate in these areas,
> and ... Killsnake fea-
> tures a good popula-
> tion of the big birds.
> The birds were first
> stocked in the
> Manitowoc area, but
> really took off in
> Killsnake.*

Killsnake has some good stands
of oak on river bottomlands and
also on knolls throughout the property. Wild turkeys congregate in
these areas, and Nikolai said
Killsnake features a good population of the big birds.

The birds were first stocked in
the Manitowoc area, but really took
off in Killsnake. The DNR stocked
Killsnake specifically in 1989 and
1990.

Most of the turkey sightings at
the area are on the south end.
There is a winter roosting area on
the southeast portion of the property where up to 100 birds can congregate.

Waterfowlers can find opportunities at Killsnake. The Manitowoc
River and Cedar Creek flow
through the property, and these are

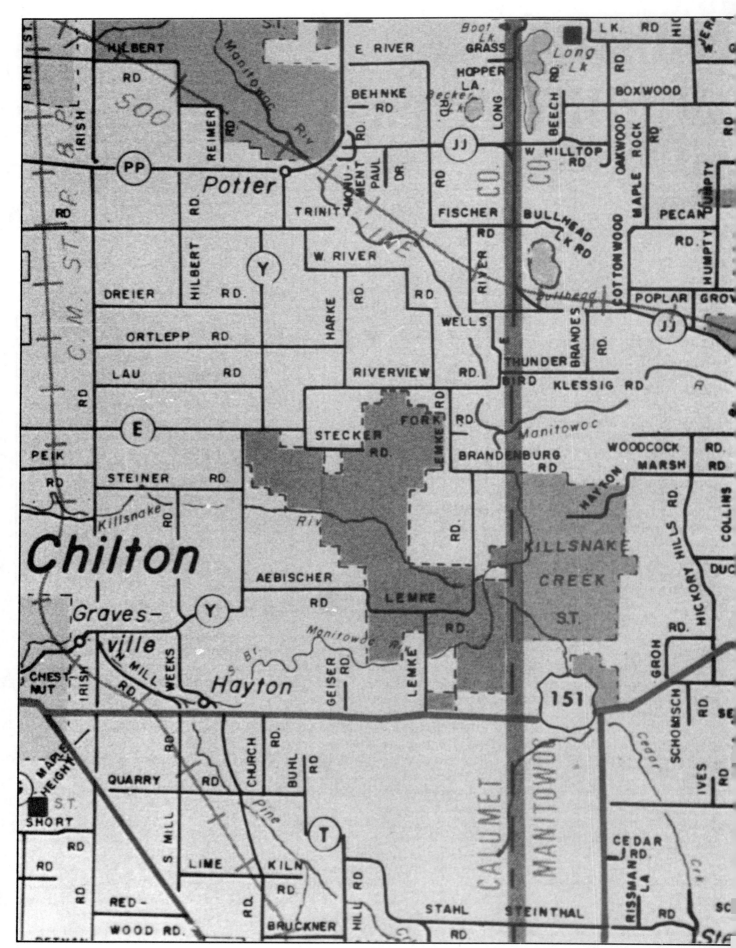

ood stands of oak at Killsnake Wildlife Area provide quality habitat for ild turkeys. The birds, which were first planted at Killsnake in 1989, are ost often sighted at the south end of the property.

good areas to look for birds, especially wood ducks. There are also numerous ponds at the area, and there is some local production there.

Experienced duck hunters know that wet falls are the best time to set decoys out at Killsnake. If precipitation is heavy enough and the area floods, it can attract scores of birds, Nikolai said. The main visitors are mallards, black ducks, and divers such as bluebills, ringnecks and redheads.

Flooding at the area seems to trigger a natural response in waterfowl, Nikolai said. When the area does flood, migrating birds are often using it the next day. Years like this are often few and far between, however: the last one was 1986.

Local deer hunters make good use of Killsnake. The area does have a good population of whitetails and, since there are some nearly inaccessible areas in the marsh, there is a chance of bagging a good buck.

Nikolai said the best time to gun hunt at the area is the Monday through Wednesday of the nine-day season. There is usually heavy hunting pressure at Killsnake on both weekends during the season, as well as Thanksgiving and the following Friday.

Small woodlots and lowland cedar or tamarack swamps seem to be the areas where hunters focus their efforts for deer, Nikolai said. However, these areas get pushed out quickly during the season.

Bow hunting season offers deer hunters a good opportunity to pursue whitetails while avoiding crowded hunting conditions.

Access to the area is simple. U.S. Highway 151 skirts the southern border of the property and intersects with Highway 32 to the east.

Collins Marsh Wildlife Area

MANITOWOC COUNTY

Canada geese ply their way skyward, greeting the morning marsh with a chorus of sound. It's one of the most treasured fall scenes to hunters, and one that's common at Collins Marsh Wildlife Area.

Collins, located in Manitowoc County, consists of about 4,100 acres of wetlands, wooded bottomlands, grasslands and flowages. It is a prime public spot for Canada goose hunting, as well as duck shooting. The area also offers good opportunities for deer, pheasants, and upland birds.

Jeff Pritzl, DNR wildlife manager, said the big story at Collins is geese. Collins has long been known as a good duck hunting area, but recently goose hunting has become more of a focus there.

The area is a perfect draw for migrating Canadas. It features large flowages in the central to southwest portion of the property, most of which are enclosed within a refuge. Pritzl said the good migrant goose hunting gets going about the second half of October and continues through November.

There is also a small resident population of giant Canada geese at Collins, Pritzl said. About 200 of the birds stayed in the area during the summer of 1992.

Collins Marsh comprises a special goose hunting zone unto itself. Hunters must apply for and receive a permit for the area to hunt there, just as they would have to for the Horicon Zone. Tags are issued and must be placed on harvested birds once they are shot.

Pritzl said that in 1992 Collins Zone hunters received about three tags apiece, slightly more than most Horicon Zone hunters did that year. That was a large cutback from previous years, caused by a freak June

TRAVEL GUIDE

NEAREST SERVICE CENTER: Manitowoc.
LODGING: There are several lodging opportunities in the Manitiwoc-Two Rivers area. The Manitiwoc Area Chamber of Commerce lists 13.
SPORTS SHOP OR HUNTING LICENSE OUTLET: Dave's Sport Center, 1806 Washington St., Two Rivers, (414) 794-7361. Louie's Sporting Goods, 809 N. 8th St., Manitowoc, (414) 684-4501.
HOSPITAL OR EMERGENCY MEDICAL CLINIC: Holy Family Memorial Medical Center, 2300 Western Ave., Manitowoc, (414) 684-2011.
EMERGENCY VETERINARY CLINIC: There are several veterinary clinics in the Manitowoc-Two Rivers area. The Manitowoc yellow pages lists 10.
AUTO REPAIR OR TOWING: There are numerous auto repair shops in the Manitowoc area. The yellow pages lists almost 50.

Collins Marsh is a perfect draw for migrating Canadas. It features large flowages in the central to southwest portion of the property.

snowstorm that wiped out most of the 1992 Mississippi Valley Population gosling hatch in Canada.

Most of the hunting done at the Collins property itself is pass shooting at birds going in and out of the refuge area, Pritzl said. There is some decoy hunting, but not much. Unlike some other areas, Collins doesn't develop problems with a firing line situation. That's because the number of people per goose hunting time period is limited. Last year, 425 people per period were allowed to hunt.

Duck hunting is still a big draw at Collins, Pritzl said. The area has actually improved in terms of duck

production, with the main specie being mallards, wood ducks an blue-winged teal.

The area also attracts quite a fe fall migrants, Pritzl said, comprise mostly of the three aforementione species. Black ducks are als unusually prominent here, h added.

"I don't advertise that," he said "I like to keep the pressure off o them."

The area can see some divin duck usage at times, Pritzl said. I 1992, however, it was poor as mos of the divers stuck to Lak Michigan.

Pritzl said duck hunting a Collins in 1992 was very good dur ing the first couple weeks o October, but wound down some what after that.

Ringneck pheasants are also very popular target at Collins Pritzl said. The area is stocke twice a week for the first two week of the season and once a week for

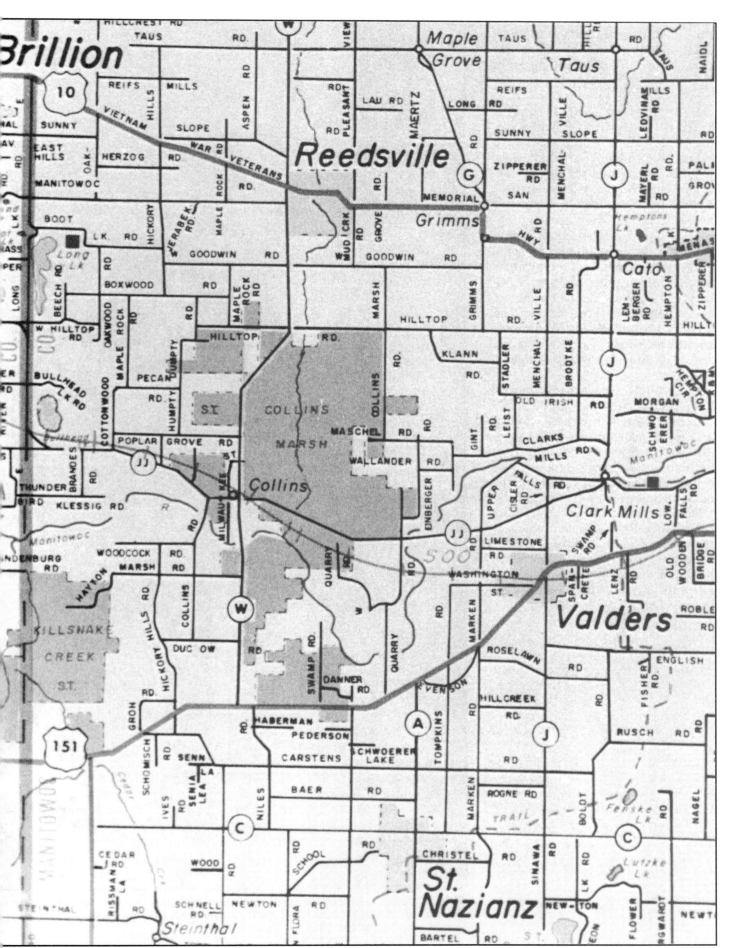

couple more weeks after that. In 1992, it had a 2 p.m. hunting closure during the first two weeks of the season. The area is open for roosters only.

Deer hunting is also a major activity at Collins, Pritzl said. Recently, deer populations in Manitowoc County were very close to goals. Pritzl said this means the area isn't overrun with deer, but supports a good population nonetheless.

With its marshy bottomlands and thick vegetation, Collins has some inaccessible spots where hunters might hold a good shot at a big buck. Pritzl said some big bucks are taken from there during the archery season. However, hunters should be willing to put in some scouting and walking in order to find them.

"Hip boots are an important item," he said.

Collins does feature some grouse and woodcock hunting, Pritzl said. The ruffed grouse shooting is very limited, but woodcock shooting can be good when the migratory flight is on, usually sometime around the middle of October.

The area doesn't feature much in the way of squirrel hunting.

Access to Collins is easy. It is bordered on the west by Highway 32, and skirted on the south by County Trunk JJ.

Collins Marsh comprises a special goose hunting zone unto itself. Hunters must apply for and receive a permit for the area to hunt there, just as they would have to for the Horicon Zone.

Gardner Swamp Wildlife Area

DOOR COUNTY

Door County offers up some of Wisconsin's most beautiful scenery, but also features a spot that DNR wildlife biologist Tom Bahti describes as "sort of an evil place."

Gardner Swamp Wildlife Area, located in southern Door County, is a 1,000-acre public hunting grounds that holds good wildlife populations in some wild habitat.

The property, located near Sturgeon Bay and Brussels, consists of a variety of habitat, including lowlands dominated by conifers — mainly cedars — and some floating bog with open water. The edges feature mixed hardwoods and some aspen. Keyes Creek runs through the center of the area.

Bahti said that the main hunting opportunities at Gardner Swamp are for waterfowl and white-tailed deer. There are also some scattered opportunities for ruffed grouse and woodcock hunting.

Gardner Swamp is not much of a waterfowl production area, Bahti said, simply for the fact that there isn't much upland nesting cover on the property. However, there is some local production of wood ducks.

The area does attract a good number of migrant birds, Bahti said. The main visitors are wood ducks, mallards, and, to a lesser extent, Canada geese and blue-winged teal. Depending on water levels, the area has been an important fall spot for wood ducks, Bahti said.

The property is very close to Lake Michigan, but Bahti said it really doesn't attract anything in the way of diving ducks. There isn't enough open water on the property for them.

With good numbers of migrating puddle ducks using the area, it

TRAVEL GUIDE

NEAREST SERVICE CENTER: Sturgeon Bay.
LODGING: There are several lodging opportunities in the Sturgeon Bay-Door County area.
SPORTS SHOP OR HUNTING LICENSE OUTLET: Mac's Sport Shop, 43 S. Madison Ave., Sturgeon Bay, (414) 743-3350.
HOSPITAL OR EMERGENCY MEDICAL CLINIC: Door County Memorial Hospital, 330 S. 16th Place, Sturgeon Bay, (414) 743-5566.
EMERGENCY VETERINARY CLINIC: Peninsula Vets, 5654 County Trunk T, Sturgeon Bay, (414) 743-7789.
AUTO REPAIR OR TOWING: Jorn's Pontiac and Buick, 224 Green Bay Road, (414) 743-4110. Bill Boettcher, 632 Green Bay Road, (414) 743-4461.

Gardner Swamp Wildlife Area, located in southern Door County, is a 1,000-acre public hunting grounds that holds good wildlife populations in some wild habitat.

might come as a surprise that Gardner Swamp sees relatively light waterfowl hunting pressure. Bahti said the reason behind that is the difficult hunting conditions that exist there.

Gardner Dam isn't an area where hunters can simply throw a boat in the water and motor out to a nearby blind. There are no trails or roads on the property. The area is tough to hunt. Waterfowlers either endure a tough walk in or utilize a small boat or skiff. Either of these options can result in a good deal of work, Bahti said.

The area used to have a much higher population of beavers, Bahti said, which made for higher water conditions.

The main access point for duck hunting at Gardner Dam is off of

Pickerel Road on the property's northeast corner. The spot offers an easier hike to the water.

Deer hunting is probably the primary activity at Gardner Dam, Bahti said. The area features a good deer population. Some nice bucks have been bagged in the Gardner Dam area in the past, Bahti said. Traditionally, the entire southern Door County area offers good deer hunting.

Many deer hunters focus on the upland areas that surround the marsh at Gardner Dam. Bahti said there generally are some hunters who seek their venison in the thick marsh areas. Together, both types of cover make for excellent whitetail habitat.

Grouse and woodcock hunting is somewhat of a secondary activity at Gardner Swamp, but Bahti said that there are birds available to

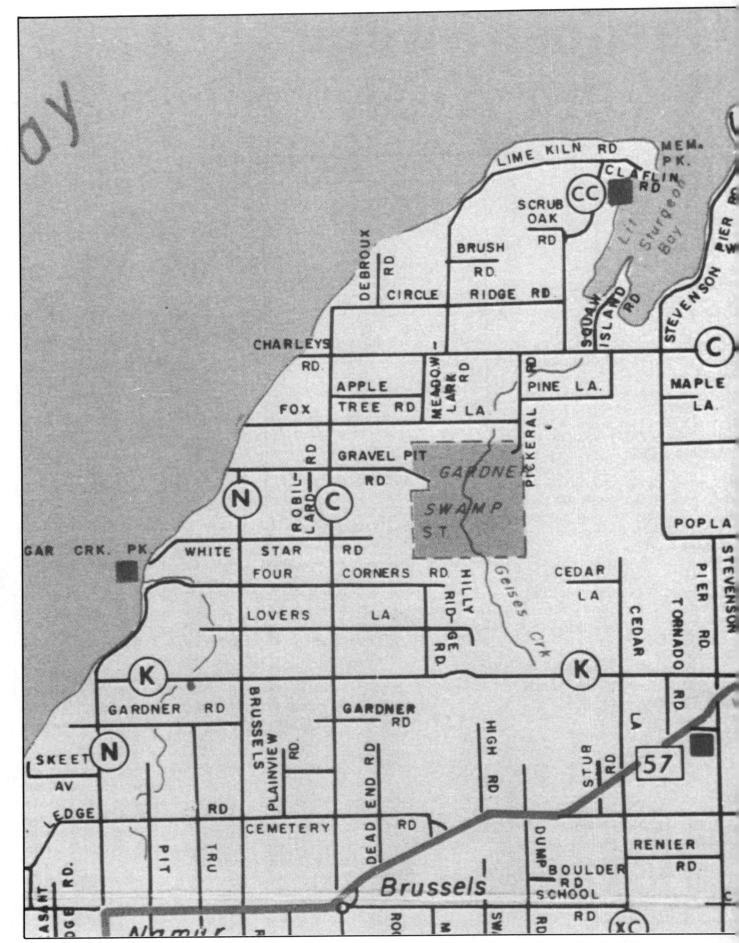

*hough Gardner Swamp is probably more widely known
r its white-tailed deer and waterfowl, the dense habi-* *tat there also supports a good number of raccoons and
other predators.*

Leonard Lee Rue III

unters.

There are some local woodcock
roduced at Gardner Dam, but
ahti said most of the timberdoo-
e shooting there will be provided
/ migrant birds. Grouse can typi-
lly be found in the aspen and
rdwoods edges in the area.

Gardner Swamp offers excellent
ccoon habitat, Bahti said. He
suspects that there is some coon
hunting, as well as some coyote
hunting, that goes on at the property.

Accessing the property is easy.
The property boundaries are
almost entirely contiguous, but
there is a small spit of private land
in the southern part. Pickerel Road
in the northeast, Gravel Pit Road
on the west and Four Corners Road
on the southwest give hunters
three convenient paths to the area.

Kettle Moraine State Forest, Southern Unit

WAUKESHA, JEFFERSON, WALWORTH COUNTIES

Sportsmen from the urban southeast corner of Wisconsin may look northward when planning their latest hunting venture, but may not have to look any farther than out their own back door.

The Southern Unit of the Kettle Moraine State Forest offers people about 18,000 acres of land, 85 percent of which is huntable. And while the area is right next to the Milwaukee metropolitan area, it still offers good hunting for a variety of game species.

The property consists mainly of upland forest, but also features grassy fields, lowland timber, marshes and about 100 small "kettle" lakes, from which the area gets its name. Mark Andersen, wildlife manager for the DNR, said that white-tailed deer and wild turkeys are probably the most sought-after game species here, while pheasants, waterfowl and small game species round out the opportunities.

Access to the area is very good. There are many state and county roads that run around and through the property. So, the forest sees a great deal of deer hunting activity during the firearms and archery seasons. Andersen said that a hunting pressure survey recently indicated that there is about one hunter for every 25 acres of huntable land in the forest. There are two small designated wildlife refuges on the property.

Whitetails are found throughout the property, Andersen said. Bow and gun hunters will likely want to scout ahead to find relatively remote areas that hold concentrations of deer.

The mature timber and grassy uplands of the forest make for very good turkey habitat. Andersen said there is a very good population of the big birds here, and hunting opportunities at the property are increasing.

TRAVEL GUIDE

NEAREST SERVICE CENTER: Whitewater.

LODGING: New Diplomat, 1262 W. Main St., Whitewater, (608) 473-6006. Super 8 Motel, 917 E. Milwaukee St., Whitewater, (608) 473-8818. Victoria on Main Bed and Breakfast, 622 W. Main St., Whitewater, (608) 473-8400. Greene House Country Inn, Whitewater, (608) 495-8771. Oak Terrace, Box 26, Whitewater, (608) 473-2121.

SPORTS SHOP OR HUNTING LICENSE OUTLET: Crummey's Sport and Marine Shop, 207 Elkhorn Road, Whitewater, (608) 473-5960. Ed's Guns and Range, 7631 Lima Center Road, Whitewater, (608) 473-4678.

HOSPITAL OR EMERGENCY MEDICAL CLINIC: Mercy-Whitewater Medical Center, 507 W. Main St., Whitewater, (608) 473-0400.

EMERGENCY VETERINARY CLINIC: Whitewater Veterinary Hospital, 527 S. Janeseville St., Whitewater, (608) 473-2930.

AUTO REPAIR OR TOWING: There are numerous automobile repair shops in the Whitewater area.

> *Access to the area is very good. There are many state and county roads that run around and through the property. The forest sees a great deal of deer hunting activity during the firearms and archery seasons.*

During the first spring hunt at the area, held in 1992, about 450 permit-holders bagged 102 birds. Andersen expected the number of permits and birds harvested to double in the spring of 1993.

Scouting at Kettle Moraine will be a necessity. Prospective turkey hunters should get out and tromp around the areas they want to hunt. Try to "roost" birds in the evening and locate areas where they feed and spend the day.

Because of the area's easy accessibility, turkey hunters will want to pay particular attention to safety measures. Accidents happen nearly every year because hunters did not make sure of their target before pulling the trigger.

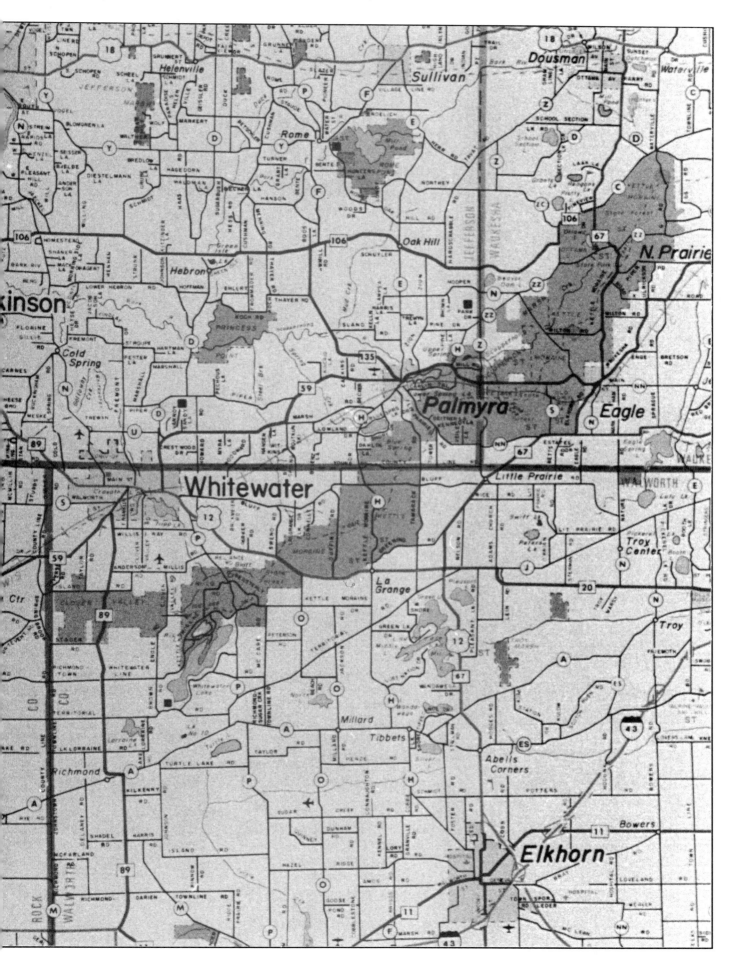

White-tailed deer are found throughout the Southern Unit of the Kettle Moraine State Forest. Hunters who *seek out remote areas will stack the odds in their favor.*

Ringneck pheasants are stocked in the southern unit. Andersen said the Scuppernong area of the property sees a great deal of stocking attention.

Birds are stocked twice a week through much of the season, then once a week almost up to the end of the hunt. There is not a 2 p.m. closure at the area.

Andersen said hunters will want to focus their pheasant chasing efforts on the available grassy uplands throughout the forest. Birds are planted in areas that look like good habitat that don't have hiking, skiing or horse trails on them.

There is also some waterfowling available to forest hunters, Andersen said. Some of the larger kettle lakes — those of 10 acres or more — can offer up some decoy

hunting. However, jumpshooting these small bodies of water is the most commonly employed method of duck hunting. Lake LaGrange, which features 80 acres of open water, also allows for some decoy hunting.

Wood ducks and mallards are the most commonly seen species in the forest. Some Canada geese are also taken from time to time. Shooting is usually good for the first two weeks of the season, then tends to slack off as the hunt progresses.

Rabbit hunters also like the forest. Andersen said many bunny chasers focus their efforts around areas near the bases of moraines or marsh edge areas that feature brushy cover. Many rabbits are taken incidentally by pheasant hunters.

There is a great deal of squirr hunting activity in the fores Andersen said, mainly around oa and other hardwood stand Anderson noted that squirrel hun ing opportunities are probably be ter in the forest's northern uni but the southern unit remains po ular.

Hunters should be aware th the forest is managed as a mult use area, and is heavily utilized non-hunters throughout much the year. There are many cam grounds in the area, as well trails for hiking, skiing, backpac ing, horse riding and nature watc ing. Sportsmen should pay partic lar attention to safety.

Kettle Moraine State Forest, Northern Unit

WASHINGTON,
FOND DU LAC AND
SHEBOYGAN COUNTIES

When it comes to hunting in southeast Wisconsin, the northern unit of Kettle Moraine State Forest is often the first choice of many sportsmen.

The forest offers about 28,000 acres of public land, most of which is open to hunting. And since the area stretches about 20 miles north and south, from Fond du Lac and Sheboygan counties into Washington County, it's only minutes away from several large population centers.

DNR wildlife manager Dale Katsma said Kettle Moraine's northern unit features a good variety when it comes to wildlife habitat. The majority of the forest, as its name implies, consists of deciduous hardwoods. There are some areas of lowland hardwoods, some patches of cedar and some pine plantations. There are some grasslands scattered throughout the public property, as well as some cropland areas. Some marshy areas can be found on the property, and the Milwaukee River runs through the area.

Kettle Moraine is immensely popular with non-hunters at all times of the year. Sightseers, hikers, pickers, equestrians and nature lovers all use the property heavily. As a result, hunters should be extra careful when pursuing game at the area. Some recreation areas in the forest are closed to hunting, and it's important to note that there is a good deal of private land within the forest's boundaries.

Deer hunting is probably the most popular activity at the forest, Katsma said. With such a variety of

TRAVEL GUIDE

NEAREST SERVICE CENTER: Sheboygan.

LODGING: There are numerous bed and breakfasts, inns, motels and hotels in the Sheboygan area. The Sheboygan County Chamber of Commerce lists more than 20.

SPORTS SHOP OR HUNTING LICENSE OUTLET: The Good Sport, 1946 N. 15th St., Sheboygan, (414) 459-7070. The New Wharf Inc., 733 Riverfront Drive, Sheboygan, (414) 458-4406. Brunette's Ace Hardware, 2825 S. Business Drive, Sheboygan, (414) 457-7787. Trilling True Value Hardware, 901 Michigan Ave., Sheboygan, (414) 457-5541.

HOSPITAL OR EMERGENCY MEDICAL CLINIC: Sheboygan Memorial Medical Center, 2629 N. 7th St., Sheboygan, (414) 457-5033. St. Nicholas Hospital, 1601 N. Taylor Drive, Sheboygan, (414) 459-8300. Valley View Medical Center, 901 Reed St., Plymouth, (414) 893-1771.

EMERGENCY VETERINARY CLINIC: There are several veterinary clinics available in the Sheboygan area. The Sheboygan County Chamber of Commerce, via the Yellow Pages, lists 10.

AUTO REPAIR OR TOWING: There are numerous auto repair or towing shops available in the Sheboygan County area.

With such a variety of whitetail habitat in close proximity to agricultural areas, deer abound at Kettle Moraine. The property is in deer management unit 69A, which features a good deer population, including some big bucks.

whitetail habitat in close proximity to agricultural areas, deer abound at Kettle Moraine. The property is in deer management unit 69A, which features a good deer population, including some big bucks.

Katsma said that during the 1992 firearms season, about 65 percent of the bucks harvested in the unit were yearlings. That compares favorably to previous years, when 75 or 80 percent of the bucks taken were 1.5-year-old animals. Several 2.5 and 3.5-year-old bucks were taken in 1992, he added.

Whitetails are fairly spread out across the property, especially during the gun deer season, Katsma said. Brushy cover, especially those areas next to or within wetland

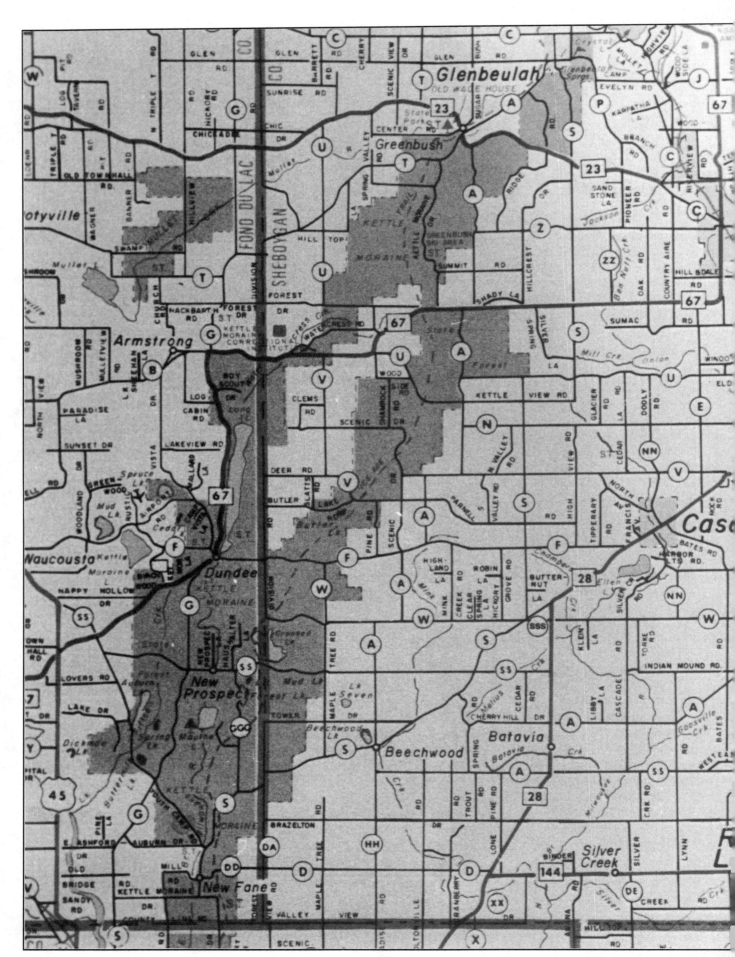

The Northern Unit of the Kettle Moraine State Forest features an abundance of small game, such as cotton- tail rabbits, as well as plenty of white-tailed deer and wild turkeys.

...eas, and stream corridors tend to ...tract more deer than upland ...ots, he added.

Archery hunting has become ...creasingly popular at Kettle ...oraine, Katsma said. Access to ...e forest is excellent, and bow ...nters should find plenty of likely ...king spots to wait out deer.

Wild turkeys have also become a ...ominent species at Kettle ...oraine. Because of its makeup, ...e property is ideal for birds. It is ...e of the few large, continuous ...ots of forest land in the area, and ...atures plenty of mature timber ...mbined with open fields and ...riculture. The forest makes up ...e core of Zone 30, and features a ...y good population of birds.

The forest will have its first fall ...nt in 1993, and is also open to ...ring hunting. Hunters who do ...ir scouting should have no trou- ...locating birds.

Pheasant hunters can find ...ortunities for a quality hunt at ...ttle Moraine, Katsma said. The ...ea is stocked, but not heavily. ...e DNR plants birds in open grassy areas around the property, and also at some of the share- cropped areas where there is standing corn. The birds aren't concentrated. Katsma said the agency tries to spread them out.

Kettle Moraine does attract a lot of pheasant hunters, especially when considering the relatively low number of stocked birds there. However, Katsma said that, since the birds are scattered, hunters can find spots that aren't hunted heavily.

Duck hunters can find quite a bit of jumpshooting around the forest, Katsma said. There are quite a few potholes around the area and, depending on water levels, they can hold early season mallards, wood ducks and teal. The Milwaukee River also offers some chances at ducks.

Some of the better jumpshooting opportunities at Kettle Moraine can be had on the small "kettle" lakes around the area.

Katsma said a couple of lakes in the property have undeveloped shorelines and can offer some shooting. Some marsh areas, including the 250-acre Bear Lake marsh, offer some decoy hunting opportunities.

Small game hunters will find plenty to keep them occupied at Kettle Moraine. The property's large stands of mature timber har- bor good squirrel populations, and hunters should have no problem finding good shooting.

Katsma said gray squirrels dom- inate the area, but a few fox squir- rels are present. Also, squirrel hunting pressure at the forest seems to have dropped off over the past 10 years, he added.

Rabbits are also common at the property, Katsma said. He suggest- ed checking brushy areas around the forest edge.

There is also some grouse and woodcock hunting at the property, Katsma said.

Sheboygan Marsh Wildlife Area

SHEBOYGAN COUNTY

Sheboygan Marsh Wildlife Area offers waterfowlers an old-time hunting experience smack dab in the middle of modern day eastern Wisconsin.

The entire marsh complex is about 13,000 acres, according to DNR wildlife biologist Dale Katsma. Sheboygan County owns about 7,500 acres of this, and an additional 700 acres is owned by the state. The remainder is privately owned.

Katsma said the area is primarily a wetlands complex. Although marshes are common in the southeastern part of the state, Sheboygan is unique in that it has many characteristics of a northern swamp area.

Cedar and tamarack areas along with brushy tag alder and dogwood areas surround the marsh proper, Katsma said. Closer to the water, cattails and open marsh areas predominate. A maze of ditches runs more than 20 miles.

At the center of the area is Sheboygan Lake, a 350-plus acre body of water that is primarily 3 feet deep or less. The Sheboygan River and a couple of its tributaries also run through the area. The marsh does have a closed refuge area near the southern portion of the property. It is closed to entry from Oct. 1 until Nov. 15, when it opens for any hunting besides waterfowl.

Waterfowling is very popular at Sheboygan Marsh. Katsma said the area features some fairly good production of wood ducks and mallards. This is sort of a mystery, however. Katsma said he still

Although marshes are common in the southeastern part of the state, Sheboygan is unique in that it has many characteristics of a northern swamp area. Cedar and tamarack areas along with brushy tag alder and dogwood areas surround the marsh proper.

hasn't figured out where the birds nest successfully.

The area is also a very good stag-

ing area and migration stop for ducks. Katsma said the mars[h] starts to see increasing numbers o[f] ducks around late August as bird[s] start to stage for the annual jour[-] ney south.

The most common ducks a[t] Sheboygan during the fall are ma[l-] lards, woodies, green-winged an[d] blue-winged teal and some widgeo[n.] Also, the area can attract ring[-] necks, bluebills and an occasiona[l] canvasback.

As is the case with many large[,] open-water marsh area[s,] Sheboygan can act as sort of [a] "home base" to migrating bird[s]

TRAVEL GUIDE

NEAREST SERVICE CENTER: Sheboygan.

LODGING: There are numerous bed and breakfasts, inns, motels and hotels in the Sheboygan area. The Sheboygan County Chamber of Commerce lists more than 20.

SPORTS SHOP OR HUNTING LICENSE OUTLET: The Good Sport, 1946 N. 15th St., Sheboygan, (414) 459-7070. The New Wharf Inc., 733 Riverfront Drive, Sheboygan, (414) 458-4406. Brunette's Ace Hardware, 2825 S. Business Drive, Sheboygan, (414) 457-7787. Trilling True Value Hardware, 901 Michigan Ave., Sheboygan, (414) 457-5541.

HOSPITAL OR EMERGENCY MEDICAL CLINIC: Sheboygan Memorial Medical Center, 2629 N. 7th St., Sheboygan, (414) 457-5033. St. Nicholas Hospital, 1601 N. Taylor Drive, Sheboygan, (414) 459-8300. Valley View Medical Center, 901 Reed St., Plymouth, (414) 893-1771.

EMERGENCY VETERINARY CLINIC: There are several veterinary clinics available in the Sheboygan area. The Sheboygan County Chamber of Commerce, via the Yellow Pages, lists 10.

AUTO REPAIR OR TOWING: There are numerous auto repair or towing shops available in the Sheboygan County area.

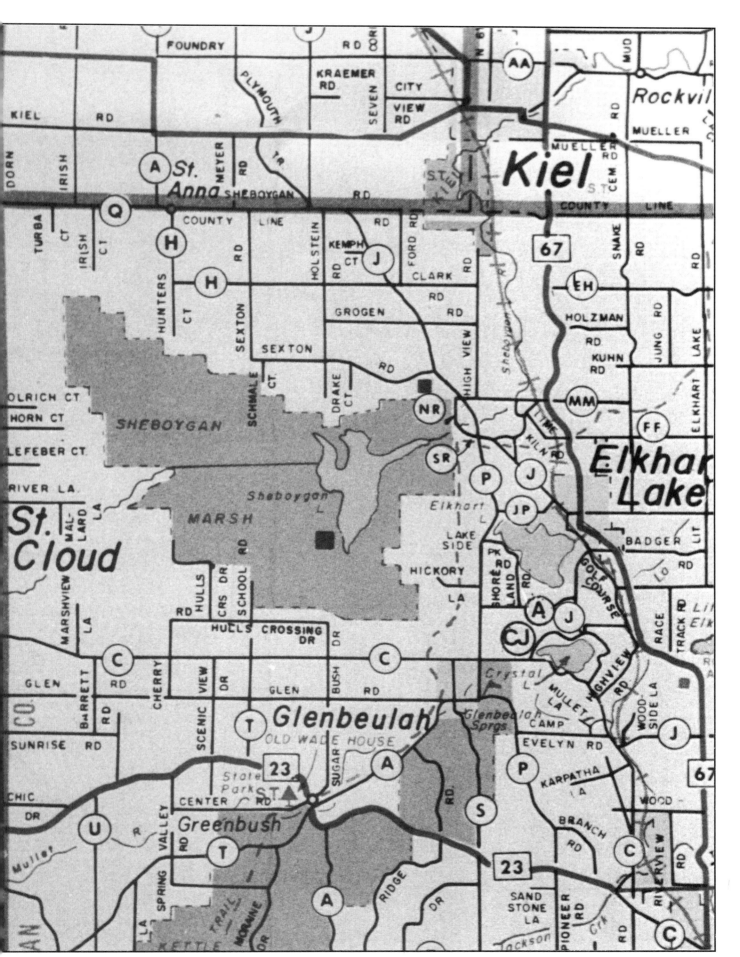

That is, they will roost in the area at night, then fly off in the morning to feed, then return in at various times during the day or evening. Nonetheless, Katsma said there are always some ducks around during the day in autumn.

Most of the waterfowling at Sheboygan is done from boats, Katsma said. There are more than 600 acres of open water that hunters can use a boat in, and boats or skiffs can also be pushed into cattail openings. The main boat landing in the area is at Broughton Sheboygan Marsh Park off of County Trunk P near the east end of the main lake.

Many hunters utilize portable blinds with their boats, then call for ducks over a decoy spread. There are very few permanent blinds that are put up at Sheboygan, Katsma said.

Some hunters use marsh skis to push through bog areas and jumpshoot birds, Katsma said. Also, there might be some jumpshooting opportunities available on the Sheboygan River. Much of the marsh area is too thick and wet for conventional jumpshooting tactics.

Despite the area's obvious attraction to waterfowlers, Katsma said that hunting pressure there really isn't overpowering. After opening weekend, especially during the week, hunting pressure tends to die down.

"If you're willing to go a little bit farther in, there are some areas where you can get away even on the busiest days," Katsma said.

Deer hunting is also popular at Sheboygan Marsh, Katsma said. The area features a good population of whitetails, especially in the brushy areas and tamarack-cedar swamp patches.

The Sheboygan Marsh is a waterfowler's paradise. The area produces a fair number of local ducks each year and attracts flocks of migrating birds because of its large areas of open water and available plant foods.

Also, deer tend to concentrate in the area in late fall and early winter as crops from the surrounding farmlands are harvested. Katsma said the area tends to be almost like a northern deer yard some winters, especially around the cedar areas.

Many hunters will walk into likely deer hunting spots from the uplands surrounding the marsh. Katsma said that some hunters will use boats to access out-of-the-way portions of the property.

Ruffed grouse and woodcock hunting is also available at the property, Katsma said. These gamebirds are mainly found around the brushy edges bordering the marsh.

Woodcock shooting is dependent mainly on the fall migration, Katsma said. There are some local birds produced here, but migrant still provide the bulk of the shooting.

Ruffed grouse numbers at the area are relatively good, and Katsma said that's probably because hunting at Sheboygan can be a tough prospect.

Access to good spots is difficult Katsma said. Hunters might find some tough walking, including spots where they can sink up to their knees, in their search for birds. It will take a tough hunter and a tough dog to get at old ruffed Sheboygan Marsh.

Mike Vogel

Allenton Wildlife Area

M ilwaukee-area hunters can consider themselves lucky. There are several quality public hunting areas in their vicinity, including Allenton Wildlife Area in Washington County.

Allenton provides sportsmen with a mixture of hunting opportunities. White-tailed deer, pheasants, ducks, geese, rabbits and squirrels are all pursued here.

Wildlife manager Tom Isaac said the area consists of about 1,200 acres of state-owned land and about 2,000 acres of leased land. Much of the property features brushy cover and wetlands. This lends itself to the multiple uses that hunters enjoy.

Ringneck pheasants are stocked heavily at Allenton, Isaac said. The property is stocked once or twice a week, and has a 2 p.m. closing time during the first two weeks of the season.

Isaac said that birds are planted in likely looking cover areas, mainly grassy uplands throughout the property. Switch grass is a common cover here, and there are some canary grass areas. The area also features some thicker willow and dogwood-type habitat, which can congregate birds that are pushed by hunting pressure.

There is also some sharecropping done at Allenton. Local growers raise crops, which are then left to stand and provide food and cover for wildlife. Pheasants benefit directly from this practice, and Isaac said many birds congregate in these areas.

White-tailed deer are abundant at Allenton. Because of this, and its close proximity to Milwaukee, the property can receive heavy pressure during the November firearms season. Sportsmen who can hunt on weekdays stand a better chance of

TRAVEL GUIDE

NEAREST SERVICE CENTER: Hartford.
LODGING: Reef Point Resort, 3416 Lake Drive, Hartford, (414) 673-9952 or 628-1258. Erin Motel and Restaurant, 911 Highway 83 South, Hartford, (414) 673-2721. Silver Bell Motel, 720 Grand Ave., Hartford, (414) 673-2232. Super 8 Motel, 1539 E. Sumner St., Hartford, (414) 673-7431.
SPORTS SHOP OR HUNTING LICENSE OUTLET: There are numerous sporting goods stores in the Hartford area. The yellow pages provided by the Hartford Area Chamber of Commerce lists eight.
HOSPITAL OR EMERGENCY MEDICAL CLINIC: Hartford Memorial Hospital, 1032 E. Sumner St., Hartford, (414) 673-2300.
EMERGENCY VETERINARY CLINIC: Algiers Veterinary Services, 1471 E. Sumner St., Hartford, (414) 673-2990. The Animal Doctors, 1528 E. Sumner St., Hartford, (414) 673-5355.
AUTO REPAIR OR TOWING: There are numerous auto repair places in the Hartford area.

WASHINGTON COUNTY

Local growers raise crops, which are then left to stand and provide food and cover for wildlife. Pheasants benefit directly from this practice, and ... many birds congregate in these areas.

not going shoulder to shoulder with other hunters.

Likely areas for deer at Allenton are edge zones where marsh and upland cover meet, as well as spots where croplands meet thick marsh cover. These places can be especially productive during the archery season, when there probably won't be heavy pressure to move deer out of the spots.

Isaac said waterfowling does receive some attention from sportsmen visiting Allenton. The area fea-

tures two small flowages, and hunters often concentrate their efforts here.

Also, there are some jumpshooting opportunities available to hunters on creeks that run through the Allenton.

The main duck species using the wetlands will be puddle ducks, mainly mallards, wood ducks and blue-winged teal. Isaac said the area also sees some usage by geese. However, hunting opportunities on adjacent private lands will probably offer better chances at the birds.

Rabbit hunters will find Allenton's brushy cover to their liking. The animals also benefit from habitat improvements done for pheasants or waterfowl.

Looking for rabbits while toting a shotgun can make for an enjoyable

Allenton Wildlife Area consists of about 1,200 acres of state-owned land and about 2,000 acres of leased land.

Much of the property features brushy cover, and ring-neck pheasants are stocked heavily at the area.

day. Although many hunters would count themselves as rabbit hunters, the animals don't receive intensive pressure at most areas.

Look for tracks, scat and areas where rabbits feed. If you find a good spot, enjoy it for a day and then let it rest for a while. Rabbits generally take some time to resume their normal routines after being disrupted by hunting pressure.

There are also some opportunities for woodcock at Allenton. Brushy plant species such as alder and dogwood give the birds good cover. Areas that lie next to wetlands usually offer the moist, heavy soils that the birds prefer to probe for earthworms, their favorite food.

Access to Allenton is easy. U.S. Highway 41 runs through the property's east end. Highway 33 crosses north of the area's boundary, and Highway 175 runs through the west portion of the land. Also, there are several town roads that run through Allenton.

Hunters who travel to Allenton might also want to check out Hartford Public Hunting Grounds, which lies just north of Hartford on both sides of Highway 83.

Hartford Public Hunting Grounds is entirely composed of leased land. Sportsmen can find opportunities here for pheasants, deer, rabbits, squirrels and varmint species.

Jackson Marsh Wildlife Area

WASHINGTON COUNTY

Jackson Marsh Wildlife Area, located in Washington County, offers some real "swamp rat" type hunting within a few minutes of the state's largest population center.

Tom Isaac, DNR wildlife manager, said the 3,000-acre area consists mainly of wooded, lowland swamp mixed with some uplands. Hunting opportunities here consist mainly of white-tailed deer, pheasants, rabbit and some waterfowl.

The area features a very good deer population, Isaac said. Since it is so close to the Milwaukee area, it's also quite popular with hunters. Nonetheless, hunters do manage to pull some pretty decent bucks out of the area year after year.

Isaac said the key seems to be the amount of effort expended by hunters. People who are willing to trudge back through the thick stuff into the heavy cover will likely stand a better chance of seeing a big rack, especially after the guns of opening morning have sounded.

There are some relatively inaccessible areas at Jackson Marsh. Hunters should use hip boots to walk back into the marsh area, Isaac said. If they're willing to put in the effort, they can get a good distance off the road.

Many deer, including experienced, older bucks, will use wet or remote areas as a refuge, especially during the heavy pressure period of the gun deer season, since most hunters won't bother them in these areas. Often, bucks will utilize seemingly small, isolated patches of cover to hide themselves during the season.

Ringneck pheasants also offer some very good hunting opportunities at Jackson Marsh. The DNR stocks the area with plenty of birds during the season. Stockings are

TRAVEL GUIDE

NEAREST SERVICE CENTER: West Bend.
LODGING: Mayer-Pick Haus Bed and Breakfast, 710 Beech St., West Bend, (414) 335-1524. Americinn Motel of West Bend, 2424 W. Washington St., West Bend, (414) 334-0307. Best Western, 2520 W. Washington St., West Bend, (414) 338-0636.
SPORTS SHOP OR HUNTING LICENSE OUTLET: Tennies True Value Hardware Stores, 869 S. Main St., West Bend, (414) 334-5891, and 112 S. 5th Ave., 338-2316.
HOSPITAL OR EMERGENCY MEDICAL CLINIC: St. Joseph's Community Hospital of West Bend, 551 S. Silverbrook Drive, West Bend, (414) 334-5533.
EMERGENCY VETERINARY CLINIC: Nancy E. Bauman, Decorah Animal Hospital, 555 E. Decorah Road, West Bend, (414) 334-5551. Parkdale Pet Care, 615 N. Main St., West Bend, (414) 334-2550. West Bend Animal Hospital, 1020 E. Washington St., West Bend, (414) 334-4443.
AUTO REPAIR OR TOWING: Hilltop Services Inc., 1410 N. Main St., West Bend, (414) 338-0028. Hoffert's Auto Service Center, 449 S. Main St., West Bend, (414) 334-5841. Bob's Auto Repair, 1200 N. Main St., West Bend, (414) 338-3670.

done on upland areas around the marsh once or twice a week. The area is a rooster-only property, and there is a 2 p.m. closure in effect during the first two weeks of the season.

Identifying good places to hunt at Jackson Marsh shouldn't be diffi-

People who are willing to trudge back through the thick stuff into the heavy cover will likely stand a better chance of seeing a big rack, especially after the guns of opening morning have sounded.

cult. Grassy areas that will provide good cover for the big birds are the ticket. Isaac said that hunting pressure doesn't really push a lot of birds toward the thick, marshy areas, so hunters should concentrate the bulk of their efforts on the upland zones.

Since the area is close to Milwaukee, hunting pressure can be high. In this case, a good dog will prove invaluable. Flushing dogs, such as Labradors or spaniels, are preferred by many wingshooters who ply thick cover. Pointing dogs often perform best in lighter, grassy cover.

Isaac said there isn't a great deal of waterfowling done on the property. However, there are some small flowages on the property, and

Leonard Lee Rue III

Cedar Creek runs through the Jackson Marsh, and the territory is usually rather wet. Raccoons are plentiful in the area and hunting pressure is next to nothing com-pared to that on other species like white-tailed deer and ducks.

Cedar Creek runs through the area, offering some opportunities.

Wood ducks will likely offer the best possibilities for wing-shooting. Hunters can often find the colorful birds by slowly wading creeks or walking along their banks. Experienced waterfowlers will try to peer as far down the creek as they can, then sneak up carefully on bends or oxbows, which are often natural congregating spots for ducks.

Isaac said Jackson Marsh can be a good spot to hunt cottontail rab-bits. Of course, hunters will have to identify likely looking brushy areas that will hold animals. Their chances of success will be bolstered if they hunt immediately after a snowfall. Fresh rabbit tracks leave little doubt as to what areas the animals are using.

There are some woodcock avail-able to hunters on the property, but it's safe to say that there are better areas at which to chase tim-berdoodle. Because of the habitat at the area, grouse hunting oppor-tunities are next to nil.

Because of the nature of the property's habitat, raccoons are very abundant. There aren't too many coon hunters around nowa-days, but those who do choose to chase the bandits can often do so with good success and no competi-tion.

Honey Creek Wildlife Area

RACINE AND WALWORTH COUNTIES

Pheasants and waterfowl are the "big wheels" in terms of hunting at Honey Creek Wildlife Area, located in Racine and Walworth counties.

The property, which is actually composed of three separate, unconnected properties, features 1,082 acres of rolling terrain. Tom Becker, DNR wildlife manager, said the habitat at Honey Creek is varied. Upland areas feature some grasslands, timber, hedgerows, brushy areas and crop fields. The property also features marsh and lowland areas.

Two lakes, Frieda Lake and Brock Lake, are contained within the property boundaries. Also, a portion of the shoreline of Long Lake is also in the wildlife area. Honey Creek itself winds through the western portion of the area.

Ringneck pheasants are the main hunting attraction here. The DNR stocks the area often during the pheasant season. Since the property is very close to large population centers, these birds see intense hunting pressure from the opening day bell right on through the last day of the season in December.

Becker said there are no real hotspots for the put-and-take pheasant hunting offered here. The DNR usually plants its pen-raised birds in grassy areas around public wildlife areas, but hunting pressure at Honey Creek leaves no stone unturned — literally.

Nearly every inch of the property is hunted hard by pheasant hunters, Becker said. That includes weekdays, which are normally more serene on many public lands.

Roosters are the only legal targets at Honey Creek, Becker said.

Duck hunters also make good use of Honey Creek. There is some local production of mallards, wood ducks and teal, and migrating waterfowl do utilize the area to some extent. Becker said hunting opportunities at the property are varied.

Frieda Lake, Brock Lake and Long Lake all offer waterfowl hunting opportunities. There are both public and private blinds on Long Lake, but the competition for space is hot and heavy.

Hunters can also check out a couple of natural flowages located on the north end of the northernmost parcel. In addition, jumpshooters can try to walk up ducks along Honey Creek itself.

Like pheasant hunting, waterfowl hunting pressure is heavy. Becker said there really aren't any times during the season that are better than others in terms of escaping crowds.

Upland bird shooters will also find some woodcock at Honey Creek. The area does produce some local birds, and migrating woodcock will also use the property, especially during wet falls.

Becker said woodcock hunting success varies from year to year.

White-tailed deer are common a

TRAVEL GUIDE

NEAREST SERVICE CENTER: Burlington.

LODGING: AmericInn, 205 Browns Lake Road, Burlington, (414) 534-2125. Beachview Motel and Lounge, 30427 Durand Ave., Burlington, (414) 763-8892. Rainbow Motel, 733 Milwaukee Ave., Burlington, (414) 763-2491. Hillcrest Inn and Carriage House, 540 Storle Ave. Burlington, (414) 763-4706. Meadowlark Acres Campground, 346 North Road, Burlington, (414) 763-7200.

SPORTS SHOP OR HUNTING LICENSE OUTLET: Reineman's Sporting Goods Center, 417 Milwaukee Ave., Burlington, (414) 763-3577. Spring Brook Sports, 5821 S. Pine St., Burlington, (414) 763-3848.

HOSPITAL OR EMERGENCY MEDICAL CLINIC: Memorial Hospital, 252 McHenry St., Burlington, (414) 763-2411, or for emergencies, 763-0575.

EMERGENCY VETERINARY CLINIC: Country Veterinary Service, 2007 S. Browns Lake Drive, Burlington, (414) 763-2254. Molitor Pet and Bird Clinic, 108 N. Pine St., Burlington, (414) 763-8113. Burlington Longview Animal Hospital, 688 McHenry St., Burlington, (414) 763-6055 or 763-3838.

AUTO REPAIR OR TOWING: Merten's Service Station, 389 Milwaukee Ave., Burlington, (414) 763-5155.

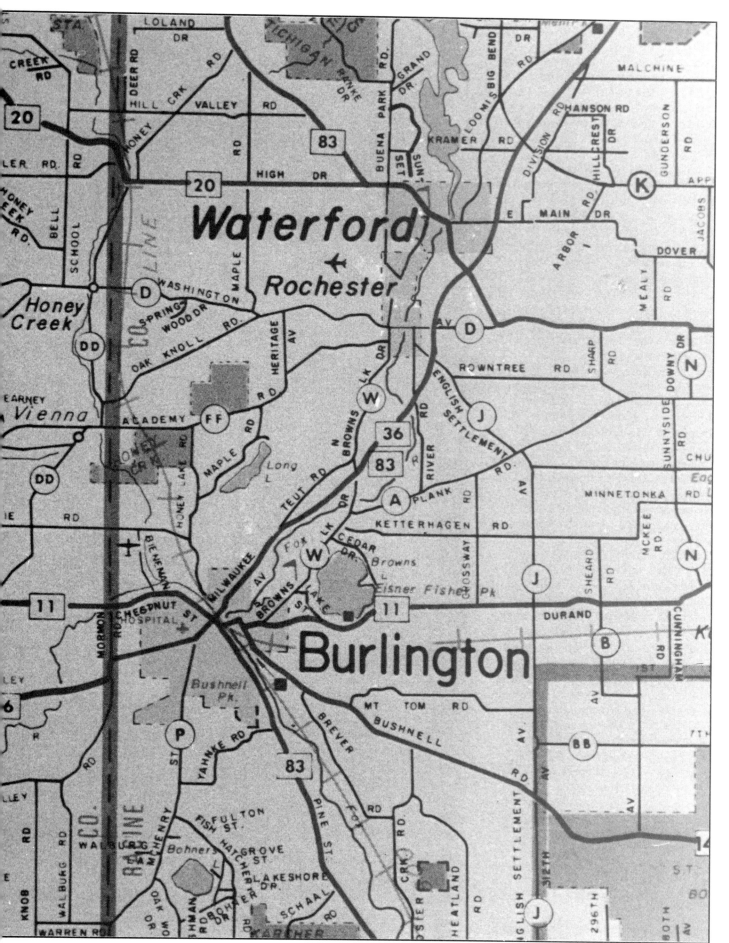

Honey Creek, but, again, hunting pressure on the animals is very heavy. Becker said even bow hunters can find conditions crowded during the week.

Archers will find the most crop fields in the northern parcel of Honey Creek. Spots where crop fields meet brush or other thick cover are good places for deer hunting. These fields are sharecropped by growers, and the crops are left standing in fall and winter to provide food and cover for wildlife.

Gun hunting calls for a different set of strategies. Intense pressure from the moment the season opens moves deer out of likely looking habitat areas and scatters them. As a result, whitetails might be found anywhere during the firearms season.

Small game hunters also have opportunities at Honey Creek. The area features some oak stands, mainly on the eastern parcel of the property. Squirrels are present in these areas, although Becker said opportunities for them are limited.

Rabbits are also found at Honey Creek, Becker said. Naturally, the hedgerows around the property are very good spots to start looking for rabbits.

Red and gray fox, as well as raccoons are common in the area, Becker said. However, little predator hunting is done at the property.

Access to Honey Creek is easy. There are three major parking lots available to hunters. The lot at the western parcel is located off of County Trunk DD. The lot on the eastern parcel is off of County Trunk W. And the northern parcel lot is off of a town road between county trunks D and FF.

Archers will find the most crop fields in the northern parcel of Honey Creek. Spots where crop fields meet brush or other thick cover are good places for deer hunting. These fields are sharecropped, and the crops are left standing in fall and winter to provide food and cover for wildlife.

Horicon Marsh Wildlife Area

DODGE COUNTY

Horicon Marsh Wildlife Area means hunting, pure and simple. The property, nestled at the heart of one of America's most famous flyways, offers excellent opportunities for waterfowl and deer hunters.

Horicon is a 10,991-acre state-owned area that lies directly south of the well-known Horicon National Wildlife Area. Together, the two areas comprise one of the largest freshwater marshes in the United States.

Naturally, waterfowl are a premiere attraction here. DNR wildlife biologist Maureen Rowe said the state-owned property consists mainly of marsh and open water.

The area attracts Canada geese by the hundreds of thousands. There is some hunting within the public area itself and around its edges, but Rowe said that neighboring private lands usually offer the better opportunities.

"To be a successful goose hunter now, you can't always count on securing a blind that borders the wildlife area," she said. "The geese have learned to fly high out of the marsh to avoid being shot at. They'll fly quite far from the marsh to land and feed."

Therefore, scouting for and locating concentrations of birds in corn or other crop fields and then securing permission to hunt is often the preferred method. Many landowners rent blinds to hunters. Others may grant permission if asked.

Many hunters pass-shoot at geese as they fly in and out of refuge areas. One prominent area is the border of the closed area on the northeast side of the property.

When pass shooting, make sure that geese are well within the effective killing range of your shotgun. Skybusting has become a major

TRAVEL GUIDE

NEAREST SERVICE CENTER: Mayville
LODGING: Audubon Inn, 45 North Main St., Mayville, (414) 387-5858. Hillcrest Inn, W1124 Hwy 33, Mayville (414) 387-2125. Iron Ridge Motel, Hwy 67, Iron Ridge (414) 387-4090. Royal Oaks Motel, W4419 Hwy 33, Horicon (414) 485-4489.
SPORTS SHOP OR HUNTING LICENSE OUTLET: West Side Beverage, 1024 Horicon St., (414) 387-3440.
HOSPITAL OR EMERGENCY MEDICAL CLINIC: Fond du Lac Clinic SC-Mayville Medical Center, 410 Short, Mayville (414) 387-2111.
EMERGENCY VETERINARY CLINIC: Mayville Animal Clinic-SC, N7860 Hwy. 67, (414) 387-4191.
AUTO REPAIR OR TOWING: Glenn's Service, 15 Bridge, Mayville (414) 387-3838. Wiese Auto Recycling Inc., W1421 Hwy. TW, Theresa (414) 488-3030.

problem in the Horicon area in recent years. This practice results mainly in crippled and wounded birds, not a quality hunting experience.

Hunters can see interior Canada geese as well as the giant Canada strain in the area. Some snow and blue geese also migrate through the area, as do tundra swans. Rowe stressed that hunters need to be able to identify swans from snow geese, as many swans have been shot during recent years. Swans are about twice as large as snow geese, and lack the black-tipped wings of the smaller birds.

Hunters should also be on the

> *Horicon is a 10,991-acre state-owned area that lies directly south of the well-known Horicon National Wildlife Area. Together, the two areas comprise one of the largest freshwater marshes in the United States.*

lookout for trumpeter swans, which have recently been reintroduced in Wisconsin. Also, there were some white pelicans in the area during the fall of 1992.

Ducks also represent a major hunting opportunity at Horicon, Rowe said. Production around the area has been up recently. The main nesting species are mallards, wood ducks and blue-winged teal.

Also, redheads nest in the area. In fact, the federal portion of the property was originally purchased to benefit the nesting birds. In addition, the area is the only place in Wisconsin listed as a ruddy duck production area.

Nesting cover and food patches have been established around Horicon to benefit waterfowl.

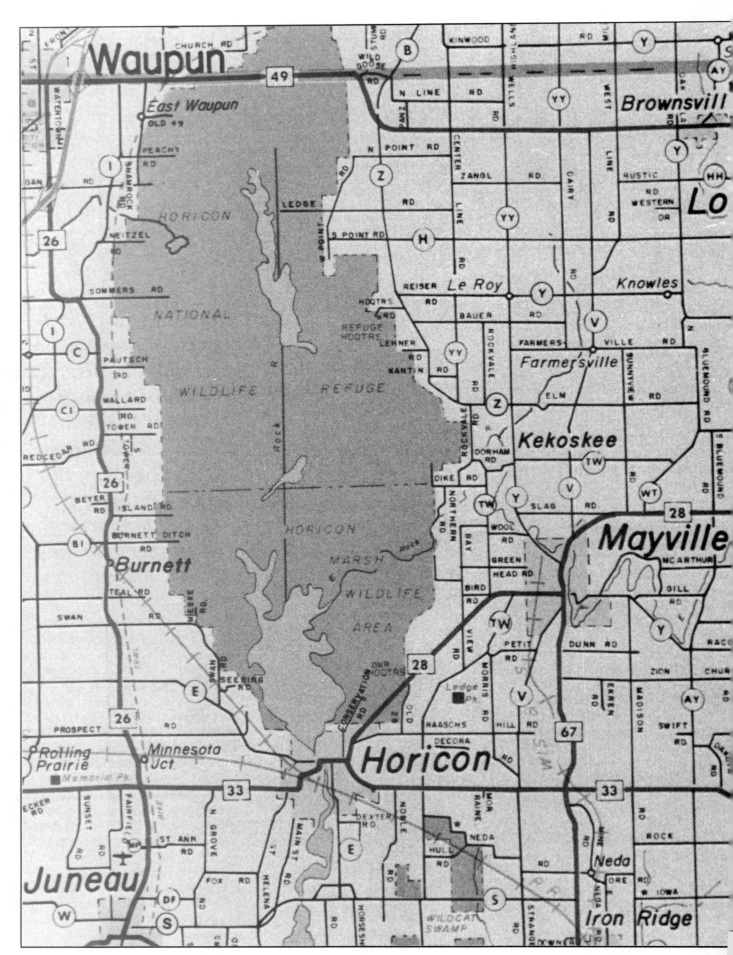

Horicon attracts great flights of migrating ducks during the hunting season. Mallards, black ducks, green-winged teal, pintail, widgeon and gadwall represent some of the major dabbling duck visitors, while redheads, canvasback, ringnecks, bluebills, buffleheads and goldeneyes represent the major diver species.

Duck hunters won't lack for spots at Horicon. The area is full of sloughs, rivers, ditches, potholes and impoundments. Parking lots on the east and west sides of the marsh offer easy access to these areas.

Many hunters use duck skiffs or canoes to push back into the dense marsh, then throw out decoys and call for birds. Others jumpshoot with marsh skis or waders. A word of caution, however: The vast, flat expanse of marsh makes it easy for hunters to get lost. Scout ahead, use caution and carry a compass.

Also, hunters need to be aware of the public land's boundaries. There are several closed areas at Horicon.

Archery hunting for deer is another popular activity at Horicon, Rowe said. There are scattered upland areas throughout the marsh, but whitetails utilize the marsh areas as well.

Hunters seem to like the thick cover that the area provides. Many use hip boots, waders or even boats to reach likely spots. Deer will use these relatively inaccessible spots as mini-refuges.

Gun hunting pressure at the marsh — especially in the fringe upland areas — can be heavy.

There is also a pheasant stocking program at Horicon. Quite a few birds are released here every fall for put-and-take hunting, Rowe said. Plantings are done in grassy uplands around the property. Only roosters can be shot.

Rabbit hunters can also have good days here by working edgerows and brushy areas, which are present at the property.

Scouting for and locating concentrations of birds in corn or other crop fields and then securing permission to hunt is often the preferred method. Many landowners rent blinds to hunters. Others may grant permission if asked.

Eldorado Marsh Wildlife Area

FOND DU LAC COUNTY

During the 1992 waterfowl season, one spot was consistently mentioned among hunters as the place to be: Eldorado Wildlife Area.

This 6,500-acre property, located in Fond du Lac County, offers good opportunities for goose, duck, pheasant and deer hunters each fall.

The area is dominated by cattail marsh and lowland brush. The West Branch of the Fond du Lac River flows through the area, and there is one major flowage within its boundaries.

In recent years, Canada geese have become the most sought-after species at Eldorado. The property features a large refuge on its northern third, and birds use this area heavily.

Much of the goose hunting done at Eldorado is pass-shooting around the refuge boundaries. The northeast part of the area attracts a great deal of this activity, and often leads to a firing line situation.

Pass-shooting here can be productive, especially if hunters correctly gauge wind and weather conditions and can conceal themselves in natural cover. However, many hunters take shots at geese that are well out of range, often crippling or wounding birds. Goose hunters should make sure that birds are close enough for a clean kill before pulling the trigger.

The area around Eldorado is heavily farmed, and geese use harvested fields as feeding areas. Scouting for concentrations of birds on private lands and then obtaining permission to hunt from landowners can be very productive.

Duck hunting at Eldorado can be very good. DNR wildlife manager Maureen Rowe said mallard and blue-winged teal production at the

TRAVEL GUIDE

NEAREST SERVICE CENTER: Fond du Lac.
LODGING: Budgetel, 77 Holiday Lane, Fond du Lac, (414) 921-4000. Country Woods Holidome, 625 Rolling Meadows Drive, Fond du Lac, (414) 923-1440. Fond du Lac Super 8, 391 N. Pioneer Road, Fond du Lac, (414) 922-1088. Sheraton Fond du Lac Hotel, One N. Main St., Fond du Lac, (414) 923-3000.
SPORTS SHOP OR HUNTING LICENSE OUTLET: Mill's Fleet Farm, 1508 Rogersville Road, Fond du Lac, (414) 922-7540.
HOSPITAL OR EMERGENCY MEDICAL CLINIC: St. Agnes Hospital, 430 E. Division St., Fond du Lac, (414) 929-2400.
EMERGENCY VETERINARY CLINIC: Dr. Fred Born, 961 S. Main St., Fond du Lac, (414) 922-3133.
AUTO REPAIR OR TOWING: There are several automotive shops in the Fond du Lac area. The Fond du Lac Area Association of Commerce lists more than 20.

The area around Eldorado is heavily farmed, and geese use harvested fields as feeding areas. Scouting for concentrations of birds on private lands and then obtaining permission to hunt from landowners can be very productive.

area is fairly good.

Eldorado can attract good flights of migrating birds, especially during higher water years. During dry years, there might not be enough water throughout the marsh to hold large numbers of ducks.

There are two boat landings at the property. One is located on the east side of the area on a town road just north of Highway 23 and County Trunk I. The other is located on a town road off of County Trunk C north of the community of Eldorado. These landings are best accessed with skiffs or canoes.

Many hunters push their way

back into the marsh and call for ducks over decoy spreads. This can be very productive, but competition can be fierce, especially during the opening days of the waterfowl season. There are also some jump shooting opportunities.

In addition, there are several small ponds around the area, which can attract birds and make for a quality hunt when the main marsh is crowded.

Mallards probably represent the most popular species for duck hunters. The area also attracts other common puddle duck species and can hold some diving duck depending on weather conditions. Some Canada geese are also taken

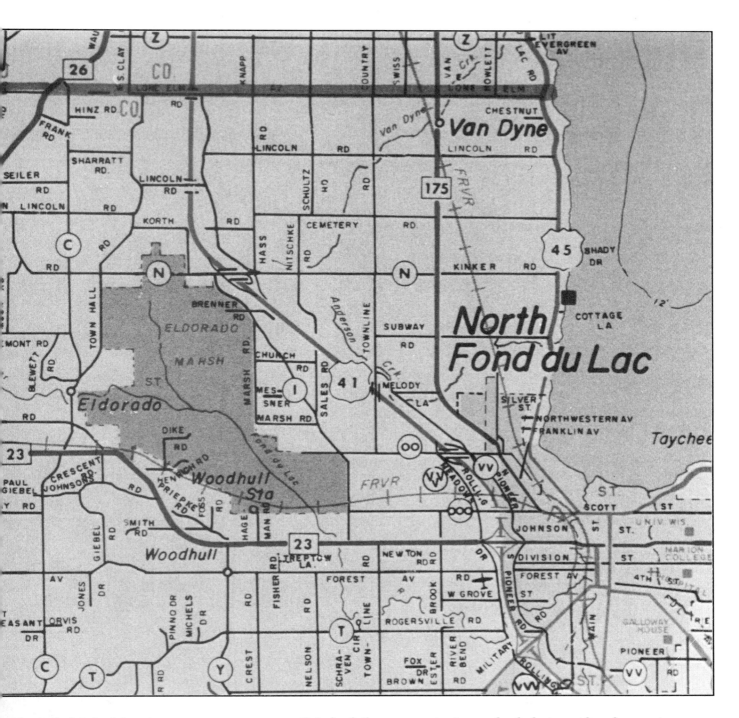

incidentally by duck hunters.

Eldorado is also a popular spot with bow and gun deer hunters. Many deer are attracted to food patches that are planted around the property. Bow hunters often find edges around these plots to be particularly good places to hunt.

Because of the area's close proximity to the Fox River Valley and Milwaukee, gun deer hunting pressure at Eldorado can be heavy. Deer tend to often seek heavy, isolated patches of cover during the gun season. The closed area on the north-ern one-third of the property is open for hunting during the gun deer season.

Pheasant hunting is also very popular at Eldorado. There are many areas of grassy upland cover around the wetland and marsh areas, and the DNR plants birds at these spots every fall. The area is open for shooting only roosters.

Eldorado's large size gives birds plenty of room to run, so hunting here can be a challenge. Experienced bird dogs are a must, and large groups of hunters can also help to outfox pheasants.

Rabbits are often taken incidentally by pheasant hunters. Cottontails benefit from the grassy areas that are planted for water-fowl production and pheasant use. Eldorado features many edge and hedgerow areas where rabbit hunters can find bunnies.

Geese are the best bet at Eldorado Marsh, but during years of high water the area can also attract terrific flights of migrating ducks in addition to the number of "local" birds it produces annually.

New Munster Wildlife Area

KENOSHA COUNTY

New Munster Wildlife Area offers sportsmen opportunities at upland birds, waterfowl, deer and small game.

Tom Becker, area DNR wildlife manager, said the property is about ,048 acres, located south of the community of New Munster. The habitat there is varied.

Most of the property features rolling ground. New Munster consists of uplands, including some grasslands and some share-cropped agricultural land. Crops in these fields are left unharvested over the winter to provide food and cover for wildlife species. About half of the property consists of lowlands, including marsh, lowland timber and shrub swamp.

Pheasant hunting for stocked birds is the biggest hunting opportunity at New Munster, Becker said. The area is stocked frequently. Becker won't say exactly when and where birds are planted, mainly because this can lead to unethical hunting practices among some hunters.

Since the property is located so close to the Milwaukee, Racine and Kenosha metropolitan areas, hunting pressure here can be extremely heavy, especially during weekends.

Pheasants on state wildlife areas are typically planted in grassy areas, but Becker reports that nearly every square inch of New Munster is hunted hard for pheasants, so there won't be any out-of-the-way honey holes there.

New Munster is a rooster-only property. There is a 2 p.m. closure in effect.

Woodcock will offer shotgunners some shooting opportunities during the fall at New Munster, Becker said. There are some local birds that are reared on the property, and migratory timberdoodle will also

TRAVEL GUIDE

NEAREST SERVICE CENTER: Burlington.

LODGING: AmericInn, 205 Browns Lake Road, Burlington, (414) 534-2125. Beachview Motel and Lounge, 30427 Durand Ave., Burlington, (414) 763-8892. Rainbow Motel, 733 Milwaukee Ave., Burlington, (414) 763-2491. Hillcrest Inn and Carriage House, 540 Storle Ave. Burlington, (414) 763-4706. Meadowlark Acres Campground, 346 North Road, Burlington, (414) 763-7200.

SPORTS SHOP OR HUNTING LICENSE OUTLET: Reineman's Sporting Goods Center, 417 Milwaukee Ave., Burlington, (414) 763-3577. Spring Brook Sports, 5821 S. Pine St., Burlington, (414) 763-3848.

HOSPITAL OR EMERGENCY MEDICAL CLINIC: Memorial Hospital, 252 McHenry St., Burlington, (414) 763-2411, or for emergencies, 763-0575.

EMERGENCY VETERINARY CLINIC: Country Veterinary Service, 2007 S. Browns Lake Drive, Burlington, (414) 763-2254. Molitor Pet and Bird Clinic, 108 N. Pine St., Burlington, (414) 763-8113. Burlington Longview Animal Hospital, 688 McHenry St., Burlington, (414) 763-6055 or 763-3838.

AUTO REPAIR OR TOWING: Merten's Service Station, 389 Milwaukee Ave., Burlington, (414) 763-5155.

Since the property is located so close to the Milwaukee, Racine and Kenosha metropolitan areas, hunting pressure here can be extremely heavy, especially during weekends.

use the spot.

Woodcock hunting varies from year-to-year, Becker said. Relatively few hunters go after the birds.

Good woodcock habitat won't be hard to identify, Becker said. Thick alder areas near or adjacent to wet areas provide ideal locations.

There is a limited amount of duck hunting available at New Munster, Becker said. Some local mallards, wood ducks and blue-winged teal are present, and some migrating birds utilize the property each autumn.

Becker said that most of the waterfowling at New Munster is done at some of the small puddles around the property. There is also a 20-acre flowage on the southeast portion of the area. However, these spots get pretty well burned out after the first two days of the season.

Palmer and Bassett creeks also run through the property, so duck hunters might be able to get some jumpshooting in.

Of course, deer hunting is very

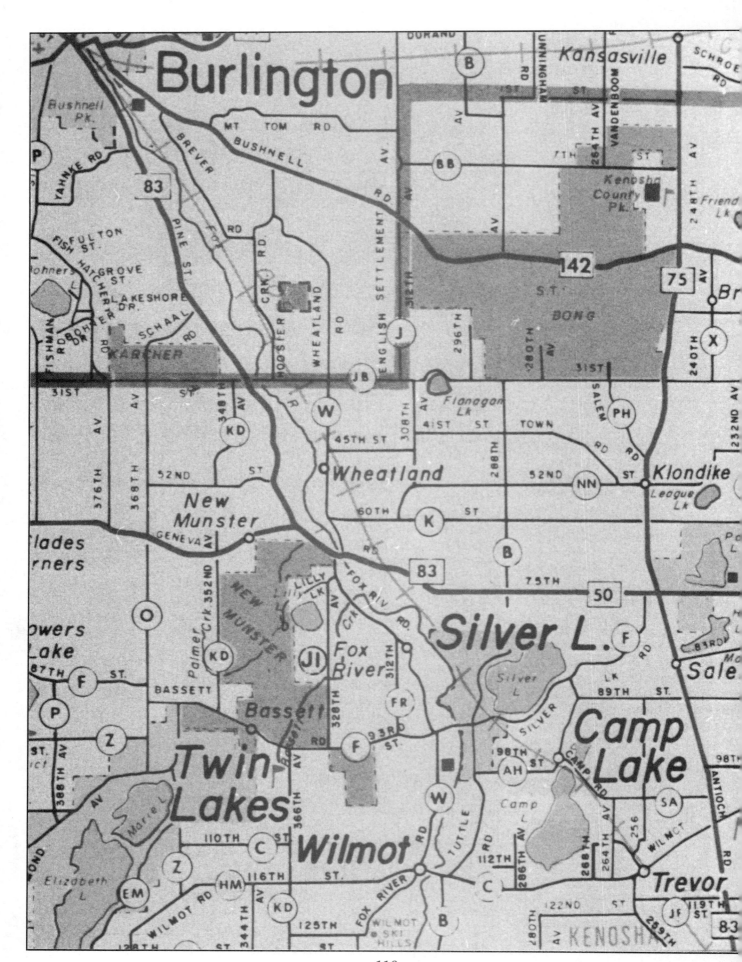

popular at New Munster. Becker said the area receives very heavy pressure, and even archery hunters may have to compete for space.

Unharvested crop fields next to thick cover on the property will be likely spots for bow hunters to stake out. However, gun hunters will likely find deer scattered throughout the area after the opening bell of the season sounds.

There are more than 100 acres of oak upland areas in New Munster, so squirrel hunters can probably find some hunting opportunities here. Gray and fox squirrels are common in these spots.

Hunters will also find cottontail rabbits in the area. Becker said brushy hedgerow areas offer the best spots for sportsmen to beat the brush for bunnies.

As is the case with many state wildlife areas, varmints are very common at New Munster. When compared to deer or pheasant hunting, very few sportsmen seek out species such as coyote, red fox or raccoon.

For some hunters, coyote and fox hunting is a great winter activity and sort of a way to make the hunting season last longer. Die-hard coon hunters can run their dogs at night with virtually no competition in most spots.

Access to New Munster is easy. The boundaries are well-marked, and there are five parking lots at the property. Two are on the west side of the area off of County Trunk KD. Another two are on the east side of the property and can be accessed by town roads. The fifth parking lot lies on New Munster's north side, off of Highway 50.

Hugh McAloon

New Munster is heavily stocked with pheasants, but it is also heavily hunt-ed because of its proximity to metropolitan areas near Milwaukee.

117

Tichigan Wildlife Area

Tichigan Wildlife Area in Racine County offers hunters pheasant and waterfowl hunting opportunities within easy driving distance of Racine and Milwaukee.

Tom Becker, area wildlife manager for the DNR, said Tichigan has about 1,200 acres of land. The area is comprised of rolling land, and includes grassy cover, wetlands, and food patches. The Fox River flows through the area, and Tichigan Lake lies on the eastern part of the property.

Put-and-take pheasant hunting is probably the No. 1 hunting attraction at Tichigan. The area is frequently and heavily stocked, Becker said. Typically birds are planted in likely grassy areas around the property.

The high bird numbers and nearby population centers make for heavy pheasant hunting pressure, Becker said. No one time is better than another, since there is almost always someone utilizing the area. There aren't any real secret hotspots, since hunters make use of virtually the entire property.

The area is open only for rooster hunting. Hens are protected. Also, there is a 2 p.m. closure in place, Becker said.

Waterfowling is also a very popular hunting activity at Tichigan, Becker said. Most of the shooting is for puddle ducks, such as mallards, wood ducks and teal.

Many hunters use boats or skiffs to hunt waterfowl on the property, Becker said. A great deal of hunting activity takes place in blinds along the shore of Tichigan Lake. Some jumpshooting is available along a series of long ditches that were created in the marsh on the western portion of the property.

Becker said waterfowling pressure, much like pheasant hunting activity, can be heavy at Tichigan.

The area mainly features migration habitat for the birds. However, local nesting of ducks has been improved since the first Ducks

TRAVEL GUIDE

NEAREST SERVICE CENTER: Burlington.
LODGING: AmericInn, 205 Browns Lake Road, Burlington, (414) 534-2125. Beachview Motel and Lounge, 30427 Durand Ave., Burlington, (414) 763-8892. Rainbow Motel, 733 Milwaukee Ave., Burlington, (414) 763-2491. Hillcrest Inn and Carriage House, 540 Storle Ave. Burlington, (414) 763-4706. Meadowlark Acres Campground, 346 North Road, Burlington, (414) 763-7200.
SPORTS SHOP OR HUNTING LICENSE OUTLET: Reineman's Sporting Goods Center, 417 Milwaukee Ave., Burlington, (414) 763-3577. Spring Brook Sports, 5821 S. Pine St., Burlington, (414) 763-3848.
HOSPITAL OR EMERGENCY MEDICAL CLINIC: Memorial Hospital, 252 McHenry St., Burlington, (414) 763-2411, or for emergencies, 763-0575.
EMERGENCY VETERINARY CLINIC: Country Veterinary Service, 2007 S. Browns Lake Drive, Burlington, (414) 763-2254. Molitor Pet and Bird Clinic, 108 N. Pine St., Burlington, (414) 763-8113. Burlington Longview Animal Hospital, 688 McHenry St., Burlington, (414) 763-6055 or 763-3838.
AUTO REPAIR OR TOWING: Merten's Service Station, 389 Milwaukee Ave., Burlington, (414) 763-5155.

RACINE COUNTY

> *Put-and-take pheasant hunting is probably the No. 1 hunting attraction at Tichigan. The area is frequently and heavily stocked. ... Typically birds are planted in likely grassy areas around the property.*

Unlimited project in Wisconsin wa completed in 1988. DU spent abou $60,000 to create a 50-acre flowag The reservoir is drained ever spring, and then millet is plante there. After Labor Day, the water i brought back into the flowage.

The DU project is in a refuge are on the north half of the property and was developed so that a firin line didn't develop around th flowage.

Woodcock fanciers will find som local birds at Tichigan, Becker sai Migrating timberdoodle will als use likely looking habitat here dur ing their fall flight. Thick alder o similar areas adjacent to wetland are generally good spots to check.

There are white-tailed deer hunt ing opportunities at Tichigan, bu

Predator hunting might be one of the least popular hunting activities at Tichigan. However, there are plenty of predators for shooters to pursue there. Red fox, coyotes and raccoons are all abundant and competition might not be heavy.

the property is heavily hunted, especially during the firearms season. Once the shooting starts, whitetails will become scattered and may be found anywhere.

Archery hunters also make heavy use of the property, Becker said, although their numbers probably won't rival those of the gun season.

Rabbits can also be found at Tichigan. Often, bunnies are taken incidentally by pheasant hunters, which gives you an idea of their habitat at that time of year.

Hunters who wait for the snow to fall may find they can easily locate good cottontail spots. Also, Tichigan may be less crowded during the winter than in fall.

Squirrel hunters can also find some opportunities at Tichigan, but they are limited since stands of mature hardwoods are relatively scarce there.

Predator hunting might be one of the least popular hunting activities at Tichigan. However, there are plenty of predators for shooters to pursue there. Red fox, coyotes and raccoons are all abundant, and competition might not be heavy.

Access to Tichigan is very good. The property is located between County Trunk F and Highway 83 just southwest of the community of Tichigan. There are several town roads that run through or around the property, and there are six parking lots at the area.

Theresa Wildlife Area

WASHINGTON, DODGE, FOND DU LAC COUNTIES

Anyone driving along U.S. Highway 41 during October or November could vouch for it: Theresa Wildlife Area is a great spot for waterfowl.

Whether it's migrating Canada geese, locally produced puddle ducks or late flights of northern birds, Theresa has it. And since it lies between two heavily populated areas — Milwaukee and the Fox River Valley — it's an incredibly popular spot to wave a shotgun over decoys.

Theresa, located in Washington, Dodge and Fond du Lac counties, is about 6,000 acres. It features a large main flowage that is controlled by a dam, about 20 sub-impoundments and two refuges, each about 1,000 acres. These are closed to hunting except during the gun deer season. The area consists mainly of wetlands, but does feature some grassy and other upland areas.

Tom Isaac, wildlife manager for the DNR, said Theresa's main draw for hunters is the annual flight of Canada geese it attracts. During the peak of the fall migration, up to 10,000 geese can be on the property. Highway 28, which cuts through the property, is a prime viewing spot for much of the activity.

Naturally, lots of geese draw lots of hunters. Isaac said that much of the goose hunting activity is pass shooting concentrated around the refuge boundaries. Geese generally fly off of the refuges to the north, west and east.

However, the DNR doesn't encourage this type of activity. Rather, Isaac said that hunters can enjoy a better quality and more productive hunt by either renting a blind or gaining permission to hunt on private lands throughout the area and using decoys and calling

TRAVEL GUIDE

NEAREST SERVICE CENTER: Hartford.
LODGING: Reef Point Resort, 3416 Lake Drive, Hartford, (414) 673-9952 or 628-1258. Erin Motel and Restaurant, 911 Highway 83 South, Hartford, (414) 673-2721. Silver Bell Motel, 720 Grand Ave., Hartford, (414) 673-2232. Super 8 Motel, 1539 E. Sumner St., Hartford, (414) 673-7431.
SPORTS SHOP OR HUNTING LICENSE OUTLET: There are numerous sporting goods stores in the Hartford area. The yellow pages provided by the Hartford Area Chamber of Commerce lists eight.
HOSPITAL OR EMERGENCY MEDICAL CLINIC: Hartford Memorial Hospital, 1032 E. Sumner St., Hartford, (414) 673-2300.
EMERGENCY VETERINARY CLINIC: Algiers Veterinary Services, 1471 E. Sumner St., Hartford, (414) 673-2990. The Animal Doctors, 1528 E. Sumner St., Hartford, (414) 673-5355.
AUTO REPAIR OR TOWING: There are numerous auto repair places in the Hartford area.

Aside from its permanent water, the property features several hundred acres of nesting cover. Ducks Unlimited has been a major contributor to the area with its funding of various habitat projects.

to lure geese into effective shooting range.

Theresa is a good duck production area, Isaac said. Aside from its permanent water, the property features several hundred acres of nesting cover. Ducks Unlimited has been a major contributor to the area with its funding of various habitat projects.

The big three — mallards, wood ducks and blue-winged teal — are the main nesting ducks, Isaac said.

The area usually produces several hundred ducks each year.

During the migration, other common North American duck species show up. Several thousand ducks generally use the area when the migration is on.

Isaac said the area gets hit pretty hard on the opening day of duck season. Hunters generally use duck skiffs, canoes or chest waders to access the water. No motor boats are allowed. Hunting over decoys is the most common method used.

Hunters who experience the best success are most often those who go the extra mile for their ducks, Isaac said. Sportsmen willing to push far back into the marsh or who will gain permission to hunt cornfields

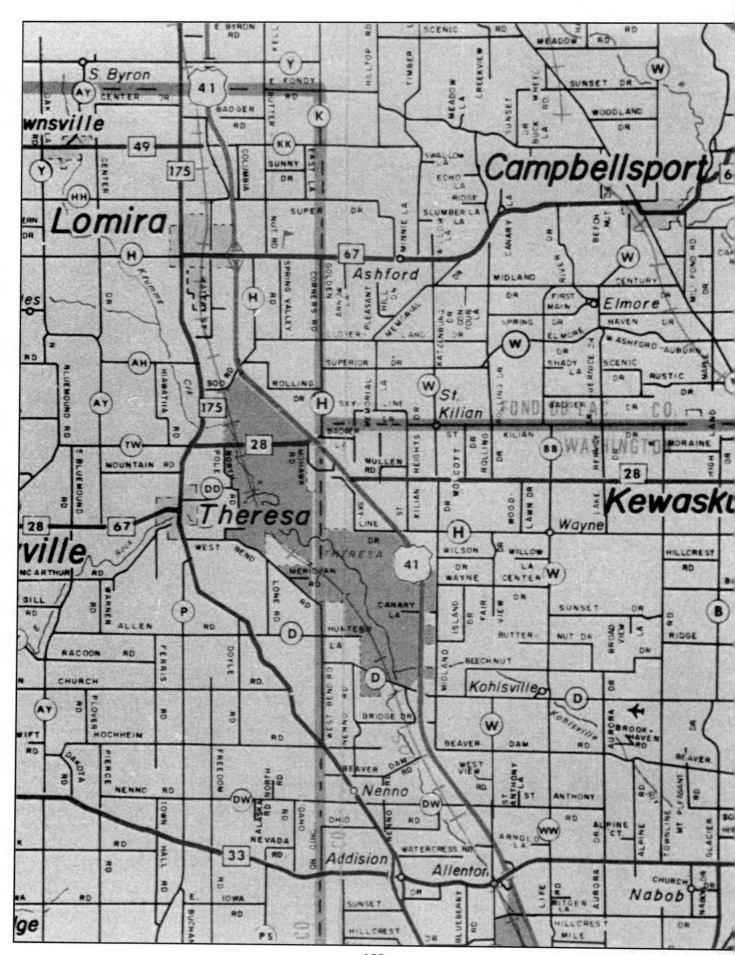

here birds feed can have good shooting.

If a wingshooter's mood switches from webbed feet to 20-inch tails, there are also good pheasant hunting opportunities at Theresa. The DNR does heavy stockings of the area; birds are planted once or twice a week in grassy areas that are easily accessible to hunters.

The area is open for roosters only. There is a 2 p.m. closure during the first two weeks of the season.

Isaac said there are also some leased lands around Theresa where hunters pursue ringnecks.

Deer hunting is also a very popular activity at Theresa. Isaac said the area features a good population of deer, and it receives heavy hunting pressure during the bow and gun seasons.

Theresa features a few wooded upland areas, but Isaac said whitetails are basically everywhere. Hunters should look for natural deer funnel areas as well as fresh sign to increase their chances of bagging an animal.

Rabbits are also common on the property. Hunters should concentrate on brushy areas around the marsh.

Woodcock are also present at the area. Their habitat is limited, but Isaac said that the property does see a fair number of birds that move through during the peak October migration. Alder and other brushy thickets adjacent to marshy areas are the most likely spots to look for the tiny gamebirds.

There are also some squirrel hunting opportunities at Theresa but areas with mature oak trees are limited.

Mallards, wood ducks and teal are the main attractions during the early part of the hunting season at Theresa, but many other species of ducks visit when the fall migration kicks in.

Hugh McAloon

Bong State Recreation Area

KENOSHA COUNTY

To many, hunting at a public area in southeast Wisconsin conjures up images of pheasant hunters walking arm-in-arm across a grassy field.

Bong Recreation Area, in Kenosha County, offers plenty of hunting opportunities minus the crowded conditions. The property gives sportsmen a chance to hunt in an area where hunter numbers are regulated.

No more than 300 hunters are allowed on the 4,515-acre property at any time. In addition to a state hunting license and a state park sticker, hunters must also purchase a daily hunting permit before being allowed to proceed to the parking lot. Hunting permits are sold each day at the property's entrance station, located just off of Highway 142. The cost is $3 per day for pheasant hunting and $1 per day for all other forms of hunting.

Gary Patzke, superintendent of Bong, said hunters can make reservations for hunting on specific dates at the property. A drawing is held around the end of August for reservation applications submitted since Aug. 1 of that year. Applications received after that are treated on a first-come, first-served basis. Applications must be received a minimum of two days prior to a hunting date.

In 1992, reservations were $3 for each date. No more than one application can be submitted for a single date, and hunters cannot make more than five waterfowl and five pheasant reservations per season. Pheasant hunters who do not arrive by the opening of shooting will forfeit their regulations. Also, waterfowl hunters who do not arrive one-half hour before shooting will forfeit their reservations. In 1992, pheasant reservations were only accepted

TRAVEL GUIDE

NEAREST SERVICE CENTER: Union Grove
LODGING: Esmond Motel, 4900 S. Colony Ave., Union Grove, 414-878-2060. Bong Motel, 1700 - 200th Ave. Union Grove, 414-878-1245. Bristol Motel, 4510 - 200th Ave., Bristol, 414-857-2396.
SPORTS SHOP OR HUNTING LICENSE OUTLET: Swantz Hardware/Ben Franklin, 1002 Main St., Union Grove. Kansasville Quick Mart, 203010 Durand Ave., Kansasville.
HOSPITAL OR EMERGENCY MEDICAL CLINIC: Burlington Memorial Hospital, Burlington. St. Mary's Medical Center, Racine. St. Luke's Hospital, Racine.
EMERGENCY VETERINARY CLINIC: Information not available.
AUTO REPAIR OR TOWING: Bob's Mobil Service, 740 Main St., Union Grove, 414-878-1359. Drinkwine's Auto Service, 19030 Spring St., Union Grove, 414-878-4575. Martin's Chrysler-Plymouth, 1422 Main St., Union Grove, 414-878-1226.

for weekends, Nov. 26 and 27 and Dec. 9.

Some sportsmen forgo reservations and simply show up at the Entrance Station on the day they want to hunt and try for non-reservable permits, which are available on a first-come, first-served basis.

Stocked pheasant hunting is the biggest draw at Bong, Patzke said. The property is stocked daily, so literally thousands of birds are released here over the course of the pheasant hunting season.

As with the rest of the state,

No more than 300 hunters are allowed on the 4,515-acre property at any time. ... The property is stocked daily, so literally thousands of birds are released here over the course of the pheasant hunting season.

pheasant hunting at Bong begins at noon on opening day and runs through the normal small game hunting hours. Aside from opening day, pheasant hunting opens at 9 a.m. for the first two weeks of the season, Patzke said. After the first two weeks, pheasant hunting opens at normal hours and runs until 2 p.m. During the pheasant season all hunting closes at 2 p.m. so the area can be safely restocked.

Hens and roosters are legal game at Bong, Patzke said. One bird of either sex may be bagged during the first two weeks of the season, while two birds of either sex may be harvested for the remainder of the season.

When pheasant hunters pay their $3 daily permit fee, they will

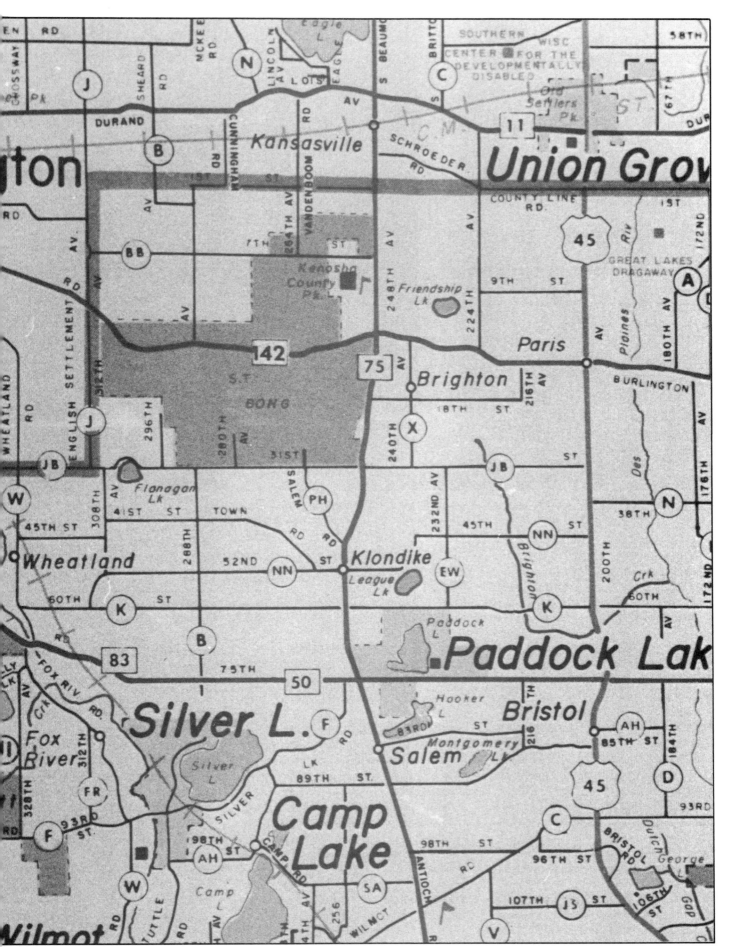

Hens and roosters are legal game at Bong. One bird of either sex may be bagged during the first two weeks of the season, while two birds of either sex may be harvested for the remainder of the season.

receive an arm band. Included with the band are dated leg tags, which must be attached to harvested birds.

Patzke said pheasant season is the only time of the year that hunters need to make reservations for. Also, it's the only time when hunting demand may exceed the available permits. After the first two weeks of the pheasant season, Bong may sell more permits after 10 a.m. even if 300 permits were sold before that time. Patzke said that it's assumed most of the early morning hunters will have left the property by that time, allowing others to purchase permits.

Probably the No. 2 attraction at Bong is waterfowl hunting, Patzke said. Again, there are special regulations on the property.

South of Highway 142, waterfowl hunting is restricted to a state blind. There are more than 25 of the blinds on the area, and there is a limit of two hunters per blind. One blind is reserved for disabled hunters, and features a ramp that allows wheelchair-bound sportsmen to reach the spot.

North of Highway 142, only jumpshooting is allowed, and a maximum of 16 waterfowl hunters are allowed in this area during the pheasant hunting season.

Patzke said there are more than 70 water bodies on Bong, ranging from a 150-acre lake to small potholes. Puddle ducks are the main targets here.

Deer are present at Bong and offer some hunting opportunities. Patzke said not many sportsmen pursue whitetails on the property, even during the November firearms season.

The opening weekend of gun season usually sees about 15 to 20 hunters at Bong, Patzke said. After that, about six to 10 hunters use the property. Hunters do have some success here, he added.

Squirrels and rabbits offer small game hunters some opportunities at Bong, Patzke said, and not many people pursue these species.

Bong is managed for prairie habitat, Patzke said. Controlled burning is used to help regenerate grassland areas. The property also features hedgerows and some scattered hardwood stands.

There are three closed areas at Bong, as well as a game refuge. The areas are identified on a map of the area.

Vernon Wildlife Area

WAUKESHA COUNTY

If there were a most-improved public hunting grounds award given out each year, Vernon Wildlife Area would have been a runaway winner in 1992.

The 3,775-acre property, located in Waukesha County near metropolitan Milwaukee, is a true conservation success story.

DNR wildlife manager Mark Andersen said Vernon has always been popular among hunters and non-sportsmen alike. The property featured some good duck hunting for locally produced wood ducks, mallards and teal close to a huge population center. And whether it was hunters or the local cross-country running team, someone was almost always utilizing this area. That hasn't changed.

The area itself, however, has. August 1993 saw the dedication of a vast habitat improvement project at the area. The project was a Matching Aid for Restoration of State Habitat (MARSH) project of Ducks Unlimited. A 155-acre impoundment was created at the property. Thirty-five acres will be managed for brood water, while the remaining 120 acres are managed for migrating waterfowl in spring and fall. The impoundment is the centerpiece of one of the two wildlife refuges on the property.

Andersen said that, without a doubt, waterfowl hunting on the property has improved since the project was completed. Waterfowl won't be the only beneficiary either. Non-game birds and other species should also benefit.

The area, which features several flowages, the Fox River and dense nesting cover, has always been a popular spot among duck hunters. However, sportsmen reported that they liked what they saw this fall.

During the peak of the migration,

TRAVEL GUIDE

NEAREST SERVICE CENTER:
Vernon.

* The property is almost within the town, so hunters should be able to find everything without directions.

Vernon will now hold about 5,000 ducks. The area was always known as a good wood duck spot early in the year, and wood ducks, mallards and teal still make up the bulk of the birds early in the fall. As autumn rolls on, puddlers such as widgeon, gadwall and black ducks come through. Anderson said the area will also attract some divers. Usually there will be several hundred ringbills, a couple hundred bluebills and a smattering of redheads and canvasbacks during peak migration.

Even if hunters weren't bagging more birds this fall, they usually reported seeing more ducks at Vernon, Andersen said.

Many hunters don chest waders or hip boots to walk into Vernon, Andersen said. Typically, walk-in hunters will either throw out a few decoys and call for birds or pass-shoot along refuge lines. The pass shooting can result in some sky-busting problems, Andersen said, but it's not any more prevalent than at other public areas.

Some hunters do use boats for waterfowl hunting. This activity mainly takes place on the large flowage on the property's southwest portion.

Pheasant hunting is also a popular activity at Vernon, Andersen said. Stockings here are heavy, and are usually done twice a week during the early part of the season and

A 155-acre impoundment was created at the property. Thirty-five acres will be managed for brood water, while the remaining 120 acres are managed for migrating waterfowl in spring and fall.

then once a week toward the end. There is a 2 p.m. closure for pheasant hunting here during the first two weeks of the season.

Because of the wet nature of the property, pheasant hunters might want to wear waterproof boots or even hip boots at Vernon.

White-tailed deer are also a favorite target for hunters. Andersen said there aren't many upland areas around the property, but the area retains a pretty fair deer population.

Vernon is within an hour's drive of almost 2 million people, Andersen said. As you might guess, deer hunting pressure here can be heavy. The most popular spot seems to be the refuge on the property's north end, which is opened to hunting during the gun deer sea-

Vernon Wildlife Area, which features several flowages, the Fox River and dense nesting cover, has always been a popular spot among duck hunters. During the peak of the migration, Vernon will now hold about 5,000 ducks.

son. This refuge consists mainly of lowland timber — stuff wood ducks would have been sitting in during early October. Compared to this spot, pressure throughout the rest of the property is moderate.

There is some squirrel and rabbit hunting available at Vernon, Andersen said. Rabbit hunters will want to focus their efforts on marsh edge areas that provide good, thick cover for the critters.

As Andersen indicated, non-hunting usage of Vernon is quite heavy. Bird-watching, hiking and other activities here remain popular, so hunters should make an extra effort to follow safe, ethical hunting practices.

Access to Vernon is very easy. There are county and town roads that run around fringes of the property, and several parking lots are maintained.

Waterloo Wildlife Area

JEFFERSON AND
DODGE COUNTIES

There probably isn't a bird hunter alive that doesn't get a thrill when a rooster pheasant decides he can run no more and bursts from grassy cover in a flurry of color and sound.

Hunters like pheasants. And these imported "Chinese chickens" play the starring role in the past and future of Waterloo Wildlife Area, located in Jefferson and Dodge counties.

Charles Kilian, wildlife biologist with the DNR, said that the 5,500-acre area used to be known as a top-quality pheasant hunting area. The DNR used to stock about 2,000 birds a year there for put-and-take hunting opportunities. Also, the property featured some of the best pheasant hunting around. Wild pheasant production at Waterloo was about as good as anywhere in the state.

But Kilian said that ringneck populations crashed in that area of the state. Private lands around Waterloo saw steady increases in bird numbers, mainly because of the Conservation Reserve Program. Waterloo itself, however, didn't see much progress.

Still, the area attracted loads of pheasant hunters because of the large numbers of pen-raised birds that were released there, Kilian said.

Currently, the area is in transition. The put-and-take hunting was discontinued in 1992, and the area is part of a natural pheasant restoration area. Kilian said 500 birds will be stocked there for three years; 1992 was the first.

Habitat restoration is the main thrust, Kilian said. Without the necessary nesting, roosting and feeding areas, pheasants simply can't make it. If the project is successful, the DNR hopes to see

TRAVEL GUIDE

NEAREST SERVICE CENTER: Sun Prairie.
LODGING: McGovern's Motel, 829 W. Main St., Sun Prairie, (608) 837-7321. Super 8 Motel, 1033 Emerald Terrace, Sun Prairie, (608) 837-8889. Watertower Inn, 650 Schiller St., Sun Prairie, (608) 837-8970.
SPORTS SHOP OR HUNTING LICENSE OUTLET: Information unavailable.
HOSPITAL OR EMERGENCY MEDICAL CLINIC: Madison General Hospital, Madison.
EMERGENCY VETERINARY CLINIC: Countryside Animal Clinic, 3755 Highway 151, Sun Prairie, (608) 249-3232. Sun Prairie Veterinary Clinic 1512 Bristol Street, Sun Prairie, (608) 837-6252. Dr. G. Merry, 2125 McCoy Road, Sun Prairie, (608) 837-5383.
AUTO REPAIR OR TOWING: There are numerous auto repair and towing shops in the Sun Prairie area. The Sun Prairie Chamber of Commerce lists 10.

The property featured some of the best pheasant hunting around. Wild pheasant production at Waterloo was about as good as anywhere in the state.

results within a couple of years.

Pheasant hunting is still allowed at the area, Kilian said. However, the populations of natural birds there can't compete with the huge opportunities the area formerly offered. As such, the property currently can't meet the demands of many bird hunters.

However, if the project is successful, the area should offer splendid hunting opportunities in the future. Kilian said the DNR's winter flushing work at the area gave them high hopes for years to come.

While the natural pheasant populations work their way back,

Waterloo offers other quality hunting opportunities. Most of the property consists of wetlands, and there is quite a bit of waterfowl hunting done here.

Puddle ducks, such as mallards, wood ducks and blue-winged teal, are the main attraction, but Canada geese aren't uncommon, Kilian said. Three streams in the area offer duck hunters opportunities, as do areas of cattail marsh.

White-tailed deer are common at Waterloo, Kilian said, especially for the southeastern portion of the state.

Deer don't seem to favor one type of habitat over another at Waterloo, but are instead found throughout the property.

About 4,500 acres of Waterloo is owned by the state, while another 1,000 acres are leased. The area is sort of a patchwork of public and private lands, so deer hunters visit-

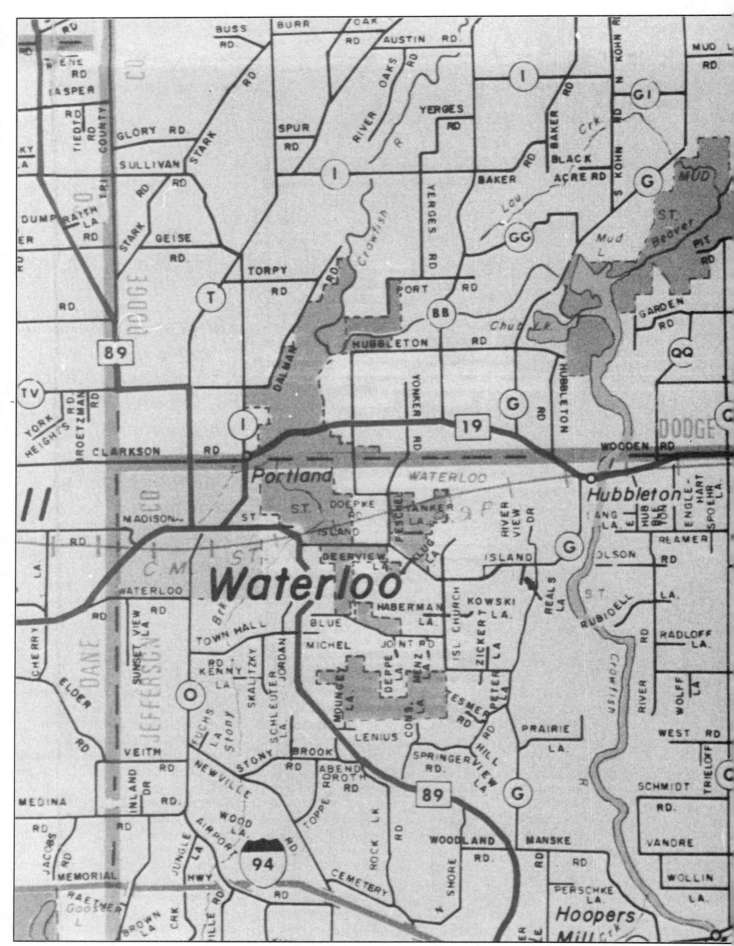

g the area will want to make sure
hat they know the property bound-
ries and respect the rights of pri-
ate landowners.

Wild turkeys are also common at
Waterloo, Kilian said. 1992 marked
he first hunting season for the big
irds on the property.

There are some upland sites of
ak and hickory on the property,
ut Kilian said the turkeys — like
he deer — at Waterloo seem to be
s happy in the area's wetlands as
s uplands. Nonetheless, hunters
ill want to do their scouting
efore planning a gobbler hunting
rip to the area.

Public access to Waterloo is
xcellent. The area is fairly close to
oth Madison and Milwaukee.
here are many town roads run-
ing through and around the prop-
rty, and there are several parking
ts in the area.

*Waterloo Wildlife Area is known mainly for its pheasant and waterfowl
hunting, but white-tailed deer are also common here.*

133

Rush Lake

WINNEBAGO AND
FOND DU LAC COUNTIES

Y ou probably won't find Rush Lake listed in a directory of Wisconsin public hunting areas.

Nonetheless, the area produces more than its share of quality waterfowling opportunities for the general public.

Located in Winnebago and Fond du Lac counties, Rush Lake is a prairie pothole type lake that serves as a breeding and migration stopover area for waterfowl and a variety of other wildlife.

Gary Jolin, area wildlife supervisor for the Department of Natural Resources, said the main attraction at Rush Lake is puddle duck hunting. Much like nearby lakes Poygan, Winneconne and Butte des Morts, the area is one of East-central Wisconsin's traditional waterfowling areas.

Rush Lake isn't classified as a "public hunting area" since its shoreline is mostly under private ownership. However, there are three DNR access points to the lake. And, unlike many water bodies in the area, Rush Lake's shoreline hasn't been developed to any great extent, mainly because of its shallow depths and marshy habitat.

Rush Lake, which covers about 3,000 acres, can see great influxes of migrating waterfowl, depending on water conditions. Jolin said that the area usually attracts more birds during dry falls, while wet falls can see birds disperse into other areas.

Mallards are the most popular species pursued on Rush Lake. Blue-winged teal are very common early, and green-winged teal and widgeon are common. Some wood ducks can be found, especially along oak-covered shoreline areas. Also, black ducks, gadwalls and pintails aren't uncommon.

Puddle duck hunters can usually find good success at Rush Lake during the early part of the season. Hunting pressure makes the birds

TRAVEL GUIDE

NEAREST SERVICE CENTER: Oshkosh.

LODGING: There are numerous lodging opportunities in the Oshkosh area. The yellow pages lists more than 30.

SPORTS SHOP OR HUNTING LICENSE OUTLET: Department of Natural Resources area office, 905 Bay Shore Drive, Oshkosh, (414) 424-3050.

HOSPITAL OR EMERGENCY MEDICAL CLINIC: Mercy Medical Center, 631 Hazel St., Oshkosh, (414) 236-2082.

EMERGENCY VETERINARY CLINIC: There are numerous veterinary clinics in the Oshkosh area. The yellow pages lists about 17.

AUTO REPAIR OR TOWING: There are numerous auto repair shops in the Oshkosh area.

tougher as time wears on, but fresh flights of Northern birds keep things interesting until freeze-up.

The area does attract some diving ducks, Jolin said. Canada goose usage is intermittent, but there are usually some birds in the area.

As a plus to hunters who hunt on the main lake body, large numbers of coots are also usually available, Jolin said.

Jolin said decoy hunting from skiffs or boats is the most prevalent form of waterfowling at Rush Lake. However, hunters need to scout the area before attempting to hunt there, he added.

Of the three landings, the one on the south end is probably the most developed. The north landing is actually nothing more than an open parking area with a trail through the rushes that leads toward a maze of potholes.

Also, the landing on the east shore was recently acquired and, at press time, hadn't been improved,

Rush Lake, which covers about 3,000 acres, can see great influxes of migrating waterfowl, depending on water conditions.

Jolin said.

Access at these two areas is usually with skiff, canoe or johnboat only. The north end features shallow water , and great mat-like growths of submergent chara can often make motor use impractical, Jolin said.

"You paddle, you push or you use a Go-devil," he said.

Some hunters choose to use the potholes along the shoreline, but most travel out to the main lake area, Jolin said. This can prove challenging, though, since they have to find their way to and from their hunting spots. The thick cattail and bulrush growths that cover the lake can result in hunters getting lost.

"It's not just a lake you can go to on opening morning," he said.

The lake is heavily utilized for waterfowl hunting, and competition can be a factor. But, like most areas, hunting pressure will be

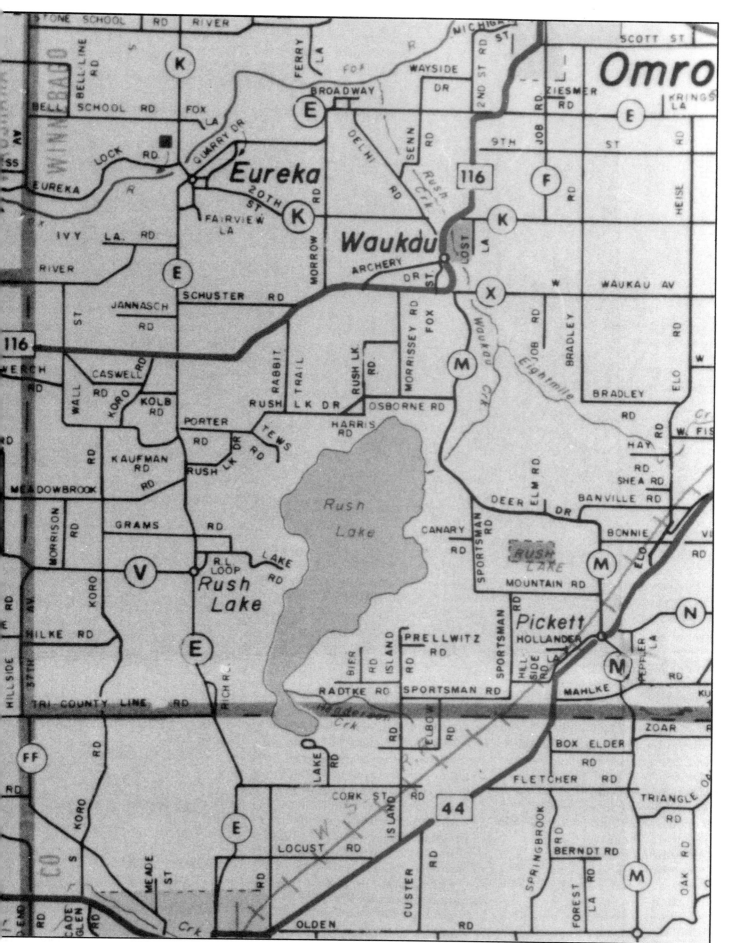

Mallards are the most popular duck species pursued at Rush Lake. Puddle duck hunters can usually find suc- *cess early in the season, but heavy vegetation makes a good retriever a necessity.*

lower during the week.

Many people construct semi-permanent blinds around vegetation on the main part of the lake. However, Jolin said he thinks more people should use portable blinds.

Not only does this eliminate the problem of having to construct a blind before the season and remove it soon after, but it also makes hunters mobile. Since blinds must legally have at least partial concealment, ducks and geese will use open water areas of the lake to avoid hunting pressure.

Some hunters avoid the crowds by pushing through the Rush Lake vegetation with marsh skis. This technique was once very prevalent in the Winnebago area, but only a

few people use it today.

Some pass-shooting opportunities are available along the shallow shoreline, but hunters should utilize the services of a well-trained retriever, as the thick vegetation can hide a bird easily.

The lake sees a good morning flight of ducks and can also offer good evening shooting as some birds return from feeding in local fields. However, many old-timers say their favorite time to be on the water is, surprisingly, at mid-day, when morning feeders often fly back into the lake.

Duck nesting production at Rush Lake is pretty good, Jolin said. A fair number of nests are generally found in the lake. Also,

Conservation Reserve Program fields that neighbor the lake have also helped provide nesting cover in recent years.

WEST

Namekagon Barrens

BURNETT COUNTY

If Wisconsin's bird hunters were lined up for a roll call, the number of sharp-tailed grouse hunters might surpass only those who chase snipe regularly.

Put simply, there are very few opportunities in the state today for the grassland birds. Namekagon Barrens, located in Burnett County, offers sportsmen one of the best shots they have.

DNR Wildlife Manager Pat Savage said the barrens, which consists of more than 5,000 acres of leased land, feature mainly brush prairie habitat with some wooded uplands around the edges and a few wetland areas. It is one of the last remnants of what was once a huge prairie that extended from Polk County up through the Bayfield Peninsula.

Burnett County took over ownership of the area in the 1920s after farming attempts there failed. An increased effort in the 1930s to plant trees resulted in a downward trend in numbers of prairie birds such as sharptails and prairie chickens. In 1953, the DNR began leasing land in Burnett County to preserve the remaining prairie.

Today, the barrens exist as one of the few areas in the state where sharptails can be hunted. The major management emphasis for the area is the prairie bird life there, including sharptails, upland sandpipers and various types of sparrows.

In order to keep forest plants from encroaching on the prairie, the DNR uses fire as its main management tool. Savage said about 800 to 1,000 acres of the barrens are burned every year in order to rejuvenate the prairie.

Savage said the sharp-tailed grouse population at the barrens is good, although the state's overall

TRAVEL GUIDE

NEAREST SERVICE CENTER: Minong.
LODGING: There are several resorts and motels in the Minong area. The Washburn County Tourism Association lists eight.
SPORTS SHOP OR HUNTING LICENSE OUTLET: Link Recreation, Highway 53, Minong, (715) 466-2272. Sportsman's Headquarters, highways 77 and 53, Minong, (715) 466-2171.
HOSPITAL OR EMERGENCY MEDICAL CLINIC: Spooner Community Memorial Hospital, Spooner.
EMERGENCY VETERINARY CLINIC: Information unavailable.
AUTO REPAIR OR TOWING: There are several auto repair shops in the Washburn County area.

population of the birds has declined.

By nature, sharptails are a low-density species, Savage said. That is, there won't be as many of them per acre as there would be of other birds, such as their cousins, the ruffed grouse. Generally, there is about one bird per 40 acres of habitat.

Sharp-tailed grouse hunting in this area is somewhat of a tradition, Savage said. Usually, there are about 50 to 100 hunters on the property during opening weekend. Many of these sportsmen grew up hunting sharptails and carry on the tradition today. Others are newcomers who want to give the elusive bird a try.

"It's kind of a trophy species to those who pursue it," he said.

Savage said sharp-tailed grouse

Namekagon Barrens is one of the last remnants of what was once a huge prairie that extended from Polk County up through the Bayfield Peninsula.

hunters must be dedicated. During a hunt, it's not unusual for sportsmen to walk five to 10 miles. The birds typically offer tricky, long-range shots, and a good dog is a necessity. The bag limit on sharptails is one per day, and the season is three weeks long.

Sharp-tailed grouse hunters are required to fill out free DNR report cards. Savage said that anyone who plans on traveling to the area is encouraged to contact him. His telephone number is 715-635-4091.

Deer hunting is also very good at the barrens, Savage said. The area has become known as a hotspot during the archery season. Deer populations are good throughout the area, and hunters tend to concentrate their efforts along the edges of the property, where wooded county forest land meets the open prairie.

Hunting pressure actually lets up a bit during the firearms deer sea-

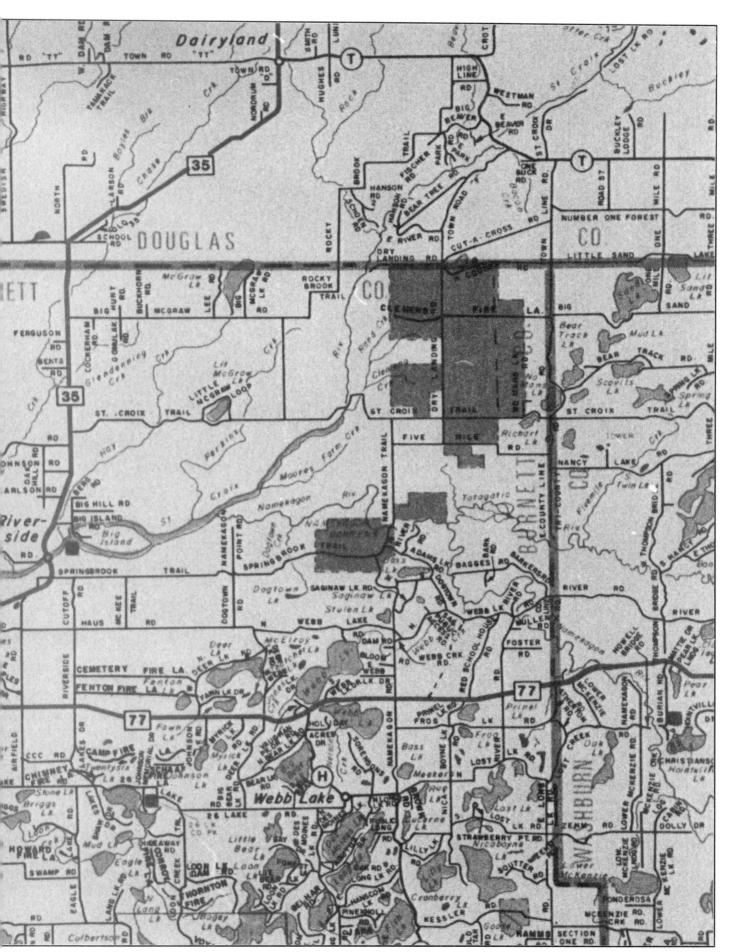

Bow hunters at the Namekagon Barrens tend to concentrate their efforts along the edges of the property, where wooded county forest land meets the open prairie.

son, Savage said. Still, the area holds deer and hunters can have good success here.

The property's fringe areas also offer good wingshooting opportunities for ruffed grouse, Savage said. Of course, hunters should look for aspen areas or similar cover types to locate birds.

Woodcock shooting can also be good at the area, Savage said. Aspen and alder thickets will attract migrating birds, and the bottomlands of the St. Croix River, which runs through the western part of the property, can also be a good spot.

The barrens also offers some duck hunting opportunities. Savage said there are some small slough areas around the property that see some waterfowl usage. These spots can offer shooting, but Savage said they will probably burn out quickly from hunting pressure.

The barrens are relatively remote. They lie about 18 miles west of Minong and about 20 miles east of Danbury. Access to the main portion of the property can b gained through Dry Landing Roa north of its intersection of the S Croix Trail.

Tiffany Wildlife Area

BUFFALO AND PEPIN COUNTIES

T o a waterfowler, there might be nothing more pleasurable than settling into a unique wetland area before dawn and listening to the invisible whistling of wings overhead. The promise of a new hunting day in a wild place is paramount.

Tiffany Wildlife Area, located in Buffalo and Pepin counties, offers duck hunters more than 13,000 acres of public land on which to pursue quackers. The northern portion of the property contains oak forest and some prairie grasses. The southern part of the property is basically a floodplain of the Chippewa River. It's here where most of the waterfowling is done.

The habitat here is primarily lowland hardwood, which is seasonally flooded. Common tree species include silver maple, basswood, cottonwood and river birch. The area is rich with sloughs, backwaters and beaver ponds.

Dave Linderud, assistant area wildlife manager with the DNR, said Tiffany is a big production area for wood ducks, and also produces mallards and hooded mergansers. Some geese also nest here.

Typically, the mergansers leave the area before waterfowling season starts. Wood ducks hang around into October. After the early season, the abundance of birds is dependent on migratory activity and weather patterns. Linderud said some years see good early shooting, then a lull period in between flights.

The main migratory species on the property are mallards and widgeon. Also present in good numbers are green-winged and blue-winged teal, northern shovelers, gadwalls, pintails and, on the bigger areas of water, ringnecks, scaup and buffleheads.

The main form of hunting at

TRAVEL GUIDE

NEAREST SERVICE CENTER: Durand.

LODGING: There are numerous bread and breakfasts, guest houses, motels and hotels in Durand. The Pepin County Economic Development Corp. lists eight total in their brochure.

SPORTS SHOP OR HUNTING LICENSE OUTLET: Pepin County Clerk, Government Center, 740 7th Ave. West, Durand, (715) 672-8857. Dick's Sporting Goods, 406 W. Main St., Durand, (715) 672-4218. Durand Hardware, 217 W. Main St., Durand, (715) 672-8687. Handy Mart, Conoco, 300 Third Ave. West, Durand, (715) 672-8935.

HOSPITAL OR EMERGENCY MEDICAL CLINIC: Chippewa Valley Hospital, 1220 3rd Ave., Durand, (715) 672-4211.

EMERGENCY VETERINARY CLINIC: Animal Health Care, 207 E. Main St., Durand, (715) 672-8609. Chippewa Valley Vet Clinic, highways 25 and 10, Durand, (715) 672-4459. Durand Veterinary Clinic, Box 9, Durand, (715) 672-8106.

AUTO REPAIR OR TOWING: Bauer Bros. Motor Service, 119 W. Madison St., Durand, (715) 672-5217. McMahon Motors, 100 E. Main St., Durand, (715) 672-8953. Polzer Garage, highways 10 and 25, Durand, (715) 672-5933.

Tiffany is jumpshooting, Linderud said. Many hunters park on the road and use hip boots or chest waders to walk into the sloughs and backwaters.

Some hunters use boats to run up the Chippewa River, then park their crafts and walk into likely

---

The southern part of the property is basically a floodplain of the Chippewa River. It's here where most waterfowl hunting is done.

areas. However, there aren't man places at Tiffany that can b reached by boat. Parking lots an boat landings can be found at th south end of the property o Highway 35 and on Highway 25 the east.

Most of the major sloughs Tiffany can be waded in years normal water, Linderud said. Son running sloughs might have wat that is too deep for waders, bu hunters can usually get aroun these by carefully skirting th edges.

Decoy hunting is also utilized Tiffany. Chippewa Dark Slough Beef Slough are two tradition. areas where this takes place.

Water levels have a profoun effect on waterfowling at Tiffan Linderud said. Hunting is best du ing years of high water. Howeve this also changes the profile of th property, sometimes allowing f boat travel through the lower on third of the property.

Tiffany is a big production area for wood ducks, and also produces mallards and hooded mergansers. Some geese also nest here. Typically, the mergansers leave the area before waterfowling season starts, while the wood ducks hang around into October.

During high-water periods, hunters will want to seek out newly flooded or shallow water areas. These are the spots that will hold ducks, especially the puddlers. Linderud suggests that hunters look farther north on the property to find areas like this.

Archery and firearms deer hunting on the uplands surrounding Tiffany's water is good, Linderud said. The area is big, but it does receive a fair amount of pressure. However, compared to some areas it is relatively light.

There are some remote areas on the property where hunters probably stand a better chance of seeing a bigger buck. Some dandy racks have come out of the area in the past. However, Linderud points out that much of the soil here is of the sandy outwash variety, which won't provide bucks with the quality of nutrition that they would receive in more fertile agricultural areas.

Typically, hunting success at the area is pretty good, Linderud said. Deer populations aren't as high here as they have been in the past, but there should still be plenty of opportunity.

Grouse hunting at the area is fair when the population cycle is up. The property doesn't feature a great deal of top-notch partridge habitat, but hunters can find birds here, especially in aspen and oak areas toward the north end of the property.

Squirrels are abundant a Tiffany in the mature stands of oa that lie on bluffs throughout th area. Linderud said this is on hunting opportunity that is unde utilized.

The mix of hardwoods and wate also makes for a substantial popu lation of raccoons. Unlike othe areas of Wisconsin, coon huntin remains very popular her Hunters who work dogs by moo light can no doubt find wha they're looking for.

Whitman Dam Wildlife Area

BUFFALO COUNTY

The two D's — deer and ducks — can really monopolize a person's fall activity. If you're one of those hunters who can't be reached from early October through November, you could probably spend the entire fall at Whitman Dam Wildlife Area.

Filled with lowland hardwoods, sloughs, backwaters and creeks, Whitman Dam offers waterfowlers and deer hunters exactly what they're looking for. The area, which covers about 2,160 acres in Buffalo County, gives sportsmen a unique opportunity for some quality bottomlands hunting.

Because of all the water at Whitman, duck hunting is the activity primarily associated with the property. The area consists mainly of floodplain, some coulee country and highland bluffs. Dave Linderud, assistant area wildlife manager for the DNR, said lowland hardwoods, such as silver maple, basswood, cottonwood and river birch, are common throughout the lowland areas.

Because of the hardwood trees in the area, it is a good production spot for wood ducks. Mallards are also raised locally, Linderud said.

Most hunting at Whitman Dam is done through jumpshooting, Linderud said. The maze of sloughs and backwaters here offers hunters a chance to sneak from spot to spot in search of puddle ducks. In years of normal water, most sloughs are accessible with hip boots or chest waders.

Some hunters walk back into slough areas, then set out decoy spreads and call for passing birds. This also works well, especially if hunters can find a relatively secluded area that won't be disturbed.

Of course, some spots are more popular than others. Indian Slough

TRAVEL GUIDE

NEAREST SERVICE CENTER: Winona, Minnesota.
LODGING: There are several lodging opportunities in the Winona area. The Winona Convention and Visitors Bureau lists 11.
SPORTS SHOP OR HUNTING LICENSE OUTLET: Buffalo County Courthouse, Alma.
HOSPITAL OR EMERGENCY MEDICAL CLINIC: Community Memorial Hospital, 855 Mankato Ave., Winona, (507) 454-3650.
EMERGENCY VETERINARY CLINIC: Central Animal Hospital, 78 Center St., Winona, (507) 454-2600. Town and Country Veterinary Clinic, 479 Mankato Ave., (507) 452-8665. Winona Veterinary Hospital, 4136 W. 6th St., Winona, (507) 452-4811.
AUTO REPAIR OR TOWING: There are numerous auto repair shops in Winona. The Convention and Visitors Bureau lists 13.

The maze of sloughs and backwaters here offers hunters a chance to sneak from spot to spot in search of puddle ducks. In years of normal water, most sloughs are accessible with hip boots or chest waders.

is a traditional place to duck hunt.

Some areas of the property are accessible by boat.

Water levels play an all-important role in duck hunting opportunities at Whitman. High water can make for good flights of migrating or staging birds, but it also poses a quandary for hunters. They must find shallow water areas — areas that ducks like to associate with — in order to meet with success. Just because there's lots of water in a given year doesn't mean ducks will utilize all of it.

In years of low water, hunters might face a lot of walking in order to get their birds.

Wood ducks and mallards are typically the most prominent bird during the early part of the season. Mallards, widgeon and some diving ducks become the bread and butter for hunters as the season progresses.

Since Whitman Dam is relatively small when compared to other hunting areas, pressure here can be concentrated. However, there are some spots toward the middle of the property where hunters who are willing to walk can find seclusion.

There is some goose hunting available at Whitman Dam.

Deer hunting is also very good here. Hunters usually concentrate on wooded areas and upland fringes around the property.

Hunting pressure during the November firearms season can be

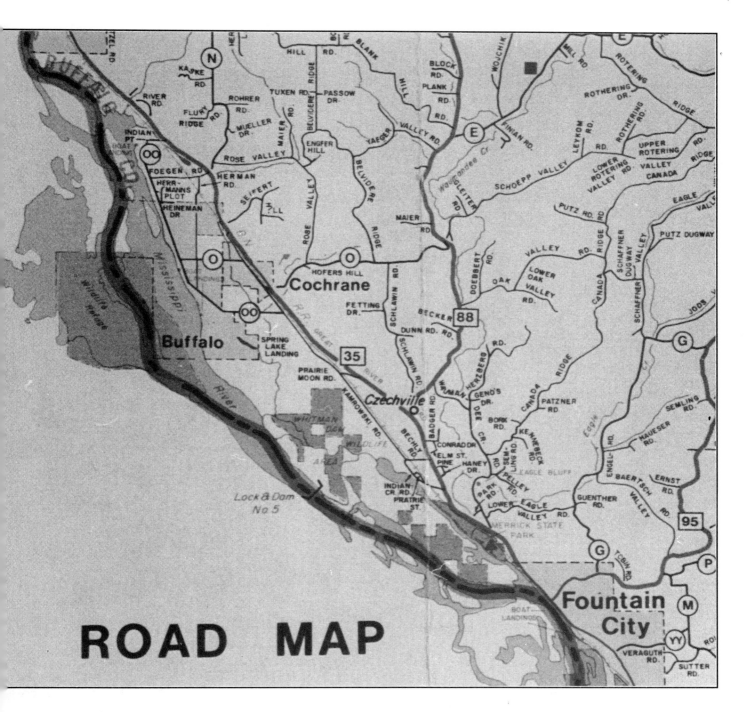

ROAD MAP

eavy, especially during the week-
nds. However, there are remote
laces on the property where
portsmen probably won't see
nother hunter. But hunters who
ag a whitetail in these spots can
ace an awfully long drag out.

Because of all the water at
Whitman Dam, trapping is also
revalent. Beavers, muskrats, rac-
oons and mink are the species
ost commonly pursued. Raccoon
unters also use the area, and find
hat the mix of water and hard-
oods offers them excellent oppor-

tunities.

Hunting opportunities for grouse,
woodcock and squirrels are minimal, Linderud said. Because of the
area's makeup, these animals simply don't have the necessary habitat
here.

Hunters should be aware that
there are private lands within the
boundaries of Whitman Dam. Many
of these areas are owned or leased
for hunting, so sportsmen on public
lands will want to pay close attention to signs marking posted areas.

Access to the area is pretty good,

Linderud said. Highways 33 and 35
are close to the property, as is
Merrick State Park.

Cylon Wildlife Area

ST. CROIX COUNTY

Cylon Wildlife Area offers sportsmen a variety of different hunting opportunities in a variety of different settings.

Located in St. Croix County, Cylon features about 2,200 acres of public land for hunters to roam.

Cylon offers a variety of wildlife habitat. The Willow River and a tributary, Black Brook, run through the property. The area is mainly flat and predominately wooded — featuring aspen, some pine areas and hardwood stands — with some fields intermixed among some scattered wetlands.

DNR wildlife manager Kris Belling said Cylon offers hunting for upland species such as white-tailed deer, ruffed grouse, woodcock, squirrels and rabbits, as well as some chances at waterfowl and pheasants.

When population cycles are up, grouse hunters can experience some good success at Cylon. As with most areas, birds at Cylon will be most abundant in young aspen areas. Grouse habitat is scattered throughout Cylon, Belling said, and hunters shouldn't have much problem identifying likely spots.

Grouse hunting pressure isn't overwhelming at the property. There are usually some hunters utilizing the area, but pressure isn't overwhelming.

Some woodcock shooting can also be had at Cylon. People probably won't come to the area specifically for timberdoodle shooting, but some birds are taken incidentally by grouse hunters. Migrant birds will provide the bulk of the gunning.

White-tailed deer are dispersed throughout Cylon. The area features good deer populations. Lots of firearms and archery hunters utilize Cylon because it is the only wooded public hunting area in the

TRAVEL GUIDE

NEAREST SERVICE CENTER: New Richmond.
LODGING: There are several campgrounds in the New Richmond area. A map provided by the New Richmond Area Chamber of Commerce lists eight.
SPORTS SHOP OR HUNTING LICENSE OUTLET: Information unavailable.
HOSPITAL OR EMERGENCY MEDICAL CLINIC: Holy Family Hospital, 535 Hospital Road, New Richmond, (715) 246-2101.
EMERGENCY VETERINARY CLINIC: Information unavailable.
AUTO REPAIR OR TOWING: Information unavailable.

Cylon offers a variety of wildlife habitat. ... The area is mainly flat and predominately wooded — featuring aspen, some pine areas and hardwood stands — with some fields intermixed among some scattered wetlands.

county, but again the pressure isn't overwhelming.

Access to the area is very good, so hunters really can't "get off the beaten path" in search of a big buck.

There are enough wetland areas throughout Cylon to provide duck hunters with some shooting. Typically, small natural wetland areas and beaver ponds provide the bulk of the shooting. There are some jump-shooting opportunities available along the Willow River and Black Brook. The streams have too many downed trees along them to allow for canoe access, so hunters will have to hoof it.

Migrant ducks make up most of the birds taken at Cylon. Wood ducks and other puddle ducks provide the main share of the shooting. Hunters may want to wait for flights of ducks in the mornings or evenings while searching out birds during the day by jump-shooting.

Although St. Croix County is at the northern edge of ringneck pheasant range, there are some natural birds at Cylon and other nearby areas. The DNR doesn't stock pheasants at Cylon. However, some local clubs stock birds at other locations in the county.

Pheasants at Cylon tend to stick to brushy wetland areas. Also, there are some share-cropped fields at the property, which offer the birds cover and food all at once.

Belling said Cylon doesn't receive a great deal of hunting pressure. Other public hunting grounds in the area seem to have better pheasant cover, and they tend to draw more wingshooters.

Mature timber stands at Cylon provide squirrel hunters with

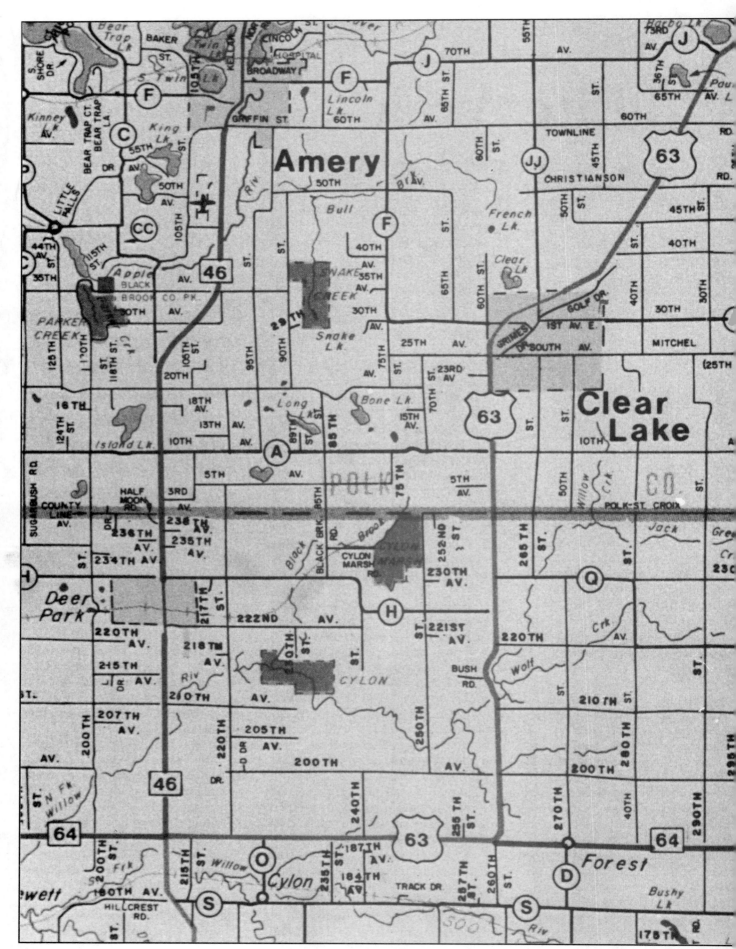

mple hunting opportunities. quirrels don't receive a lot of ttention from hunters here, so portsmen can likely enjoy a morn-g of bushytail hunting in relative eace.

Cylon also features huntable umbers of cottontail rabbits.

Access to Cylon is excellent. own roads run along three sides f the property, and there are three arking lots in the area. Some unters will also simply pull off e road and walk into the proper-. Two roads — Deer Road and wamp Road — enter the property oundary from the north.

Many firearms and archery hunters utilize Cylon because it is the only wooded public hunting area in the county. Yet, the pressure isn't over-whelming.

Kickapoo Wildlife Area, Wauzeka Unit

CRAWFORD COUNTY

Surprisingly, several public hunting areas in Wisconsin feature good turkey hunting opportunities. Perhaps foremost among them is the Wauzeka Unit of the Kickapoo Wildlife Area.

Good relationships with private landowners is no doubt the key to wild turkey hunting. But what about hunters who, for one reason or another, cannot secure permission to hunt on private land?

Surprisingly, several public hunting areas in Wisconsin feature good turkey hunting opportunities. Perhaps foremost among them is the Wauzeka Unit of the Kickapoo Wildlife Area.

Located in Crawford County, this 5,700-acre property features large wooded highlands among cropland areas. In other words, it's fantastic turkey habitat.

The Wauzeka Unit is part of the Zone 2 turkey management unit, which is one of the top turkey hunting areas of the state. In fact, the entire southwestern portion of the state is known for its excellent turkey hunting. However, the Wauzeka Unit remains sort of a secret when it comes to turkeys. DNR wildlife manager Dave Matheys said some turkey hunters use the area, but you probably won't see more than one or two other parties there during a hunting day.

Turkeys are spread throughout the property. There are plenty of mature oaks and other hardwood trees, which provide roosting areas for the birds. The alfalfa and other food crops that are share-cropped at the area provide good feed for the big birds. Open fields around the property give gobblers plenty of places to display for hens.

Matheys said reaching much of the property can take some effort

TRAVEL GUIDE

NEAREST SERVICE CENTER: Prairie du Chien.
LODGING: There are numerous lodging opportunities in the Prairie du Chien area. The Prairie du Chien Area Tourism Council lists almost 20.
SPORTS SHOP OR HUNTING LICENSE OUTLET: Stark's Sport Shop, Prairie du Chien, (608) 326-2478. Sports World, Prairie du Chien, (608) 326-5118.
HOSPITAL OR EMERGENCY MEDICAL CLINIC: Prairie du Chien Memorial Hospital, 705 E Taylor St., Prairie du Chien, (608) 326-2431.
EMERGENCY VETERINARY CLINIC: Information unavailable.
AUTO REPAIR OR TOWING: Halpin Tire Service, Prairie du Chien, (608) 326-6488.

and a good set of legs. The only true flat land at Wauzeka is directly adjacent to the Kickapoo River, which flows through the area. Otherwise, hills are the name of the game. Anyone who's been to Crawford County knows that hills here can be some real monsters. In other words, they're steep.

Keeping this in mind, hunters willing to trudge back a ways from the parking lot can probably find some relatively untouched spots. Of course, scouting is an absolute necessity when it comes to turkey hunting. If you can locate birds, as well as areas where they roost, feed and strut, your chances of success are far greater than those of some-

one who goes in cold.

The Wauzeka Unit also features a very good population of white tailed deer. Like the turkeys, deer are spread throughout the property mainly because the entire area features good habitat.

Share-cropped corn and alfalfa areas draw quite a few deer during the fall and winter, Matheys said. Many other hunters focus their efforts on ridgetops and edges between forest and open lands.

Like turkey hunters, deer hunters could be in for some tough climbing if they decide to hunt here.

There are a few aspen areas at Wauzeka, which attract ruffed grouse. However, oak areas that feature a good understory of dogwood, hazel or new oak will also attract birds and offer up some

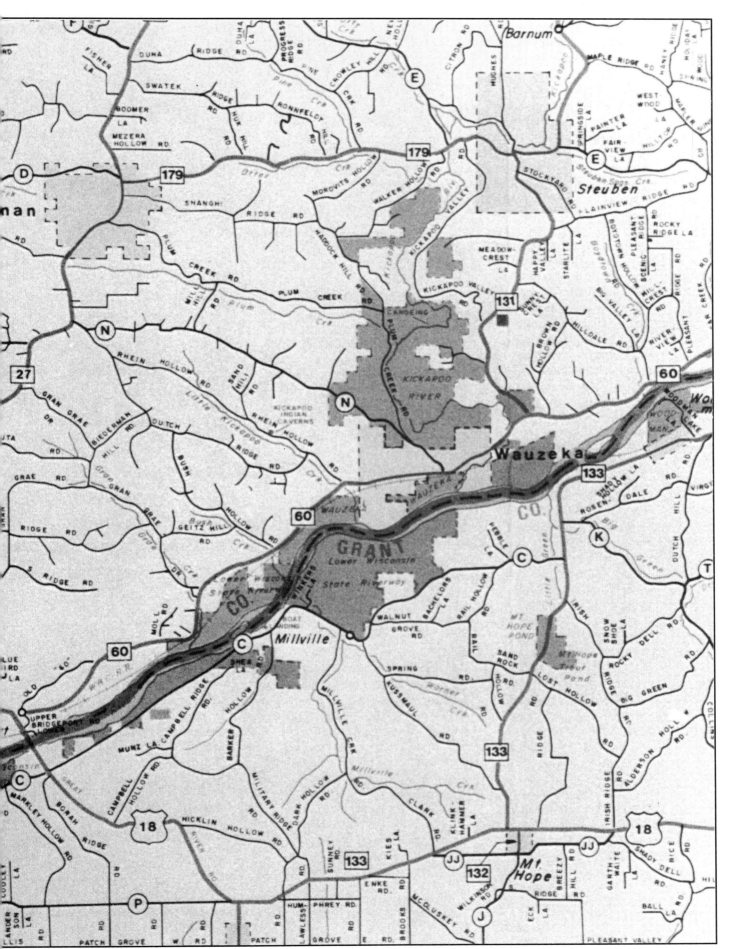

wing-shooting.

Because of all the mature hardwoods at Wauzeka, squirrel hunting here can be good. There is a good population of bushytails at the property, and hunting opportunities will be best during years of plentiful acorn crops.

There is some waterfowling available to hunters at Wauzeka. The Kickapoo River itself will hold some birds every year, and there are a number of wetland areas associated with the river.

Matheys said the river can offer tremendous hunting early in the season. However, a good deal of work will be required. There are dozens of oxbows and old meandering areas that will attract puddle ducks. Often, hunters will hike back in along the river channel and try to jump-shoot birds here. Other waterfowlers will paddle the river with a canoe in hopes of seeing ducks.

Mallards and wood ducks are the main species bagged, although some teal and Canada geese are also taken.

Some of the land at Wauzeka is owned by the DNR, while part of it is available under perpetual hunting and fishing easements. There are several parking lots located around the property.

The Wauzeka Unit is part of the Zone 2 turkey management unit, which is one of the top turkey hunting areas of the state. In fact, the entire southwestern portion of the state is known for its excellent turkey hunting.

LaFarge Reservoir Project

VERNON COUNTY

Stalled construction projects are often cursed. However, one such project has actually proven to be a blessing to Wisconsin hunters.

A 9,600-acre property north of LaFarge, in Vernon County, was to have been flooded as a reservoir by the U.S. Army Corps of Engineers. However, the project stalled. Today, the area is open for public hunting, and provides good opportunities for a variety of game species.

DNR wildlife manager Dave Matheys said the spot features a good mix of habitat types. It's comprised mainly of uplands, hardwood stands, lowlands, share-cropped land and water. Neither the DNR nor the Corps does much in terms of wildlife management here, but the DNR does extensive pheasant stockings each year.

Matheys said hens and roosters are stocked around the property twice a week during the early portion of the fall season, and then once a week almost up until the season closes in December. Hens and roosters are legal targets here, but Matheys reminds hunters that they need a free permit in order to pursue the birds at LaFarge.

Hunting pressure is really only heavy during the first two weeks of the season, Matheys said. After that, the weather usually takes a turn for the worse, and the white-tailed deer rut beckons many hunters to abandon their shotguns for compound bows. However, opportunities to harvest a bird exist right up until the season closes.

Birds are stocked primarily in grassy upland areas around the

TRAVEL GUIDE

NEAREST SERVICE CENTER: Viroqua.

LODGING: There are several lodging opportunities available in the Viroqua area. The Viroqua Area Chamber of Commerce lists seven.

SPORTS SHOP OR HUNTING LICENSE OUTLET: Vernon County Courthouse, (608) 637-3569.

HOSPITAL OR EMERGENCY MEDICAL CLINIC: Vernon Memorial Hospital, 507 S. Main St., Viroqua, (608) 637-2101.

EMERGENCY VETERINARY CLINIC: Dr. David Brown, 507 Rockview Lane, Viroqua, (608) 637-7300. Piper Veterinary Clinic, 731 S. Main St., Viroqua, (608) 637-3333. Veum Veterinarians Ltd., 739 St. Main St., Viroqua, (608) 637-2741. Viroqua Veterinary Center, Highway 14 North, Viroqua, (608) 637-2001.

AUTO REPAIR OR TOWING: There are numerous auto repair shops in the Viroqua area.

> *A 9,600-acre property north of LaFarge, in Vernon County, was to have been flooded as a reservoir by the U.S. Army Corps of Engineers. ... Today, the area is open for public hunting, and provides good opportunities for a variety of game species.*

property, Matheys said. There are also some marshy areas that see some action. Despite the heavy stockings, the area, as of 1992, did not have a 2 p.m. closure for pheasant hunting.

LaFarge also offers some quality duck hunting opportunities, Matheys said. The Kickapoo River runs the length of the area, and there are also several ponds and sloughs around the property.

LaFarge usually attracts good

numbers of ducks — typically puddle ducks — each year. The birds seem to prefer oxbow and meandering areas along the Kickapoo River. Hunters can either jump-shoot these areas or paddle the river with a skiff or canoe. Another opportunity, which is often overlooked, is to scare birds off a slough or oxbow, then set out decoys in anticipation of their return. It's surprising how often this proves effective, especially if the ducks haven't been pressured too much.

LaFarge is located within the state's Zone 3 turkey management area. There are good populations of

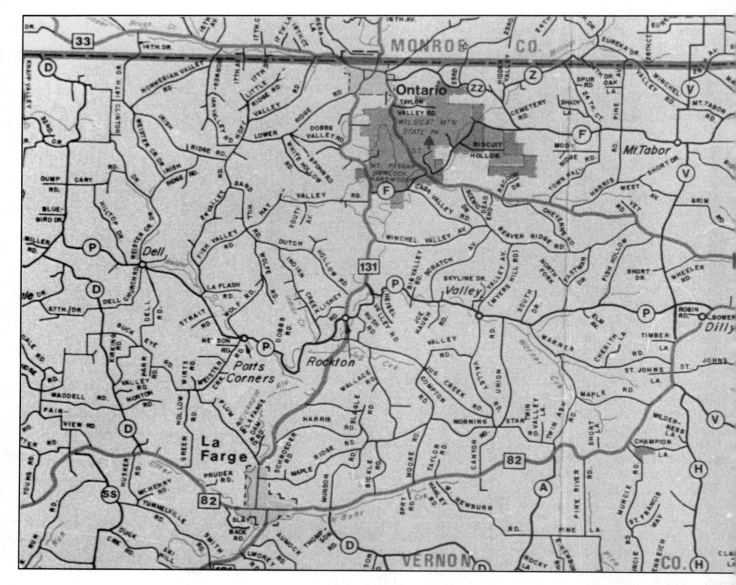

wild turkeys here. The wooded oak hills and other hardwood areas at the property make good habitat.

Turkey hunting success at LaFarge isn't as high as at some other places, Matheys said. For one thing, the area receives greater pressure than some spots, mainly because of its close proximity to La Crosse.

Matheys said LaFarge features very good deer hunting. White-tailed deer populations here are very good, and are higher than some other nearby public areas.

Some nice bucks have been taken from the property in recent years. The area is no secret to firearms deer hunters, but LaFarge's large size can offer people good hunting once they outdistance the "parking lot crowd" of hunters.

Grouse and woodcock are also available to hunters here. Naturally, habitat that features predominately aspen or alder, as well as spots with hazel or dogwood, will hold the most birds. Woodcock hunting is best near brushy areas associated with moist soils or adjacent to streams or wetlands.

Matheys said another wingshooting opportunity at LaFarge is offered by jacksnipe. The swift little birds, which to the inexperienced eye may resemble woodcock, like to hold near creeks and wet areas during their fall migration. Although they're not typically thought of during the bird season, they can offer excellent shooting.

Squirrels can be found throughout hardwood stands at LaFarge. Hunters should look for acorn and

other nut cuttings around the base of standing or fallen trees. The squirrels won't be far away.

Furbearers, including fox, mink, muskrat and beaver, are also common at LaFarge, Matheys said.

Van Loon Wildlife Area

LACROSSE COUNTY

Most Wisconsin duck hunters count mallards and wood ducks as their bread and butter. Van Loon Wildlife Area provides wingshooters with both.

Van Loon consists of about 3,800 acres in La Crosse County. Essentially, the property is on an island. The Black River forks at the north end of the area and rejoins at the south end.

Habitat at Van Loon consists mainly of bottomland hardwood stands, sloughs, ponds and associated uplands. Naturally, waterfowling is the type of hunting most often associated with this place.

DNR wildlife technician Roger Anderson said the area is a very good stopover spot for migrating birds. The most common species seen here are wood ducks and mallards.

Van Loon is close to the Mississippi River, and can see sort of a spillover effect from that great flyway. Anderson said that when waterfowl hunting pressure on the big water is heavy, ducks may utilize Van Loon with greater frequency. This is especially true in years when there is a good acorn crop.

The property isn't much of a waterfowl production area, Anderson said, but some local wood ducks, hooded mergansers and mallards are raised here. There are also some local Canada geese in the area.

One of the reasons Van Loon can offer quality duck hunting is that it can be very difficult to get into. There are several access points on the property — including ones of highways 93 and 53. However, much of the interior of the property is wild country.

Some waterfowlers with boats use the Black River as a way to

TRAVEL GUIDE

NEAREST SERVICE CENTER: La Crosse.
LODGING: There are numerous lodging opportunities available in the La Crosse area.
SPORTS SHOP OR HUNTING LICENSE OUTLET: Monsoor's Sport Shop, 517 Copeland Ave., La Crosse, (608) 784-0482.
HOSPITAL OR EMERGENCY MEDICAL CLINIC: Lutheran Hospital, 1910 South Ave., La Crosse, (608) 785-0530. St. Francis Medical Center, 700 West Avenue South, La Crosse, (608) 785-0940.
EMERGENCY VETERINARY CLINIC: Thompson Animal Medical Center, 4540 Mormon Coulee Road, La Crosse, (608) 788-8820. Hillside Animal Hospital, W5706 Highway 33, La Crosse, (608) 788-3425.
AUTO REPAIR OR TOWING: T&H Auto Body Shop Inc., 2520 Ward Ave., La Crosse, (608) 788-0380. Hinnie's Auto Body, 2145 Ward Ave., La Crosse, (608) 788-6464.

Essentially, the property is on an island. The Black River forks at the north end of the area and rejoins at the south end.

reach hunting spots. Many other hunters walk into the area. This can be difficult. Anderson said some hunters may have to walk more than two miles into the property to reach hunting spots.

Most of the hunting done here is jump-shooting around the potholes and sloughs, Anderson said. There are some larger expanses of open water, such as Van Loon Lake, that offer hunters some decoy shooting opportunities.

Scouting the property before the season is essential, Anderson said. Because getting into the property is difficult, finding your way back out

can be twice as tough. Hunters need to know where they are going, and should also carry a compass.

The forested uplands at Van Loon support a good population of wild turkeys, Anderson said. Of course, areas with good, mature stands of oak will be likely spots for prospective gobbler chasers.

Because of the limited access at Van Loon, turkey hunting can also be a tough proposition. However, the limited access can make for good hunting when sportsmen put in extra effort to reach out-of-the-way spots.

White-tailed deer are also very common at Van Loon. Many hunters associate these animals with the forested uplands here, but Anderson said that waterfowlers report seeing deer far out into the marshes.

Again, deer hunting can be tough because of limited access. During years when the Black River floods, deer will be pushed out of the lowlands, making them, in theory,

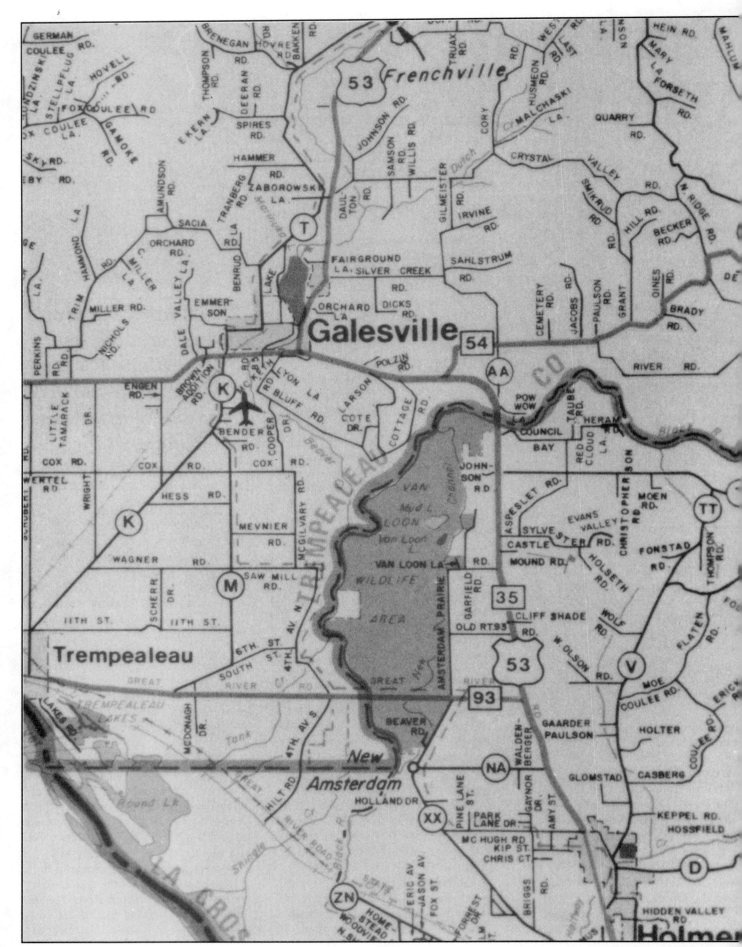

'an Loon is close to the Mississippi River, and can see ort of a spillover effect from that great flyway. When

waterfowl hunting pressure on the big water is heavy, ducks may utilize Van Loon with greater frequency.

Dave Larsen

ore accessible to hunters. Also, ears that feature good acorn crops ill also draw deer to oak stands.

Anderson reports that there ave been some big bucks taken at he property. Escaping the opening ay crowds can help hunters hedge heir bets for a wallhanger.

Van Loon's oak stands support a ood population of squirrels, Anderson said. There are also a ew ruffed grouse in the area.

The raccoon population at Van oon is excellent, Anderson said. However, not too many hunters nd hounds pursue the predators

because it's very difficult to do so. Hunters must know the area very well before they attempt a coon hunt. Otherwise, they might spend most of the night attempting to find their way back out of the property.

On a non-hunting note, Van Loon features several old iron bridges that run east to west through the center of the area. These are located off of what used to be called Seven Bridges Road. The bridges aren't considered safe even for pedestrians. They are listed on the National Register of

Historic Places, and there are almost no bridges such as these still in existence.

North Bend Bottoms Wildlife

JACKSON COUNTY

As its name might suggest, North Bend Bottoms Wildlife Area is a good place for duck hunters to try their luck.

But the 1,600-acre property, located in the southwest corner of Jackson County, also provides hunters with opportunities for deer, turkeys, upland birds and squirrels.

The northern border of the area is the Black River. The property itself is mainly a large floodplain, featuring lots of backwater sloughs, lowland hardwood stands, marshes and some grasslands. There are about 90 acres of open water on the property.

Eugene Kohlmeyer, DNR wildlife manager, said North Bend Bottoms is a major production area for wood ducks. Some mallards are also raised locally.

North Bend Bottoms is also a good area for migrating waterfowl. Kohlmeyer said mallard hunting on the property can be excellent, depending on conditions on the nearby Mississippi River. If there are high water conditions during fall, migrating birds will often use river corridors such as North Bend Bottoms. Also, years that feature good acorn crops also attract puddle ducks, which feast on the tender nuts.

Waterfowlers have a variety of hunting options at the property. Kohlmeyer said access is relatively difficult. Hunters park around the periphery of the property and then use chest waders to walk into areas they want to hunt.

Many of the prime potholes and other hunting areas take a good amount of walking to reach, so

---

TRAVEL GUIDE

NEAREST SERVICE CENTER: Black River Falls.

LODGING: There are numerous motels, hotels and campgrounds in the area.

SPORTS SHOP OR HUNTING LICENSE OUTLET: Pearson's Hardware, 306 E. Main St., Black River Falls, (715) 284-4815. Moe Hardware Hank, 33 Main St., Black River Falls, (715) 284-4621. Department of Natural Resources office, Highway 54, (715) 284-5301.

HOSPITAL OR EMERGENCY MEDICAL CLINIC: Black River Memorial Hospital, 711 W. Adams St., Black River Falls, (715) 284-5361.

EMERGENCY VETERINARY CLINIC: Hart Veterinary Service, 310 Highway A, Black River Falls, (715) 284-4424.

AUTO REPAIR OR TOWING: Nortman's Inc., Highway 54, Black River Falls, (715) 284-2511. Brauner's, Highway E, Black River Falls, (715) 284-4879.

---

hunters might have to put in some effort to experience success. Pre-season scouting can also be important, as hunters can locate what areas birds are utilizing.

Even though the area is comprised mainly of flat bottomlands, hunter access is primarily obtained off an escarpment adjacent to the wetlands.

Some hunters carry in decoys, then call to ducks, Kohlmeyer said. Others jump-shoot sloughs and

---

If there are high water conditions during fall, migrating birds will often use river corridors such as North Bend Bottoms. Also, years that feature good acorn crops also attract puddle ducks, which feast on the tender nuts.

backwater areas around the property.

There is quite a bit of oak on the upland edges that surround the bottoms, Kohlmeyer said. This makes for excellent wild turkey habitat.

Kohlmeyer said the area is currently open to spring and fall turkey hunting. Success rates at the property generally run around 20 percent, which is consistent with most areas throughout the state.

White-tailed deer are another big draw for hunters visiting the bottoms. Kohlmeyer said there is a good population of deer throughout the area.

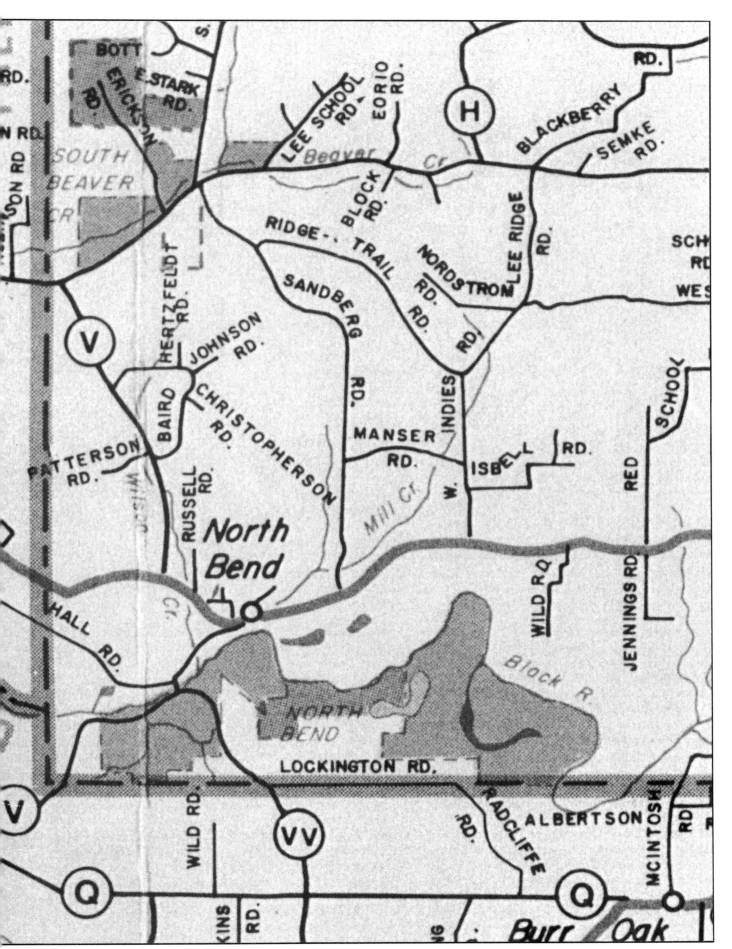

The northern border of North Bend Bottoms Wildlife Area is the Black River. The property itself is mainly a large floodplain which supports numerous ducks, turkeys, deer and small game species.

North Bend attracts quite a few deer hunters, especially during the November firearms season. "Anyplace in western Wisconsin, there are deer hunters," Kohlmeyer said.

With all of the oak stands around North Bend Bottoms, squirrels are very abundant, Kohlmeyer said. However, very few sportsmen take advantage of the opportunities provided by these game animals.

"They're one of the most underhunted species we have here," Kohlmeyer said. "There are squirrels all over western Wisconsin, and people really don't take advantage of that sport."

Upland bird fanciers will also find some opportunities at North Bend Bottoms. Kohlmeyer said there are some ruffed grouse on the property, although much of the area is too wet to be ideal for the birds. Nonetheless, a small percentage of the property is made up of upland brush and edge areas.

As with the rest of Wisconsin, grouse numbers at North Bend Bottoms were near the bottom of their cycle in the early 1990s.

There are also chances for wingshooters to get into some woodcock action. The area sees some flights of migrating birds in fall. The flight usually peaks around mid-October.

In addition to the hunting opportunities there, North Bend Bottoms also provides ideal habitat for furbearers, Kohlmeyer said. Muskrats, mink, otter and some beaver can be found on the property, and trapping can be very good.

County Trunk VV, located on the western part of the property, provides access to the area. Also Lockington Road, along the southern edge, can let hunters access the area.

Patrick Durkin

Black River State Forest

JACKSON COUNTY

I f you're a hunter who likes to explore large tracts of land while afield, Black River State Forest won't disappoint.

The 65,000-acre property, located in Jackson County, is also loaded with deer, upland birds, small game and waterfowl.

Eugene Kohlmeyer, DNR wildlife manager, said the forest features a lot of scrub oak, jack pine and aspen areas. Other features include rolling uplands, flat sand plains, marsh areas, lakes, flowages, creeks, the Black River and the East Fork of the Black River.

Kohlmeyer said the Black River State Forest is very attractive to deer hunters. Since Jackson County features so much public land, it's a natural spot for sportsmen.

The area features a very good white-tailed deer population. The population was reduced somewhat in recent seasons by high hunter harvests, but Kohlmeyer estimates there are still about 20 deer per square mile of habitat in the area.

Finding deer will require some pre-season scouting. Deer will concentrate in different areas as the seasons change, Kohlmeyer said.

"You have to scout the area to find out what the changes are from year to year," he said.

There are some large areas of land with few roads around them. Archery hunters will find these spots particularly inviting and, if they walk back far enough, might never encounter another hunter.

Of course, hunting pressure is much higher during the firearms deer season. Kohlmeyer said deer tend to scatter during this time of heavy pressure.

There is a relatively high harvest of yearling bucks in the forest. However, some years hunters take quite a few 2- and 3-year-old deer.

TRAVEL GUIDE

NEAREST SERVICE CENTER: Black River Falls.
LODGING: There are numerous motels, hotels and campgrounds in the area.
SPORTS SHOP OR HUNTING LICENSE OUTLET: Pearson's Hardware, 306 E. Main St., Black River Falls, (715) 284-4815. Moe Hardware Hank, 33 Main St., Black River Falls, (715) 284-4621. Department of Natural Resources office, Highway 54, (715) 284-5301.
HOSPITAL OR EMERGENCY MEDICAL CLINIC: Black River Memorial Hospital, 711 W. Adams St., Black Rive Falls, (715) 284-5361.
EMERGENCY VETERINARY CLINIC: Hart Veterinary Service, 310 Highway A, Black River Falls, (715) 284-4424.
AUTO REPAIR OR TOWING: Nortman's Inc., Highway 54, Black River Falls, (715) 284-2511. Brauner's, Highway E, Black River Falls, (715) 284-4879.

That could be attributable to the occasional harsh weather conditions encountered by hunters during the opening weekend of the previous season.

With so much forested land, upland bird hunting in the forest can be good. Kohlmeyer said regenerating aspen and alder drainage areas are especially attractive to ruffed grouse.

During peak cycle years, grouse hunting in the forest is very good.

Woodcock hunters will also find good opportunities at Black River State Forest. There is a lot of sandy country in the area, so woodcock hunters will want to seek out spots

---

There are some large areas of land with few roads around them. Archery hunters will find these spots particularly inviting and, if they walk back far enough, might never encounter another hunter.

---

with moist soils. Kohlmeyer recom mends that hunters concentrat their efforts on area river bottom especially those with good alde thickets.

Wild turkey hunting at Blac River State Forest remains some what of an undiscovered commodi ty. The property features a ver good population of the big birds and hunting opportunities in th area are expanding.

Spots with mature hardwoo stands combined with open field will concentrate the most turkeys With so much acreage available pre-season scouting will becom doubly important to locate birds.

Hardwood stands in the area ar also home to a decent squirrel popu lation. There are probably mor

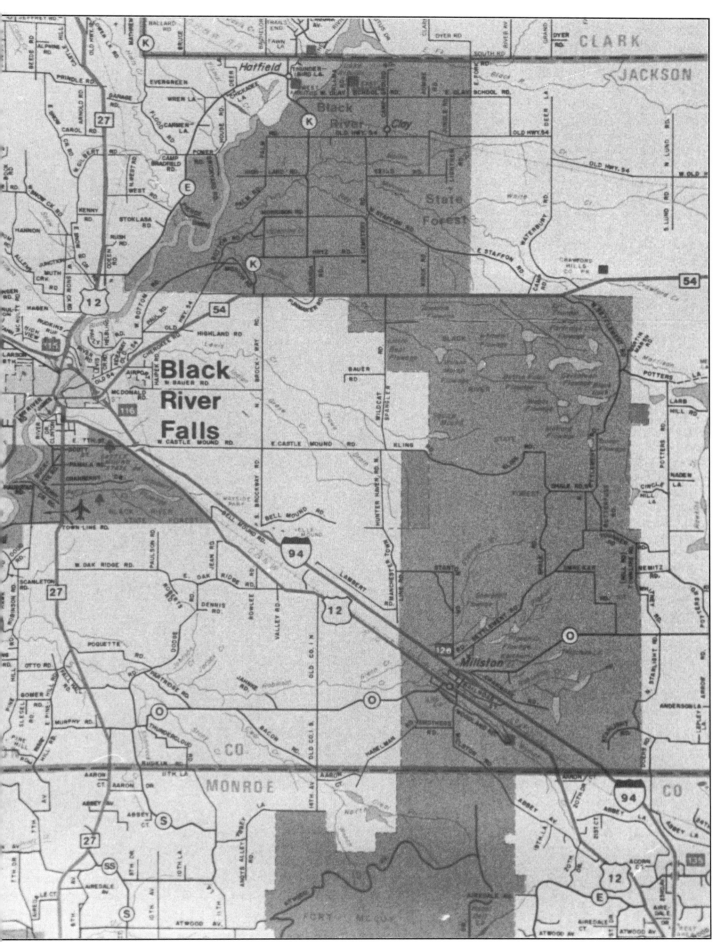

bushytails available to hunters in the western part of Jackson County, but good hunting opportunities are still available in the state forest.

Waterfowling is also possible at Black River State Forest. Much of the hunting in the area takes place at Dike 17 Wildlife Area, a 3,700-acre area in the east-central portion of the property.

Both puddle duck and Canada goose hunting is available at Dike 17. Birds tend to use this spot as a premigration staging area.

Much of the hunting at Dike 17 is done with decoys and calls. Pressure is generally the highest on weekends, but subsides during the week.

Creeks and impoundments found throughout the forest could also provide some jumpshooting opportunities for hunters who have located birds.

Varmint hunting in the forest gives hunters extra sporting opportunities. Raccoons are common on the property, as are coyotes. Red and gray foxes are also present.

Access to Black River State Forest is very good, Kohlmeyer said. There are roads throughout the area.

The forest also sees a great deal of non-hunting activity. Its massive acreage allows for plenty of picnicking, nature hikes and sightseeing.

With so much forested land, upland bird hunting in the forest can be good. Regenerating aspen and alder drainage areas are especially attractive to ruffed grouse.

Augusta Wildlife Area

EAU CLAIRE COUNTY

White-tailed deer, of course, probably attract the most hunters to Augusta. The area's variety of habitat benefits deer, and its easy access benefits hunters.

N orth country duck and goose hunters will find unique opportunities awaiting them at Augusta Wildlife Area, located in Eau Claire County.

Augusta contains about 2,100 acres of land and a combination of different wildlife habitats. Set on mainly sandy soils, the property features hardwood and conifer stands, marshes and impoundments.

John Dunn, DNR wildlife biologist, said Augusta is not a fantastic waterfowl production area, although some wood ducks and mergansers are raised here. Rather, the flowages on the property can serve as staging areas for a variety of waterfowl, including wood ducks, mallards, teal and Canada geese.

Duck hunting at Augusta is centered around the four flowages there. These impoundments are the result of damming the headwaters of Brown's Creek. They range in size from 16 to 80 acres.

Dunn said most waterfowlers at Augusta use chest waders or hip boots to walk into the edges of these flowages. These impoundments typically have a wooded fringe area, so hunters will want to work extra hard at concealing themselves. Also, a good retrieving dog will be a boon here, especially if a bird is dropped onto an area of water that might pour over your waders.

Some hunters use skiffs or canoes to reach waterfowling spots, Dunn said, but these are really only necessary on Mallard Pool, the largest and northernmost of the flowages.

Augusta draws a good deal of pressure in terms of waterfowling, Dunn said. The area is relatively easy to reach, and holds enough birds to make for good hunting throughout the season. Dunn points out that hunting pressure subsides

TRAVEL GUIDE

NEAREST SERVICE CENTER: Eau Claire.
LODGING: There are numerous lodging opportunities in the Eau Claire area.
SPORTS SHOP OR HUNTING LICENSE OUTLET: There are numerous sport shops and license outlets in the Eau Claire area.
HOSPITAL OR EMERGENCY MEDICAL CLINIC: Luther Hospital, 1221 Whipple St., Eau Claire, (715) 839-3311. Sacred Heart Hospital, 900 West Clairemont Ave. , Eau Claire, (715) 839-4222.
EMERGENCY VETERINARY CLINIC: There are numerous veterinary clinics in the Eau Claire area.
AUTO REPAIR OR TOWING: There are numerous auto repair shops in the Eau Claire area.

later in the season, especially during mid-week. Hunters should have few problems finding a secluded spot during these times.

White-tailed deer, of course, probably attract the most hunters to Augusta, Dunn said. The area's variety of habitat benefits deer, and its easy access benefits hunters. Whitetails can be found throughout the property. Old timber sale areas seem to attract quite a few animals, and there is some conifer and marsh habitat that offers seclusion for deer.

Augusta lies adjacent to the Eau Claire County Forest, a 50,000-acre property that also offers quality deer hunting. Gun and bow hunters generally utilize both properties.

With all of the forest land and timber sales in the area, you proba-bly guessed correctly that there a some opportunities for ruffe grouse hunting at Augusta. Dun said there is an active timber man agement program at Augusta an the Eau Claire County Forest tha provides new and varied age classe of aspen for grouse.

Although the partridge popula tion cycle was near its low point i the early 1990s, the quality aspe habitat promoted by these pr grams should benefit the birds a their numbers rise.

Dunn said there were a numbe of years when timber in the are was hard to sell. As a resul wildlife managers found themselve looking at some stands of over mature aspen. However, the DN successfully promoted incentives stimulate logging activity in th area, and timber harvests are no back up to snuff.

Augusta sees some woodcoc activity, Dunn said, mainly durin

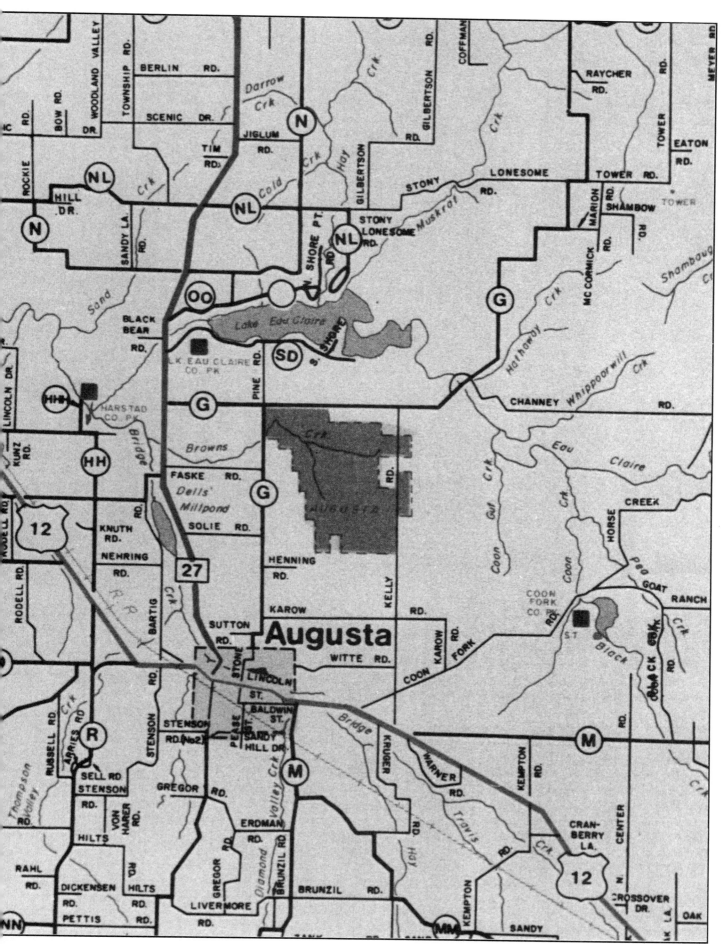

Old timber sale portions of the Augusta Wildlife Area seem to attract quite a few animals, and there is some *quality habitat that offers seclusion for deer.*

the traditional mid-October flight. The area, which has sandy, somewhat sterile soils, isn't a classic woodcock haunt, however.

There is some rabbit hunting available at Augusta. Hunters will want to check out new timber sale areas with good undergrowth and brush spots.

Dunn said there are some wild turkeys at Augusta and the Eau Claire County Forest. However, hunters won't need to worry about applying for a tag to hunt the prop-

erties: They're both outside of any established state turkey management zone.

The DNR stocked some areas near Augusta, and some turkeys apparently moved into the property, Dunn said.

Hunters will have no problem getting into Augusta. Dunn said there are very few areas on the property that are inaccessible. It is bordered by roads to the south and west, and also has good access points at the north and east ends.

SOUTH

Governor Dodge State Park

IOWA COUNTY

There are just two public hunting opportunities at Governor Dodge State Park, but hunters who use the area know that they are well worth it.

The park, located in hilly Iowa County, provides a variety of game species with plenty of good habitat. However, hunters are limited to white-tailed deer hunting with a muzzleloader, and spring wild turkey hunting.

The 5,000-acre state park is covered mainly with abandoned farmlands, wooded ridges, fields and some sharecropped agricultural areas. The topography is steep. The park features some big hills and sheer rock outcroppings. Oak and hickory make up a good portion of the park's wooded areas. There are two man-made lakes on the property, as well as several ponds. Some small wetland areas exist, but most of the area consists of uplands.

The area is simply ideal for wild turkeys, according to Bill Ishmael, wildlife manager for the DNR.

"It's excellent turkey habitat," he said. "There's lots of mature oak, fields, nesting fields and display areas. There are lots of seeds and food sources for the birds."

Governor Dodge is managed as a separate wild turkey management zone, 4A. Anyone who is successful in receiving a permit to hunt the zone should contact the park's office for information on the area.

Expert turkey hunters will tell you that scouting goes hand-in-hand with success. Governor Dodge is no exception. Prospective hunters should be willing to do their homework before grabbing their decoys and heading out into the woods.

Locating birds is a good first step. Identifying areas where they roost is ideal. Many sportsmen accomplish this by scouting likely oak

TRAVEL GUIDE

NEAREST SERVICE CENTER: Dodgeville.
LODGING: Don Q. Inn, Highway 23 North, Dodgeville, (608) 935-2321. Wildwood Lodge, Highway 23 North, Dodgeville, (608) 588-2514. Concord Inn, Highway 23 North, Dodgeville, (608) 935-3770. Pine Ridge Motel, County Trunk YZ, Dodgeville, (608) 935-3386. Super 8 Motel, 1309 Johns St., Dodgeville, (608) 935-3888.
SPORTS SHOP OR HUNTING LICENSE OUTLET: Menning Bait and Sports, (608) 935-2820.
HOSPITAL OR EMERGENCY MEDICAL CLINIC: Memorial Hospital, 825 S. Iowa St., Dodgeville, (608) 935-2711.
EMERGENCY VETERINARY CLINIC: Dodgeville Veterinary, (608) 935-2306.
AUTO REPAIR OR TOWING: Randy's Service Station, (608) 935-5424. Terry's Towing, (608) 935-2401.

areas in the evening, when the birds fly into tall trees for the night. Hunters can then stake out a nearby area the next morning and call to gobblers.

Governor Dodge State Park is also treated as a separate deer management unit, 70C. Ishmael said whitetails are distributed fairly equally throughout the park. Some areas, such as the abundant woodland edges in the park, tend to see more deer than others.

The animals thrive because of the mixture of cover throughout the area, but Ishmael said the overall population is kept fairly close to management goals.

The park sees a great deal of activity during the spring, summer

"It's excellent turkey habitat. ... There's lots of mature oak, fields, nesting fields and display areas. There are lots of seeds and food sources for the birds."

—Bill Ishmael, DNR wildlife manage[r]

and fall. However, gun deer seaso[n] here can be an experience of rel[a]tive serenity. Muzzleloaders are t[he] only weapons allowed and a limite[d] number of permits are issued [to] people to hunt the area.

Although the terrain at the are[a] is rugged, the park features a[n] extensive system of paved road[s] and good trails. Camping is permi[t]ted in the park during the gun se[a]son.

But even though access is goo[d,] the controlled level of hunting [at] the park can lead to some goo[d] shots at a trophy buck.

"There's some nice bucks tha[t] come out of there every year[,"] Ishmael said.

During recent seasons, the mu[z]zleloader deer harvest has be[en] around 100 animals, Ishmael sai[d.] Because of the limited permit nu[m]

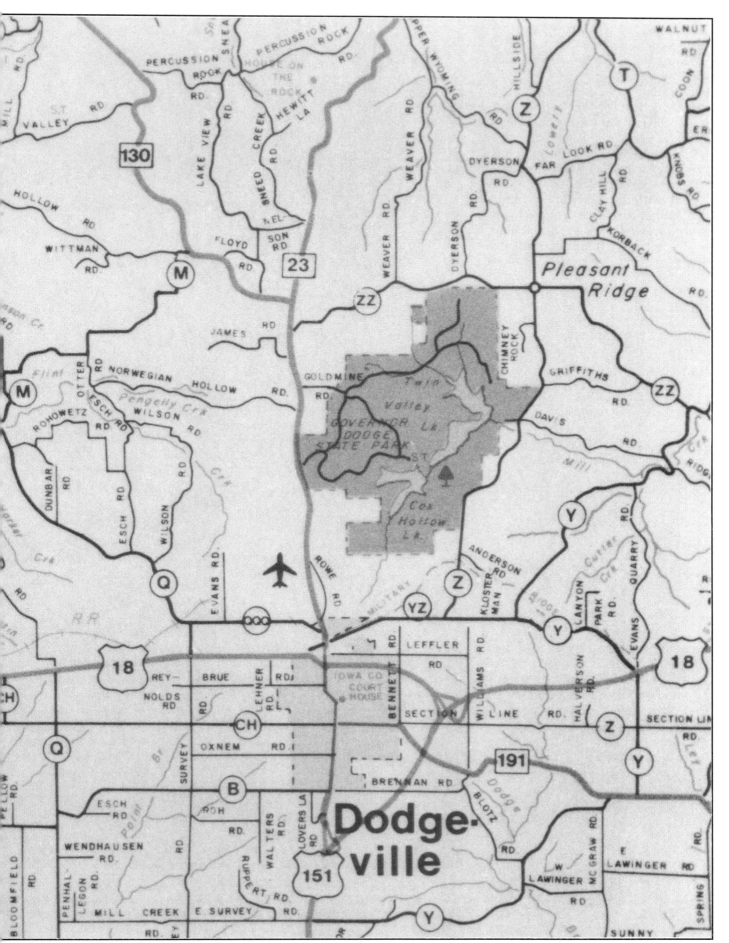

ber, success rates are generally very good.

Thanks to the high acreage and good habitat, there are very good populations of game birds, squirrels and rabbits throughout the park. However, hunting for these species is not allowed. Only legislative changes would open up seasons on these game animals, but that likely won't happen.

Still, with deer and turkey hunting opportunities like this, who could argue that Governor Dodge isn't a top-quality public hunting area?

The 5,000-acre Governor Dodge State Park is covered mainly with abandoned farmlands, wooded ridges, fields and some sharecropped agricultural areas. Only muzzleloading deer hunts and spring turkey hunts are legal on the property.

Yellowstone Lake Wildlife Area

LAFAYETTE COUNTY

To someone looking at a week-end of camping and hunting, Yellowstone Lake Wildlife Area might offer the perfect setting.

The 4,000-acre public hunting grounds, located in Lafayette County, is adjacent to Yellowstone Lake State Park. The park offers camping, beaches and docking access to Yellowstone Lake itself.

DNR wildlife manager Tom Howard said many people take advantage of the park's close proximity and stay there while on hunting trips in the area. The situation might also be ideal for families that accompany a hunter on a trip.

In terms of hunting opportunity, Yellowstone Lake offers a wide variety of game to choose from. Deer hunting is extremely popular here, as is pheasant hunting. The property also features good populations of wild turkeys, rabbits, squirrels and coyotes. Some waterfowl and upland bird hunting is also available.

The habitat at Yellowstone Lake is diverse, Howard said. The area features some good stands of mature hardwoods such as oaks and hickories, as well as open grasslands, some crop fields and very steep hills.

There are about 500 acres of prairie restoration in the area that are managed with fire, and there are also about 200 acres of young hardwood trees. There are also several miles of small streams running through the property.

White-tailed deer are probably the most sought-after game species at Yellowstone. Howard said the area is generally very crowded during the gun deer season, and hunters are everywhere.

However, the archery season is a different story. Howard said

TRAVEL GUIDE

NEAREST SERVICE CENTER: Darlington.
LODGING: Towne Motel, 245 W. Harriet St., Darlington, (608) 776-2661.
SPORTS SHOP OR HUNTING LICENSE OUTLET: Mathy's Coast to Coast, 226 Main St., Darlington, (608) 776-3729.
HOSPITAL OR EMERGENCY MEDICAL CLINIC: Memorial Hospital, 800 Clay St., Darlington, (608) 776-4466.
EMERGENCY VETERINARY CLINIC: Lax Veterinary Clinic, 342 Main St., Darlington, (608) 776-2122. Dr. Ralph Schwartz, Highway 23 South, (608) 776-3332.
AUTO REPAIR OR TOWING: Engstad Chevrolet, 109 Main St., Darlington, (608) 776-4451. Virtues Ford and Chrysler, Highway 23 South, (608) 776-4431.

Many people take advantage of the park's close proximity and stay there while on hunting trips in the area. The situation might also be ideal for families that accompany a hunter on a trip.

hunters should have no problem finding good bowhunting opportunities on the property. If sportsmen are willing to walk a mile, he added, they probably won't see another human being.

The property does feature a good population of deer. Since the area's habitat is so diverse, animals are generally spread throughout the property.

Yellowstone does provide an added bonus for gun deer hunters. The property has a shooting range where hunters can sight in their guns.

Pheasant hunting is also extremely popular at Yellowstone. Howard said that the area is heavily stocked each fall. Plantings are

done on the east end of the property in grassy upland areas. The area is a rooster-only property.

Howard said hunters shouldn't ignore the western part of the property when stalking pheasants. Some of the planted birds sneak over to that side of Yellowstone and, although action there probably won't be as heavy as on the east end, hunters can likely enjoy their sport in relative isolation.

Because the area features a nice mix of mature hardwoods, open fields and crops, wild turkeys thrive at Yellowstone. Howard said the property offers excellent hunting opportunities for the great birds.

Sportsmen really don't have to worry too much about crowded conditions during turkey hunting because hunter numbers in each management zone are controlled

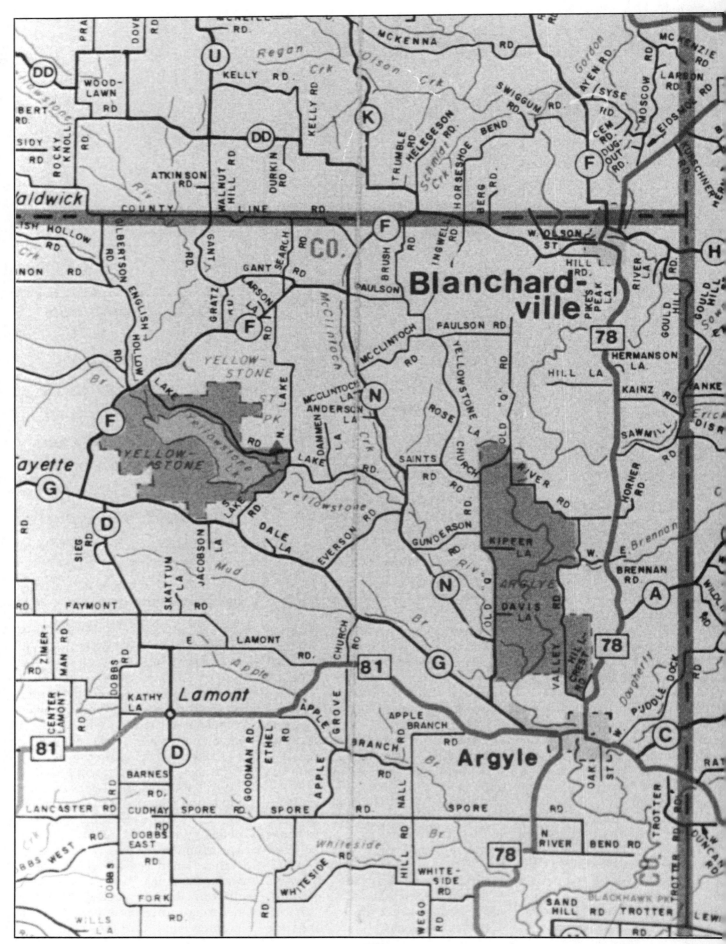

Leonard Lee Rue III

ost of the pheasant stocking at Yellowstone Wildlife
·ea is done at the east end of the property. However,
·nters who explore the west side might find birds and
less pressure. In addition to pheasants, Yellowstone is
home to turkeys, deer, various small-game animals and
a few coyotes.

a the state's permitting system. ·llowstone is in Zone 12. Howard id hunter success at Yellowstone usually pretty good.

Waterfowling opportunities at ·llowstone are limited, Howard .id. The eastern end of ·llowstone Lake proper falls in e state park boundaries. That eans hunting isn't allowed there.

There are some marshy shore-·e areas on the western end of e lake, Howard said. These spots n produce some duck shooting, pecially during the early part of e season. After that, hunting essure tends to burn these areas t quickly.

Upland bird hunting is also lim-ed at Yellowstone. There are

some grouse in the area, but Howard said their numbers aren't great. Also, the property features some bobwhite quail. However, there aren't enough of these little birds to provide consistent hunting opportunities.

Small game hunters should have no problem finding action at Yellowstone. Howard said the area's mature timber stands support good squirrel populations and, in turn, good hunting opportunities.

Also, the area features some good opportunities for rabbit hunters.

Howard said coyote hunting is fairly popular at Yellowstone. Many hunters run hounds for the

predators. An activity that is increasing in popularity is calling for coyotes. The area features ample opportunities for coyote hunters.

Vehicle travel in Yellowstone is prohibited, Howard said. However, there are miles of walking trails through the property, and parking access is good.

Leonard Lee Ru

Blackhawk Lake

IOWA COUNTY

For many hunters, Blackhawk Lake Recreation Area could be the perfect compromise.

It's far enough away from major population centers so that it isn't overrun with people, yet it won't take all day to drive there. And if you seek a variety of game species and some fantastic topography thrown in for aesthetics, Blackhawk Lake is the ticket.

Blackhawk Lake itself is nestled deep within the steep hills of Iowa County. A campground lies next to the lake, and adjacent to that are about 1,500 acres of public hunting grounds.

The wildlife management property at Blackhawk displays a good cross-section of habitat typical of the Driftless Area. Untouched by the last major glacier that rumbled across the state, the property features steep, imposing hills, oak and hickory ridges, abandoned farm fields, prairie grasses, hedgerows, corn and alfalfa fields, and brushy hillsides.

Bill Ishmael, wildlife manager for the DNR, said there is a great deal of sharecropping activity at Blackhawk. Through agreements with the DNR, local growers plant crops, which are then left standing to benefit wildlife.

As with many public hunting areas, the main attraction for many hunters visiting Blackhawk is the white-tailed deer. The crops and diversity of cover at Blackhawk benefit the animals, while the steep terrain offers deer quick and easy escape routes from hunters.

Blackhawk and the region around generally harbor high deer populations. Because the area is relatively small when compared to some public places, firearms deer hunting pressure can be heavy. Ishmael said hunter activity during the archery season is less.

Thick timber stands and crop

TRAVEL GUIDE

NEAREST SERVICE CENTER: Dodgeville.
LODGING: Don Q. Inn, Highway 23 North, Dodgeville, (608) 935-2321. Wildwood Lodge, Highway 23 North, Dodgeville, (608) 588-2514. Concord Inn, Highway 23 North, Dodgeville, (608) 935-3770. Pine Ridge Motel, County Trunk YZ, Dodgeville, (608) 935-3386. Super 8 Motel, 1309 Johns St., Dodgeville, (608) 935-3888.
SPORTS SHOP OR HUNTING LICENSE OUTLET: Menning Bait and Sports, (608) 935-2820.
HOSPITAL OR EMERGENCY MEDICAL CLINIC: Memorial Hospital, 825 S. Iowa St., Dodgeville, (608) 935-2711.
EMERGENCY VETERINARY CLINIC: Dodgeville Veterinary, (608) 935-2306.
AUTO REPAIR OR TOWING: Randy's Service Station, (608) 935-5424. Terry's Towing, (608) 935-2401.

fields are also an ideal mix for another Wisconsin big game animal: the wild turkey. Ishmael said Blackhawk features a very good turkey population.

"It offers some good opportunities for turkey hunting," he said. "There might be some pretty significant turkey hunting pressure."

Successful turkey hunters, whether spring or fall, will locate birds and areas that turkeys are likely to use. This means pre-season scouting and, perhaps, a willingness to trek back to out-of-the-way spots that aren't likely to be crowded after the opening-day bell sounds.

Ishmael said ringneck pheasants are also stocked on the property for put-and-take wingshooting opportunities. There is a lot of stocking at Blackhawk, and the area is open for

Untouched by the last major glacier that rumbled across the state, the property features steep, imposing hills, oak and hickory ridges, abandoned farm fields, prairie grasses, hedgerows, corn and alfalfa fields, and brushy hillsides.

hen and rooster shooting.

The birds are stocked mainly in grassy habitat near agricultural plots in the area. Identifying likely areas where pheasants will hide shouldn't be hard at Blackhawk. Flushing a bird after early season hunting pressure has made him wise might be more difficult. Locating roosting areas while watching birds walk or fly in during evening hours will give you a good starting place. From there, a thorough, resourceful dog might prove to be your biggest asset.

Pheasant hunters often take cottontail rabbits as an incidental

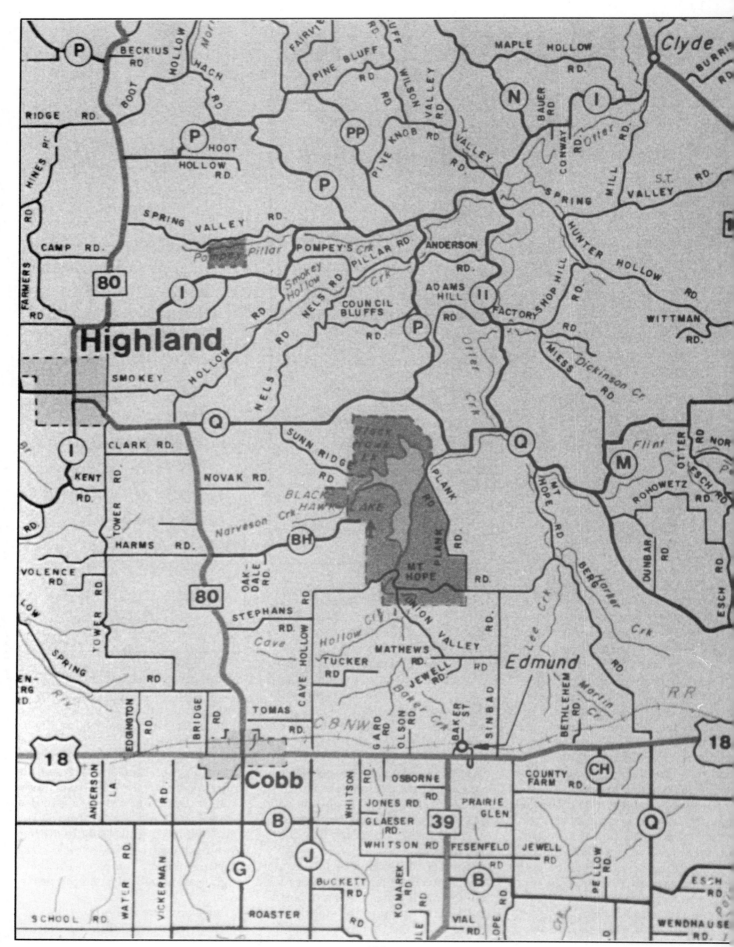

Blackhawk and the region around it generally harbor high deer populations. Because the area is relatively small when compared to some public places, firearms deer hunting pressure can be heavy.

addition to their bag. Blackhawk features good cover for bunnies: Plenty of brushy hedgerow areas run through croplands and abandoned farm fields.

"It's probably a pretty good rabbit hunting area," Ishmael said.

Hillsides and ridges covered with mature oak and hickory trees offer good opportunities for squirrel hunters. The season opens in mid-September, and early-season hunters often score well by listening and watching for squirrels rustling the still-green leaves above. When October and November roll around, the animals can be identified easily, and the patient, quiet hunter will have success.

Ishmael said the area also offers some hunting for ruffed grouse. Good areas, such as dogwood or aspen thickets, will be fairly easy to identify, but might prove hard to find. And the Blackhawk-area hills can wear a hunter's legs down quickly during the course of a hunt.

Dave Larsen

Goose Lake Wildlife Area

DANE COUNTY

Everyone enjoys hunting success, but some enjoy it more when there's a challenge involved.

Thick cover, hard walking and whispered tales of huge rafts of ducks and monster bucks. It's talk of these things that gets some sportsmen geared up for a challenge. But an area that could offer all of this probably exists only in the remote wilderness, right?

No.

In fact, Goose Lake Wildlife Area, located just north of Deerfield in Dane County, could offer hunters just that.

Goose Lake is a 2,000-acre property featuring glacial drumlins, grasslands, wooded areas, lowlands and two lakes. It's located right off of I-94, and is easily reached by Highway 73 on the west and County Trunk BB to the south. It probably sees more "non-consumptive" users — like hikers and bird watchers — than it does hunters.

Yet DNR wildlife biologist Doris Rusch said that this spot is chock-full of wildlife. And you can have a taste of it — if you're not afraid of a little work.

To start, the two lakes on the property — 133-acre Goose Lake and 34-acre Mud Lake — see a lot of use from migratory waterfowl in both spring and fall.

This is no secret among hunters. Mud Lake receives a good deal of early season attention from waterfowlers, and tends to burn out rather quickly. But Goose Lake is another story.

The lake is a shallow, tamarack-type bog, Rusch said. It supports some quality vegetation, including wild rice. The rice has gone back and forth in recent years. This quality habitat attracts loads of ducks.

"It's been reported that tens of thousands of mallards have been seen to go into Goose Lake," she said.

Sounds great, right? However, Rusch said that only the strong can hunt Goose Lake. Vehicle travel isn't allowed in the area, and it's a long walk from parking areas to the lake itself. Also, the lake's vegetation, which includes a good deal of floating bog, makes travel difficult at best.

"People who do it, do it because they like a challenge," Rusch said. "If you went through the parking lot, it's probably a mile-and-a-half to get a boat down there."

Some hunters walk into the area or use marsh skis to reach the bog, but even that doesn't guarantee success, Rusch said.

"From talking to people who have gone through that effort, if they made it to one opening, then the mallards were sitting down in the spot of open water farther out," she said.

Mud Lake is somewhat easier to hunt, Rusch said, but tends to burn out quickly after the season opener. Rusch added that Mud Lake usually attracts more in the way of diving ducks, including canvasbacks.

Goose Lake is also somewhat of a legend when it comes to deer hunting. Part of the area was once a private hunting club where bucks were allowed to mature. Although these big guys are probably long gone, the property still features some good white-tailed hunting opportunities for those not afraid of a challenge.

The area features a mix of grassy uplands, woods and wooded lowlands. Rusch said these lowland areas offer thick cover for white tails.

TRAVEL GUIDE

NEAREST SERVICE CENTER: Cambridge.
LODGING: There are several lodging opportunities available in the Cambridge area. The Cambridge Chamber of Commerce lists seven.
SPORTS SHOP OR HUNTING LICENSE OUTLET: Available in Fort Atkinson, 12 miles east of Cambridge.
HOSPITAL OR EMERGENCY MEDICAL CLINIC: Cambridge Clinic, 110 North St., Cambridge, (608) 423-3251.
EMERGENCY VETERINARY CLINIC: Clinic available on South Street.
AUTO REPAIR OR TOWING: Auto repair is easily accessible, though the chamber of commerce lists no specifics.

Thick cover, hard walking and whispered tales of huge rafts of ducks and monster bucks. It's talk of these things that gets some sportsmen geared up for a challenge.

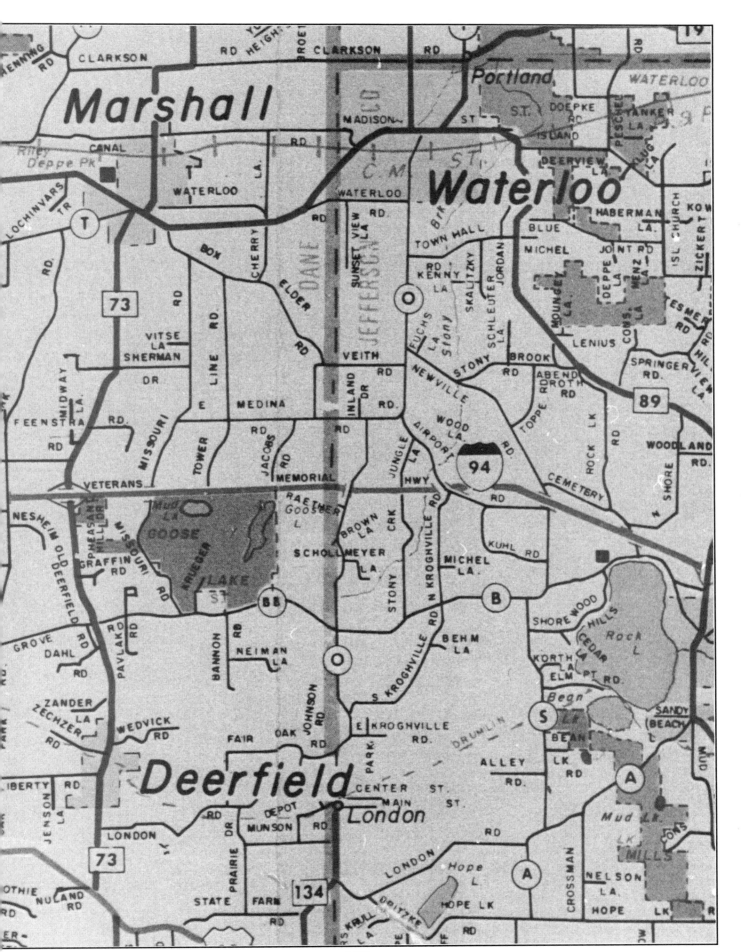

Only a driven dog and hunter will find the waterfowling treasure Goose Lake holds in store. This shallow bog lake makes travel difficult, but attracts thousands of mallards at times. The same dense habitat helps to protect white-tailed deer, and thus, produces some real trophy bucks.

"Deer are down there thick as fleas on a dog," she said. "They get down in there and nobody gets them out."

Secure spots such as these will always hold some older, larger bucks, Rusch said.

Rusch also offered a warning about these spots: They're loaded with poison sumac. Anyone who's rubbed elbows with this plant will tell you that it's not an experience to be relished.

Despite its close proximity to both Madison, deer hunting pressure at Goose Lake is never so much that a quality hunt can't be had, Rusch said. Often, it seems as if many hunters avoid public areas because they think they will be packed, when in fact this might leave the properties relatively uncrowded.

Pheasants are probably the biggest hunting draw at Goose Lake, Rusch said. The area's grassy uplands, which feature switch grass, Indian grass and big bluestem, are heavily stocked with birds during the fall.

Rusch said stockings are made two or three times a week. This tends to draw wingshooters to the property during October and November.

There are also wild turkeys on the property, Rusch said. The spring of 1992 saw the first hunt for these birds, and Rusch said opportunities should improve in the future.

Dave Larsen

Brooklyn Wildlife Area

DANE AND
GREEN COUNTIES

B rooklyn is a name you'd probably associate with busy streets
and harried commuters. But
that's New York. This is
Wisconsin, and the Brooklyn we're
concerned with features aesthetic
beauty and some first-class bird
and deer hunting opportunities.

Located in Dane and Green counties, Brooklyn Wildlife Area covers
about 2,600 acres of wooded ridges,
grassy uplands, shallow impoundments and lowlands.

DNR wildlife biologist Doris
Rusch said Brooklyn features a
great diversity in terms of habitat
and wildlife species. Also, scenic
Story Creek runs through the property. Rusch said this trout stream
was "channelized" about 30 years
ago, but has been "remeandered" so
that it now loops back and forth
along a natural course.

Rusch said deer hunting at
Brooklyn is very good. There are
numerous whitetails on the property, and the wooded lowland here
offers the animals some secure hiding spots and escape routes.

Big bucks are often associated
with Northern Forest units, but
Rusch said they are not uncommon
in this area of the state, where agriculture is king. Commercial crops
offer whitetails fantastic sources of
nutrition throughout the year,
which helps to grow 'em big.

"That's an area of the country
where we have seen some trophy
antlered bucks come from," she
said.

There is a great variety of bird
hunting available at Brooklyn.
Rusch said bobwhite quail populations in the area tend to fluctuate,
but have been very good in recent
years.

Quail, which are often associated
more with prairie states than the
dairy state, no doubt benefit from

the warm season grasses planted in
areas around Brooklyn. Species
such as big bluestem and switch
grass greatly benefit quail and
other wildlife.

Pheasant hunting at Brooklyn is
also good. The area features a great
population of wild birds, but these
wary fellows seem to move out once
the opening bell of the fall season is
rung. Rusch said the wild birds
seem to re-enter the area after the
season closes, so a December hunt
might offer intrepid hunters a good
chance at the ringnecks.

"You can hear lots of birds crow-
ing in April," she said. "The roosters are there."

The DNR also stocks pheasants
on the property, and many wingshooters key in on these birds during the season.

As you move from Brooklyn's
grasslands to its wooded areas, two
other familiar species become avail-

able: Ruffed grouse and woodcock.

Rusch said the area features a
nice residential population of ruffed
grouse.

"A few isolated properties are sort
of strongholds for ruffed grouse,"
she said.

Hunters chasing the partridge at
the area should try to locate aspen
or alder areas associated with a
good understory of dogwood or
other plants.

Woodcock also use the property,
and are probably most prevalent
during the fall migration.
Traditional cover for these birds
includes young aspen and alder
edges along wet areas.

Wild turkeys are also present at
Brooklyn. Rusch said the population at the property is fantastic.

"The brood sizes are huge," she
said. "If you spot a brood, it may
have 14 to 16 birds in it."

Waterfowlers will also find oppor-

TRAVEL GUIDE

NEAREST SERVICE CENTER:
Oregon.
LODGING: Lodging is available in
the Stoughton area or the Madison
area.
**SPORTS SHOP OR HUNTING
LICENSE OUTLET:** Dorn Tru-
Value Hardware, 131 Richards
Road, Oregon, (608) 835-5737.
**HOSPITAL OR EMERGENCY
MEDICAL CLINIC:** Dean Medical
Center, 753 N. Main St., Oregon,
(608) 835-3156.
**EMERGENCY VETERINARY
CLINIC:** Village Animal Clinic, 726
N. Main St., Oregon, (608) 835-
7007.
AUTO REPAIR OR TOWING:
Gary Wille Auto Service, 704 N.
Main St., Oregon, (608) 835-7339.

*Big bucks are often
associated with
northern forest units,
but ... they are not
uncommon in this
area of the state,
where agriculture
is king.*

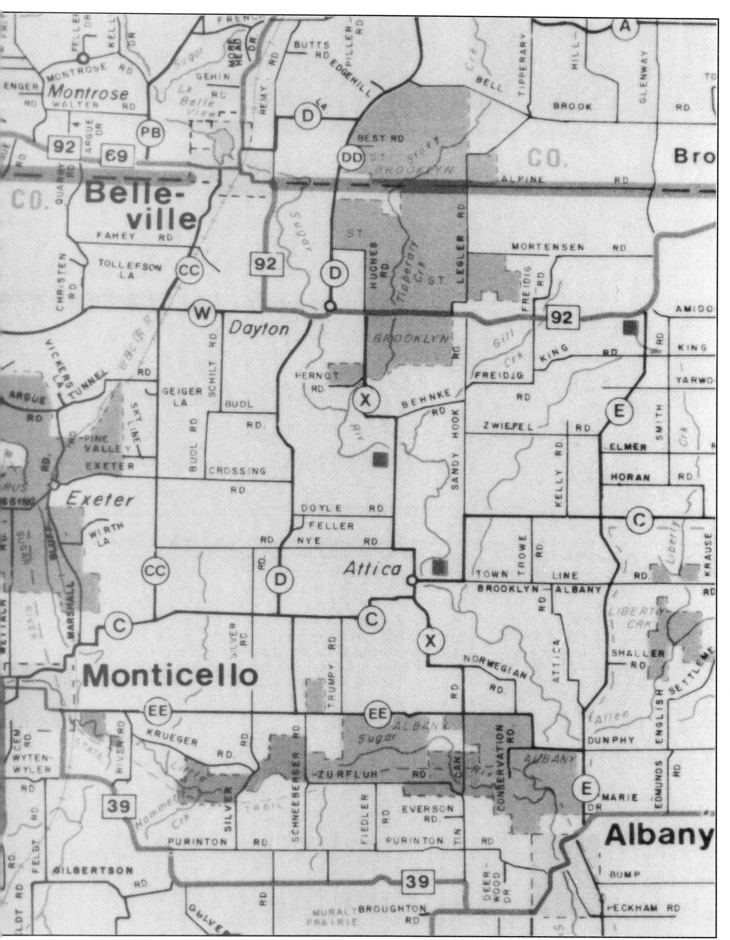

Deer hunting at Brooklyn Wildlife Area is very good. There are numerous whitetails on the property, and the wooded lowland here offers the animals some very secure hiding spots and escape routes. Wild pheasants also make this property their home, but these hardy fellows are often difficult to flush for even a seasoned dog and hunter.

tunities at Brooklyn, Rusch said. Story Creek itself gives jumpshooters a spot to seek out early-season puddlers such as wood ducks and mallards. Also, the DNR recently acquired a 200-acre parcel of land where the agency created about 50 acres of shallow water impoundments for waterfowl.

Brooklyn is easy to reach. Highway 92 runs along the south part of the property, and county trunks D and DD are also close by. There are several parking lots around the property, and an Ice Age Trail lets walkers follow the area's glacial features.

Turtle Creek Wildlife Area

WALWORTH AND ROCK COUNTIES

Turtle Creek Wildlife Area certainly has one of the most unique configurations of any public hunting area in the state, and features some unusual shooting opportunities as well.

The 1,073-acre area, located in Walworth and Rock counties, is basically a long, thin property that runs along the length of Turtle Creek itself. The area is about 10 miles long and no more than one-half mile wide.

DNR wildlife manager Mark Andersen said habitat on the public property consists mainly of lowland areas along the creek. There isn't a great deal of forest land here.

The area was originally a fisheries project, but was eventually given over to wildlife because of the flock of giant Canada geese that winters here every year.

In the early 1990s, about 3,500 of the big birds were wintering in this area, which is part of the Rock Prairie subzone of the state's Exterior Zone goose hunting area.

Numerous pothole-sized springs in Turtle Creek keep large areas of water from freezing during the winter, giving geese much-needed open water. Birds also sit in nearby Lake Geneva or Lake Delavan, and make good use of a dry land refuge in Rock County. Often, birds will fly out of these places and travel to the creek for a drink of water or a nip of watercress.

There is some goose hunting available along the course of the creek. Andersen said hunters do take birds in this manner. However, there is a rich, long tradition of goose hunting on the private land surrounding the property. Families and groups of hunters have well-established blind sites on private lands, many of which have been used by the same parties for

TRAVEL GUIDE

NEAREST SERVICE CENTER: Elkhorn.
LODGING: AmericInn of Elkhorn, 210 E. Commerce St., Elkhorn, 1-800-634-3444. Thomas Motel, 840 N. Wisconsin St., Elkhorn, (414) 723-2955. Ye Olde Manor House, Route 5, Elkhorn, (414) 742-2450.
SPORTS SHOP OR HUNTING LICENSE OUTLET: Information unavailable.
HOSPITAL OR EMERGENCY MEDICAL CLINIC: Lakeland Medical Center, located on County Trunk NN east of I-43 and U.S. Highway 12, (414) 741-2120.
EMERGENCY VETERINARY CLINIC: There are several veterinary clinics in the Elkhorn area. The Elkhorn Area Chamber of Commerce lists six.
AUTO REPAIR OR TOWING: There are several auto repair shops in the Elkhorn area. The chamber of commerce lists eight.

more than 20 years. Needless to say, obtaining permission at some of these areas can be difficult.

The goose hunting season in the Rock Prairie subzone traditionally ran longer than the Exterior Zone hunt, Andersen said. However, in 1992, for example, the Exterior Zone hunt ran longer.

There is some duck hunting available at Turtle Creek, but Andersen said there are better spots to pursue birds. Some hunters walk the creek or use a canoe or skiff to travel down the creek itself.

Stocking pheasants at Turtle Creek would likely be a waste of hunters' money. Because of its long, thin nature, it probably wouldn't take more than one gunshot to send even planted roosters scurrying for

(Geese) also sit in nearby Lake Geneva or Lake Delavan, and make good use of a dry land refuge in Rock County. Often, birds will fly out of these places and travel to the creek for a drink of water or a nip of watercress.

the relatively safe plots of private land that border the area.

Andersen said there are some wild pheasants on the property, mainly in thick grassy areas that border the creek. Populations aren't very high, but some birds are present.

Likely habitat here is easy to find, because Turtle Creek offers what is really the only usable cover in the area. In fact, it's easy to tell where the public land ends and the bordering private lands start by the cover. The area around Turtle Creek is farmed heavily.

Deer are common in the Turtle Creek area. However, again, the property's nature makes hunting

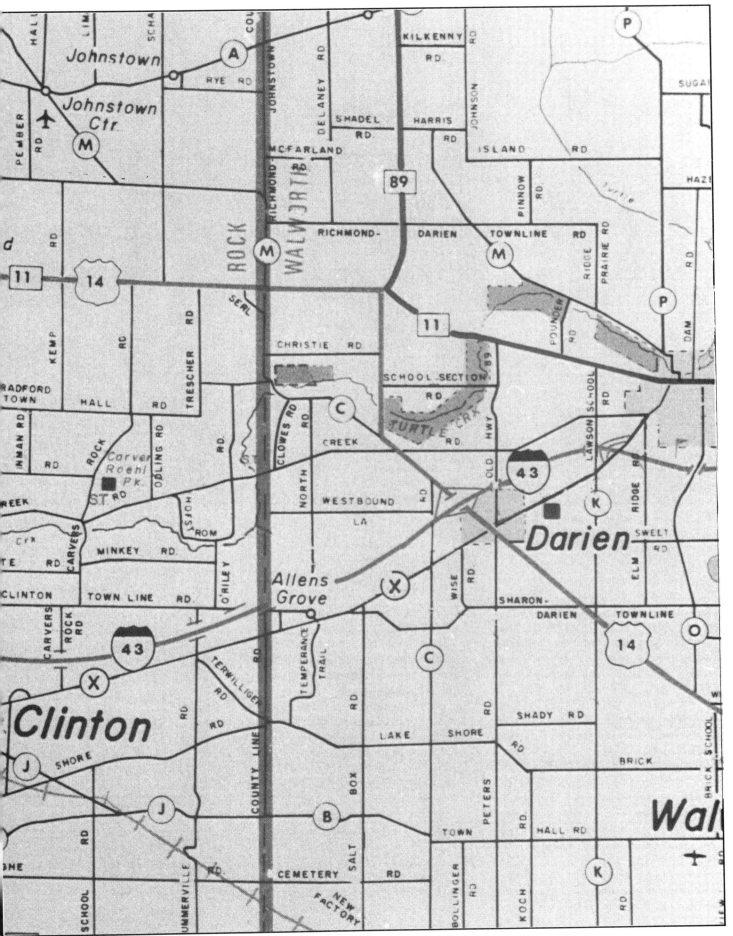

The Turtle Creek Wildlife Area was originally a fisheries project, but was eventually given over to wildlife *because of the flock of giant Canada geese that winters here every year.*

them a difficult proposition. Bow hunters may find their opportunities a little easier, because heavy pressure probably won't be pushing deer off the property as quickly as during the gun season.

Rabbit hunting at Turtle Creek is generally good, Andersen said. Good habitat lies along brushy edges and crop field edges around the creek.

Because the sanctuary of private land is so easy for flushed rabbits to reach, hunters may want to try "eyeballing" bunnies. This technique, which requires infinite patience and a good deal of practice, calls for one or two hunters to walk slowly along likely cover while looking intently for hiding rabbits. Once spotted, they can be bagged with a .22-caliber rifle.

Andersen said there is also some squirrel hunting available at Turtle Creek, but it is limited because of the limited forest land at the property.

Turtle Creek is easy to reach. The public land starts immediately west of the city of Delavan. Many state, county and town roads skirt or cross the area, and parking lots are available to hunters.

192

Lower Wisconsin State Riverway

CRAWFORD, GRANT
AND IOWA COUNTIES

Imagine you're a hunter with a wide variety of interests — ducks, deer, upland birds and even squirrels or raccoons.

You also don't like crowds. You long to go off the beaten path and see some really wild country.

It's hard to imagine many places that would suit your needs. But the Lower Wisconsin State Riverway is probably one of them.

There are 92 miles of river included in the state riverway. Included along them are several public wildlife management areas and a great deal of newly acquired public land. Put simply, hunting opportunities abound here.

Many of the wildlife areas now incorporated under the roof of the Lower Wisconsin State Riverway are well known to sportsmen. They include: Mazomanie, Helena Marsh, Lone Rock, Bakken's Pond, Avoca, Blue River and Lower Wisconsin River.

The DNR has tried to maintain the individual identities of the areas because they form the core of the riverway program. However, about 10,000 acres of land have been acquired under the new riverway program, so some of the boundaries are now blurred.

Much of the hunting done here is waterfowling. Because the riverway is in the Driftless Area, which wasn't touched by the last great glacier, it features a great deal of the wetlands in the southwest part of the state. These wetlands take the form of river flood plains, backwaters, marshes and flooded timber.

Mention the area to waterfowlers

**TRAVEL GUIDE
SAUK CITY-
PRAIRIE DU SAC**

LODGING: Cedarberry Inn, 855 Phillips Blvd., Sauk City, (608) 643-6625. Skyview Motel, S9645 U.S. Highway 12, Prairie du Sac, (608) 643-4344. The Graff House, 393 Water St., Prairie du Sac, (608) 643-6978.
SPORTS SHOP OR HUNTING LICENSE OUTLET: Ace, Sauk Prairie, 500 Water St., Sauk City, (608) 643-2433.
HOSPITAL OR EMERGENCY MEDICAL CLINIC: Sauk Prairie Memorial Hospital, 80 First St., Prairie du Sac, (608) 643-3311.
EMERGENCY VETERINARY CLINIC: Sauk Prairie Small Animal Clinic, 807 Phillips Blvd., Sauk City, (608) 643-2451. Sauk Prairie Veterinary Clinic, 1010 North, Prairie du Sac, (608) 643-6050.
AUTO REPAIR OR TOWING: Ballweg Chevrolet Olds Pontiac Buick Geo, Highway 12, Sauk City, (608) 643-8571. Everett's Body Shop and Towing, 847 15th St., Prairie du Sac, (608) 643-8624.

You long to go off the beaten path and see some really wild country. It's hard to imagine many places that would suit your needs. But the Lower Wisconsin State Riverway is probably one of them.

and one bird springs to mind: the wood duck. Paul Brandt, wildlife manager for the southern portion of the riverway, said the area provides major wood duck breeding habitat. Bill Ishmael, wildlife manager for the northern portion, agreed, and said the area also sees quite a few migrant woodies.

Mallards are also quite common in the area, and Ishmael said there can also be some good flights of teal and widgeon.

There are also a few resident Canada geese in the area, Brandt said.

Hunters can have success in the area using several methods. The area features many backwaters, small sloughs and creeks that offer good jump-shooting opportunities, Ishmael said.

Decoy hunters often make use of some of the area's larger, open water areas, Ishmael said. These include Bakken's Pond, Long Lake, Cruson's Slough or Smith's Slough.

Like many places, there can be significant duck hunting pressure early in the waterfowl season. However, it declines on weekdays. And since the area is so large, hunters willing to paddle or pole can find good areas to hunt without

The southern portion of the riverway provides major wood duck breeding habitat. The area also sees quite a few migrant woodies.

Dave Larsen

TRAVEL GUIDE
PRAIRIE DU CHIEN

LODGING: There are numerous lodging opportunities in the Prairie du Chien area. The Prairie du Chien Area Tourism Council lists almost 20.
SPORTS SHOP OR HUNTING LICENSE OUTLET: Stark's Sport Shop, Prairie du Chien, (608) 326-2478. Sports World, Prairie du Chien, (608) 326-5118.
HOSPITAL OR EMERGENCY MEDICAL CLINIC: Prairie du Chien Memorial Hospital, 705 E Taylor St., Prairie du Chien, (608) 326-2431.
EMERGENCY VETERINARY CLINIC: Information unavailable.
AUTO REPAIR OR TOWING: Halpin Tire Service, Prairie du Chien, (608) 326-6488.

TRAVEL GUIDE
RICHLAND CENTER

LODGING: Riverside Motel, Highway 14 and County Trunk B, Richland Center, (608) 647-6420.
SPORTS SHOP OR HUNTING LICENSE OUTLET: Triangle Kwik Stop, 845 Sextonville Road, Richland Center, (608) 647-8067. Coast -to-Coast, 142 E. Court St., Richland Center, (608) 647-2414.
HOSPITAL OR EMERGENCY MEDICAL CLINIC: Richland Hospital, 431 N. Park St., Richland Center, (608) 647-6321. Richland Medical Center, 1313 W. Seminary St., Richland Center, (608) 647-6161.
EMERGENCY VETERINARY CLINIC: Richland Veterinary Service, 378 W. Seminary St., Richland Center, (608) 647-8944.
AUTO REPAIR OR TOWING: Herb Carter Jr. Towing Service, Richland Center, (608) 647-3185. Compton's Towing Service, Richland Center, (608) 647-8604. Ron's Spur Service, Highway 14, Richland Center, (608) 647-3150.

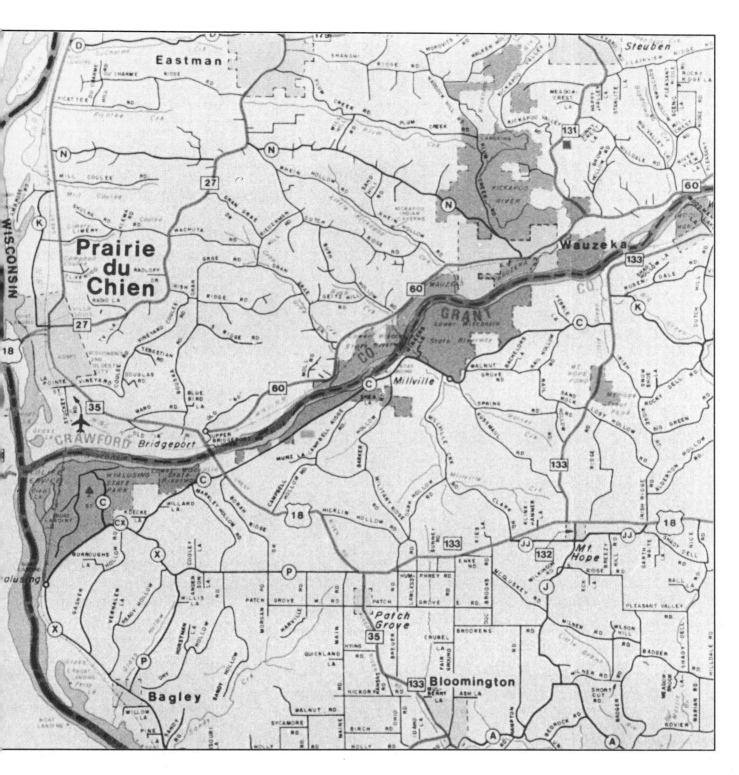

much competition.

"There shouldn't be any problem, specially during the week, in finding a good spot to set up some decoys and having a good hunt," Ishmael said.

One of the best ways to hunt the lower Wisconsin is with a canoe or skiff, Brandt said. This allows for decoy and jump-shooting. There is some walk-in hunting, but hunters should pay close attention to water levels before attempting this.

Deer hunting also receives a great deal of attention throughout the riverway, and deer are present in good numbers throughout the area.

"We've got a pretty good mix of agriculture, wetland, brush land and woodlands all the way up and down the river," Ishmael said. "So there's plenty of deer habitat down here."

The riverway — especially the traditional public hunting areas — can see some stiff hunting pressure during the gun season. However, Ishmael said hunters who do their scouting beforehand can find lightly hunted areas.

Also, new property acquisitions should provide more quality deer

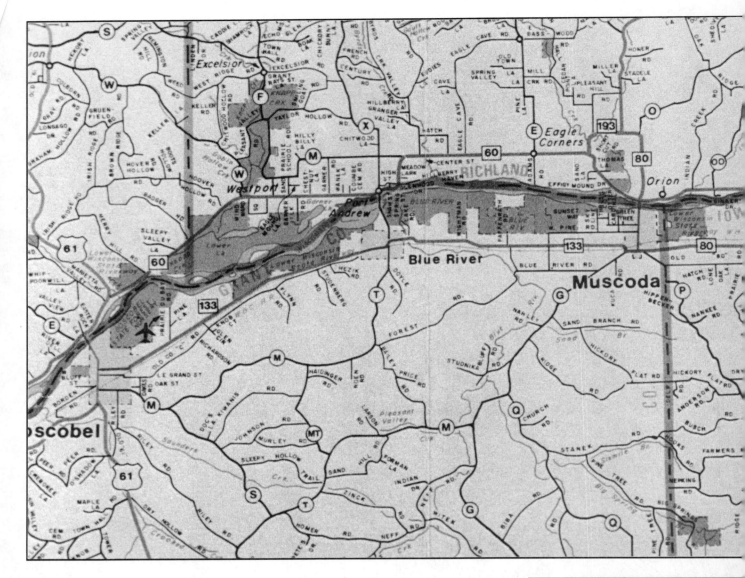

hunting areas in the future, he said.

Upland bird enthusiasts should also find the area to their liking. Hunters can chase grouse, woodcock and pheasants on various portions of the riverway.

Edge areas between the wetlands and uplands offer likely spots for grouse and woodcock chasers. Ishmael advises people to check young aspen and oak areas.

There are several spots that attract hunting pressure because they tend to hold a lot of grouse, and are attractive to migrating woodcock. But Ishmael said there is so much land now under state ownership that people should be able to find places that haven't been hit hard.

Pheasants are stocked at Mazomanie Wildlife Area and Avoca Wildlife Area, Ishmael said. Mazomanie is a rooster-only property, while Avoca offers rooster and hen shooting.

Wild turkeys are abundant throughout this part of the state, and there are some public turkey hunting opportunities along the riverway. Ishmael said more good areas will become available as the state purchases more land.

TRAVEL GUIDE
SPRING GREEN

LODGING: There are numerous lodging opportunities in the Spring Green Area. The Spring Green Area Chamber of Commerce lists 16.
SPORTS SHOP OR HUNTING LICENSE OUTLET: Mr. and Mrs. T's, Highway 14, Spring Green, (608) 588-2717.
HOSPITAL OR EMERGENCY MEDICAL CLINIC: Spring Green Medical Center, 150 E. Jefferson St., Spring Green, (608) 588-7413.
EMERGENCY VETERINARY CLINIC: Information not available.
AUTO REPAIR OR TOWING: Louis' Rainbow Shell, Highway 23, Spring Green, (608) 588-2444.

Wisconsin Deer Harvests

Year	Gun Kill	Bow Kill	Total	Year	Gun Kill	Bow Kill	Total
1897*	2,500	na	2,500	1948*	41,954	279	42,233
1898*	2,750	na	2,750	1949*	159,112	551	159,663
1899*	3,000	na	3,000	1950*	167,911	383	168,294
1900*	3,500	na	3,500	1951*	129,475	188	129,663
1901*	4,000	na	4,000	1952*	27,504	126	27,630
1902*	4,000	na	4,000	1953	19,823	*355	20,178
1903*	4,250	na	4,250	1954	24,698	*743	25,441
1904*	4,500	na	4,500	1955	35,060	nr	—
1905*	4,250	na	4,250	1956	35,562	nr	—
1906*	4,500	na	4,500	1957	68,138	nr	—
1907*	4,750	na	4,750	1958	95,234	nr	—
1908*	5,000	na	5,000	1959	105,596	nr	—
1909*	5,550	na	5,550	1960	61,005	nr	—
1910*	5,750	na	5,750	1961	38,772	nr	—
1911*	9,750	na	5,750	1962	45,835	nr	—
1912*	8,500	na	8,500	1963	65,020	nr	—
1913*	9,750	na	9,750	1964	93,445	3,164	96,609
1914*	9,850	na	9,850	1965	98,774	4,995	103,769
1915*	5,000	na	5,000	1966	110,062	5,986	116,048
1916*	7,000	na	7,000	1967	128,527	7,592	136,119
1917*	18,000	na	18,000	1968	119,986	6,934	126,920
1918*	17,000	na	17,000	1969	98,008	5,987	103,995
1919*	25,152	na	25,152	1970	72,844	6,520	79,364
1920*	20,025	na	20,025	1971	70,835	6,522	77,357
1921*	14,845	na	14,845	1972	74,827	7,087	81,914
1922*	9,255	na	9,255	1973	82,105	8,456	90,561
1923*	9,000	na	9,000	1974	100,405	12,514	112,919
1924*	7,000	na	7,000	1975	117,378	13,588	130,966
1925	Season Closed Statewide			1976	122,509	13,636	136,145
1926*	12,000	na	12,000	1977	131,910	16,790	148,700
1927	Season Closed Statewide			1978	150,845	18,113	168,958
1928*	17,000	na	17,000	1979	125,570	16,018	141,588
1929	Season Closed Statewide			1980	139,624	20,954	160,578
1930*	23,000	na	23,000	1981	166,673	29,083	195,756
1931	Season Closed Statewide			1982	182,715	30,850	213,565
1932*	36,000	na	36,000	1983	197,600	32,876	230,476
1933	Season Closed Statewide			1984	255,240	38,891	294,131
1934*	21,251	1	21,252	1985	274,302	40,744	315,046
1935	Season Closed Statewide			1986	259,240	40,490	299,730
1936*	29,676	1	29,676	1987	250,530	42,651	293,181
1937*	14,835	0	14,835	1988	263,424	42,393	305,817
1938*	32,855	1	32,855	1989	310,192	46,394	356,586
1939*	25,730	6	25,736	1990	350,040	49,291	399,331
1940*	33,138	5	33,142	1991	352,328	67,005	419,333
1941*	40,403	18	40,421	1992	288,906	60,479	349,385
1942*	45,188	15	45,203				
1943*	128,296	76	128,372				
1944*	28,537	78	28,615				
1945*	37,527	160	37,687				
1946*	55,276	256	55,532				
1947*	53,520	368	53,888				

* - Kills were estimated in these years. Mandatory registration began in 1953.

na - Not Applicable

nr - Not Reported

Source: Wisconsin Department of Natural Resources

Turkey Harvests

Spring

Year	Zones Open	Permits Issued	Harvest	Success Rate (%)
1983	4	1,200	180	15%
1984	5	1,900	308	16%
1985	5	2,125	497	23%
1986	7	3,495	793	23%
1987	7	6,040	1,482	25%
1988	10	11,071	2,490	23%
1989	16	21,280	4,406	21%
1990	19	29,887	6,532	22%
1991	20	37,171	6,862	18%
1992	36	43,972	8,794	20%
1993	42	62,160	12,343	20%
1994	47	71,610	—	—

Fall

Year	Zones Open	Permits Issued	Harvest	Success Rate (%)
1989	8	7,260	1,570	22%
1990	12	12,465	3,433	28%
1991	15	16,671	2,904	17%
1992	19	24,998	5,024	20%
1993	24	31,440	—	—

Black Bear Harvests

Year	Male	Female	Total	Permits Issued
1957	nr	nr	460	na
1958	nr	nr	811	na
1959	nr	nr	665	na
1960	nr	nr	675	na
1961	nr	nr	337	na
1962	nr	nr	617	na
1963	nr	nr	579	na
1964	nr	nr	511	na
1965	nr	nr	308	na
1966	nr	nr	475	na
1967	nr	nr	541	na
1968	nr	nr	613	na
1969	nr	nr	752	na
1970	331	341	672	na
1971	444	347	791	na
1972	nr	nr	878	na
1973	376	230	606	na
1974	224	166	390	na
1975	344	195	539	na
1976	373	206	579	na
1977	375	256	631	na
1978	426	436	852	na
1979	449	288	737	na
1980	469	386	855	na
1981	624	610	1234	na
1982	797	636	1433	na
1983	539	395	934	na
1984	617	480	1097	na

Year	Male	Female	Total	Permits Issued
1985	No Season *			
1986	308	195	503	860
1987	533	304	837	1690
1988	601	494	1125	2056
1989	584	375	978	2020
1990	705	501	1247	2825
1991	715	480	1219	2560
1992	819	655	1474	2620

nr — Not Reported

na — Not Applicable

* — No season was held in 1985 after the Department of Natural Resources determined that black bears were overshot in the preceding seasons.

Black Bear Population Estimates
Zone

Year	A	B	C	Total
1985	3349	1116	285	4750
1986	3903	1232	327	5462
1987	4418	1395	355	6168
1988	4577	1525	435	6537
1989	4412	1716	430	6558
1990	4581	1781	440	6802
1991	4424	1896	387	6707
1992	4526	1760	343	6629
1993	4261	1657	225	6143

Canada Goose Harvests

Year	Quota	Est. Kill	Year	Quota	Est. Kill
1966	14,000	27,900	1980	30,000	57,600
1967	20,000	21,300	1981	20,000	39,800
1968	20,000	25,300	1982	18,000	45,800
1969	25,000	42,800	1983	25,000	33,500
1970	35,000	28,600	1984	25,000	39,900
1971	28,000	52,500	1985	25,000	43,500
1972	28,000	35,800	1986	45,000	49,900
1973	28,000	60,800	1987	49,620	39,600
1974	28,000	77,000	1988	63,700	53,700
1975	28,000	66,400	1989	89,200	81,200
1976	28,000	45,700	1990	194,000	120,500
1977	35,000	89,900	1991	185,787	130,787
1978	50,000	85,700	1992	66,700	52,436
1979	35,000	62,200			

Pheasant Harvests

Year	Harvest	Year	Harvest
1927	First open season in parts of Waukesha and Jefferson counties.	1985	260,791
1930	Closed Season	1986	268,924
1940	482,516	1987	270,379
1950	414,487	1988	242,666
1960	274,300	1989	252,709
1970	622,656	1990	244,209
1980	365,700	1991	189,980
		1992	193,318

Spring Statewide Conservation Hearings

Year	Attendance	Year	Attendance
1993	5,331	1976	8,123
1992	9,240	1975	13,350
1991	9,598	1974	4,918
1990	4,591	1973	5,020
1989	6,622	1972	6,242
1988	7,618	1971	*5,572
1987	4,372	1970	9,340
1986	5,311	Ave.	6,530
1985	4,554		
1984	7,007		
1983	5,368		
1982	6,653		
1981	*5,276		
1980	5,672		
1979	5,160		
1978	6,446		
1977	5,249		

* — Estimate. Actual totals are probably somewhat higher.

The spring fish and wildlife hearings are conducted in each of the state's 72 counties each April. Sportsmen are invited to attend the hearings and vote on proposed changes in the rules and laws that govern hunting and fishing in Wisconsin.

DEER HUNTING BUDDIES

Name_____

Address _____

City _____

State _____ Zip _____

Phone Number _____

Name_____

Address _____

City _____

State _____ Zip _____

Phone Number _____

Name_____

Address _____

City _____

State _____ Zip _____

Phone Number _____

Name_____

Address _____

City _____

State _____ Zip _____

Phone Number _____

Name_____

Address _____

City _____

State _____ Zip _____

Phone Number _____

Name_____

Address _____

City _____

State _____ Zip _____

Phone Number _____

Name_____

Address _____

City _____

State _____ Zip _____

Phone Number _____

Name_____

Address _____

City _____

State _____ Zip _____

Phone Number _____

Name_____

Address _____

City _____

State _____ Zip _____

Phone Number _____

Name_____

Address _____

City _____

State _____ Zip _____

Phone Number _____

Name_____

Address _____

City _____

State _____ Zip _____

Phone Number _____

Name_____

Address _____

City _____

State _____ Zip _____

Phone Number _____

DEER HUNTING BUDDIES

Name_____

Address _____

City _____

State _____ Zip _____

Phone Number _____

Name_____

Address _____

City _____

State _____ Zip _____

Phone Number _____

Name_____

Address _____

City _____

State _____ Zip _____

Phone Number _____

Name_____

Address _____

City _____

State _____ Zip _____

Phone Number _____

Name_____

Address _____

City _____

State _____ Zip _____

Phone Number _____

Name_____

Address _____

City _____

State _____ Zip _____

Phone Number _____

Name_____

Address _____

City _____

State _____ Zip _____

Phone Number _____

Name_____

Address _____

City _____

State _____ Zip _____

Phone Number _____

Name_____

Address _____

City _____

State _____ Zip _____

Phone Number _____

Name_____

Address _____

City _____

State _____ Zip _____

Phone Number _____

Name_____

Address _____

City _____

State _____ Zip _____

Phone Number _____

Name_____

Address _____

City _____

State _____ Zip _____

Phone Number _____

DAILY WEATHER LOG

Date	Temp	Humidity	Moon Phase	Rain Inches	Snow Inches	Fog	Wind Speed	Wind Direction	Sun	Other

HUNTING VEHICLE MILEAGE RECORDS

Date / Vehicle	Odometer Start	Odometer Finish	Total Miles	Acc. Total Miles	Vehicle	Odometer Start	Odometer Finish	Total Miles	Acc. Total Miles

BOW HUNTING IN-WOODS TIME

DATE	TIME IN	TIME OUT	HOURS	HUNT METH.	DEER SEEN	WEAPON	TERRAIN	AIR TEMP.	SKY	WIND DIR.	WIND VEL.	PRECIP.	SNOW COVER

LEGEND

DATE: Month, Day, Year

TIME: Use 24 Hr. Clock
Ex. 2:00 P.M. = 1400

HOURS: Time In-Woods

HUNT METHOD:
Still—ST
Tree Stand—TS
Ground Stand—GS
Deer Drive—DD
Scout—SC

DEER SEEN: No. Deer Observed

WEAPON:
Bow—B   Gun—G
Camera—C   None—N

TERRAIN:
Edge of Field—FL
Conifer Forest—CF
Hardwood Forest—HF
Softwood Forest—SF
Swamp—SW

AIR TEMP.—Degrees F

SKY:
Clear—CL
Partly Cloudy—PC
Overcast—OC

WIND DIRECTION:
N NE E SE S SW W NW
Direction wind is coming from.

WIND VELOCITY:
Light—LT
Moderate—MD
Gusty—GT
Strong—ST
Calm—CM

PRECIPITATION:
Rain—RN
Snow—SN
Sleet—SL
Hail—HL
Fog—FG

SNOW COVER: Inches Snow on Ground

The Great Wisconsin Outdoors!
- Enjoy it even more, through these fine books -

FISH WISCONSIN, 2nd Edition

By Dan Small   **8½x11-in., softbound**
224 pg., illustrated, $16.95

From north to south, and east to west, noted Wisconsin outdoorsman Dan Small guides you to more than 60 productive lakes and streams. You'll discover not only where to go, but how to get there, learn local techniques, hot baits, access points, bait shop locations and guide services -- all the things you need to boost your confidence once you hit the water.

This new 2nd edition features more than 50 detailed maps to help you pinpoint the best areas. More than 20 new lakes and streams, including the Wolf River and a selection of the state's top trout streams have been newly added to round out the best companion you can have at your side when you fish Wisconsin.

WISCONSIN HUNTING By Brian Lovett

8½"x11", softcover   208 pg., $16.95

WISCONSIN HUNTING is an extensive guide to more than 60 of Wisconsin's finest public hunting grounds -- your one-stop scouting report to better deer, bear and small game hunting the next time your boots touch the Wisconsin outdoors.

Grouped into five regions statewide and compiled by Wisconsin outdoor writer Brian Lovett, WISCONSIN HUNTING lets you put your time where it's most productive -- into the hunt.

You'll find it easier than ever to locate productive areas thanks to larger expanded area maps; learn the best techniques to score in each sector; plus get a convenient list of lodging facilities, emergency services and licensing outlets for each hunting section. Statewide historical harvest data provides insight into major wildlife populations.

MUSKY MASTERY

By Steve Heiting
6x9-in., softbound
The Techniques of Top Guides   **160 pg., illustrated, $9.95**

Want a shortcut to the fish of 10,000 casts? Then listen to the tips and tactics of 11 of Wisconsin's top musky guides as presented by WISCONSIN OUTDOOR JOURNAL editor Steve Heiting in MUSKY MASTERY.

Fast-flowing narrative, liberally peppered with how-to detail and action-packed photos bring you the knowledge you'll need to coax that trophy to the end of your fishing line.

Do it under the cover of darkness; with a fly rod; on a jerk bait; or with a live sucker. With accomplished musky chasers as your on-paper guides, your odds on musky action this season are bound to go up.

GAME WARDENS VS POACHERS
Tickets Still Available

By James L. Palmer   **6"x9", softbound**
12 exciting chapters, $12.95

The light-hearted true tales of a genuine, hairy-chested northwoods game warden.

James Palmer, a 28-year Wisconsin DNR veteran, relates with insight and humor the way it was during his days as a warden, pilot, covert investigator and chief of the Special Investigations.

Containing a large dose of irreverence and plenty of anecdotes you won't find in a DNR news release. For example, what was a warden to do if he got into a car chase with a violator and another officer was too far away to help? "The most interesting option was the good old ram," Palmer writes. "Every young game warden looked forward to his first ram. You just weren't a real, hairy-chested warden until you had done it."

ORDER FORM Please print clearly

Your Name _____

Address _____

City/State/Zip _____

Qty	Title	Price	Sub Total
	Fish Wisconsin, 2nd Ed.	$16.95	
	Musky Mastery	$ 9.95	
	Wisconsin Hunting	$16.95	
	Game Wardens vs Poachers	$12.95	
	Shipping and Handling Books*		
	Subtotal Books		
	WI residents add 5.5% sales tax		
	Total Enclosed		

*Please add $2.50 for postage and handling for the first book and $1.50 for each additional book. Addresses outside the U.S., add $5.00 per title ordered for postage and handling.

( ) Check or money order enclosed payable to:
    Krause Publications

( ) MasterCard   ( ) VISA

Account Number _____

Expiration Date: Mo. _____ Yr. _____

Signature _____

MasterCard & VISA Cardholders save time by calling toll-free
800-258-0929 Dept. ZI1
Mon.-Fri. 6:30 am - 8 pm ● Sat. 8 am - 2 pm, CST.
General Business Phone: 715-445-2214
Mon.-Fri. 8:00 am to 5:00 pm

Mail to:

krause publications

700 E. State St., Iola, WI 54990-0001   ZI1